Resilient Classrooms

Creating Healthy Environments for Learning

SECOND EDITION

**BETH DOLL
KATHERINE BREHM
STEVEN ZUCKER**

THE GUILFORD PRESS
New York   London

© 2014 The Guilford Press
A Division of Guilford Publications, Inc.
72 Spring Street, New York, NY 10012
www.guilford.com

Printed in the United States of America

This book is printed on acid-free paper.

Last digit is print number: 9   8   7   6   5   4   3   2   1

Library of Congress Cataloging-in-Publication Data

Doll, Beth, 1952–
    Resilient classrooms : creating healthy environnments for learning / by Beth Doll,
Katherine Brehm, and Steven Zucker.—2nd ed.
        pages cm—(The Guilford practical intervention in the schools series)
    Includes bibliographical references and index.
    ISBN 978-1-4625-1334-5 (pbk. : alk. paper)
    1. Children with social disabilities—Education—United States.   2. Children with mental
disabilities—Education—United States.   3. Classroom environment—United States.   I. Brehm,
Katherine.   II. Zucker, Steven.   III. Title.
    LC4091.D65 2014
    371.826'94—dc23
                                                                          2013036802

To Addison, Elizabeth,
and all of the children who need classrooms
that teach them to treasure learning

About the Authors

Beth Doll, PhD, is Associate Dean for Academic Affairs and Professor of School Psychology in the College of Education and Human Sciences at the University of Nebraska–Lincoln. She has served as an officer or president of three state school psychology associations as well as of Division 16 (School Psychology) of the American Psychological Association. Dr. Doll's research addresses models of school mental health that foster resilience and enhance the well-being of students and program evaluation strategies that demonstrate the impact and accountability of school mental health services. She has published journal articles on issues of resilience, school mental health, self-determination, the identification of emotional disabilities, and students' friendships. Dr. Doll generally works within collaborative groups that include school practitioners and other community members, and involves graduate students as full members of these groups.

Katherine Brehm, PhD, is a practicing school psychologist with experience in the Ysleta Independent School District (Texas) and Denver Public Schools (Colorado). She was a member of the school psychology faculty at the University of Texas at El Paso and the University of Colorado at Denver. As a school psychologist, Dr. Brehm led her district in developing cross-disciplinary roles for school psychologists that increase the relevance of mental health services to learning, provided inservice training on teaching children with attention deficits, and planned for the district's implementation of standards-based education. She has conducted research in consultation, has coauthored a book on interventions for school emotional and behavioral problems, has published nationally on the topic of resilience, and has completed postdoctoral training in family therapy and neurological practices.

Steven Zucker, PhD, is a private consultant in school psychology in the Denver metropolitan area. He was a member of the faculty of the University of Colorado at Denver, practiced as a school psychologist for 17 years in the Cherry Creek Public Schools (Colorado), and was instrumental in creating a school environment that valued the full inclusion of students with disabilities. Dr. Zucker co-crafted Colorado's Blueprint for the Future, the state's agenda for integrated educational and mental health services for students. He has presented statewide and nationally on resilience, systems change, and inclusive practices. Dr. Zucker co-developed the ClassMaps model with Beth Doll and served as a coordinator on the first ClassMaps project. His experience as a practitioner with inclusion, systems change, and school mental health has been invaluable in the preparation of this book.

Acknowledgments

We owe special thanks to our graduate assistants Courtney Wimmer and Kimberly Alex, who found our references, checked our editing, helped prepare the figures and tables, and kept us organized and moving forward. We could not have worked through this second edition without their dedicated assistance. We also appreciate the many colleagues who have tried out our materials and concepts in their own schools and practices and returned to us with recommendations and comments. True wisdom comes from listening carefully to colleagues' responses and taking their judgments to heart. Several of them were kind enough to contribute their own case studies to this edition. Next, we must acknowledge the valuable contributions of numerous graduate students who worked alongside us over the past 12 years: Samuel Song, Stacy Kosse, Erin Siemers, Susie Fleissner, Erin Strasil, Mary Kelly Haack, Courtney LeClair, Sarah Kurien, Allison Champion, Allison Osborn, April Turner, Mindy Chadwell, Kristin Bieber, Kadie Petree, Brooke Chapla, Jonathan Sikorski, Erika Franta, and Catelyn Cantril. Many of these students have gone on to rich and rewarding education careers in research or practice. And, finally, we give heartfelt thanks to the many teachers and students who took a chance on us, shared their special insights about classrooms and student well-being, and told us how to improve our strategies. They were generous with their advice and encouraged us in our efforts.

Contents

CHAPTER 1

Introduction to
the Resilient Classroom

Resilient children are children who are successful despite the odds. Although they live their early years under harsh circumstances of deprivation, maltreatment, illness, or neglect, resilient children create successful lives for themselves. They earn advanced educational degrees, achieve successful careers, become financially stable, form happy and healthy families, and give back to their communities. Legends of resilient children are part of the fabric of American folklore. In fairy tales, Cinderella became a princess and lived happily ever after despite enduring years of her stepmother's abuse. The Horatio Alger novels inspired late 19th-century immigrants with rags-to-riches tales of impoverished youth who became wealthy entrepreneurs through diligence and hard work. A belief in personal resilience is captured in the common speech of our grandmothers who spoke of "pulling yourself up by your own bootstraps."

Developmental research on risk and resilience shows that such "bootstrap" legends are largely fictional. It is true that substantial numbers of chronically deprived children are successful despite the odds, but not because they single-handedly overcome risk. Instead, truly resilient children are vulnerable children who benefited from the caring, sustenance, and guidance of a community. In Emmy E. Werner's classic study of developmental disabilities, the children who overcame high-risk childhoods were those who had a close bond with at least one caretaker or had access to nurturing from other adults (Werner, 2013). Michael Rutter's study of the Isle of Wight showed that high-risk children were less likely to develop mental illness when they had effective parenting and positive adult models (Rutter, 2010). These resilient children had a committed and caring community pulling them upward into well-adjusted adulthood. In effect, it was the "child-in-community" who was resilient and not the child alone.

The premise of this book is that school classrooms can become resilient communities that provide essential support and guidance so that vulnerable children can learn and be successful. By drawing upon exemplary research in education, child development, and psy-

1

chology, we describe the characteristics of classrooms that comprise resilience. We explain why every school's mission of academic excellence makes it essential to embed these supports into resilient classrooms. Finally, we describe practical, data-based strategies that can infuse resilience into the fabric of classrooms' everyday routines and practices. Our ultimate goal is to reshape current understanding of the interface between schooling and children's mental health and to rethink existing strategies for supporting the success and psychological wellness of vulnerable children in schools.

WHY CHANGE CLASSROOMS INSTEAD OF KIDS?

North American schools are reeling under the pressures of meeting rising standards for academic excellence while educating large numbers of high-risk children. Of the 49 million children being educated in today's schools, 18% are living under conditions of abject poverty with the very real possibility that their family will not be able to pay the next month's rent or heating bills (Annie E. Casey Foundation, 2010). In 2008, 772,000 children were identified as physically or emotionally abused or neglected, and for 161,000 children the abuse was so harmful that the children were removed from their families and placed into foster care (Children's Defense Fund, 2010). One out of every five children meets the diagnostic criteria for at least one mental illness listed in the *Diagnostic and Statistical Manual of Mental Disorders* (DSM-IV-TR; American Psychiatric Association, 2000; Hoagwood & Johnson, 2003; U.S. Department of Health and Human Services, 1999). Given these prevalence rates, the typical school classroom with 25 students is likely to have at least five children with significant mental health needs, four students living in poverty, and one child struggling with severe abuse. Schools located in communities of concentrated poverty, unemployment, crime, and violence will inevitably show even higher prevalence rates.

> **The typical classroom probably has at least five children with serious mental health needs, four students living in poverty, and one child struggling with severe abuse.**

Traditional models would address these needs with "change-the-kid" strategies: referring needy children into individual and group mental health services where the children learn to overcome their hardships through new understandings, improved social and coping skills, and strengthened self-management strategies. Developmental risk research raises questions about whether these traditional strategies can be effective in changing the developmental trajectories of high-risk children (Doll & Cummings, 2008; Hoagwood & Johnson, 2003; Knitzer, 2005). Even more important, national statistics show that most high-risk children are not served by community mental health or social service agencies (Hoagwood & Johnson, 2003; U.S. Department of Health and Human Services, 1999). Nationwide, there is a documented gap of 12–15% of school-age children who have urgent needs for mental health services but are not receiving them through community providers. Schools cannot hire enough school mental health professionals to meet the needs of these children in change-the-kid ways. Instead, this gap requires that schools find other ways to support the social and emotional needs of vulnerable children so that they can learn and be successful despite their risk. A premise of this book is that alternative strategies will be more enduring and most successful when they are integrated into naturally occurring systems of support that are part of children's everyday lives.

Blueprints for designing natural supports can be found in existing research on risk, resilience, and effective schools. Longitudinal studies have shown that when children develop competence in the midst of adversity, it is because systems have operated to protect the child and counteract threats to development (Doll & Lyon, 1998; Werner, 2013). Characteristics of these systems are close and nurturing relationships between children and caretaking adults, access to successful adult models, support for children's self-efficacy, opportunities for children to practice self-regulation and set and work toward ambitious goals, support for warm and effective peer relationships, and "connectedness" within and among families and with formal and informal community groups that serve families. Similarly, James P. Comer's experience with impoverished inner-city schools taught him that the children need caring adults to support them and school environments that support the total development of the child (Comer, Haynes, Joyner, & Ben-Avie, 1996). Emory L. Cowen, initiator of the Primary Mental Health Project, described specific features of mentally healthy school environments: supporting secure attachments to adults, providing the child with age-appropriate competencies, exposing the child to contexts that enhance wellness, empowering the child, and preparing the child to cope effectively with stress (Cowen, 1994; Cowen et al., 1996). The tradition of Cowen's work is well represented in the activities and publications of the Collaborative for Academic, Social, and Emotional Learning (CASEL, 2003; Zins, Weissberg, Wang, & Walberg, 2004). Comer et al. (1996), Cowen et al. (1996), and CASEL have demonstrated success in raising the achievement of high-risk children by changing the social context of schooling. Subsequently, the National Research Council and Institute of Medicine's (NRC/IOM, 2004) comprehensive research review concluded that highly successful schools actively engaged their students in learning and personal growth by (1) fostering caring and supportive social communities of students and teachers, (2) maximizing students' expectations for their own success, and (3) promoting students' autonomy and self-regulation. Thus, multiple lines of inquiry across multiple research teams converge to demonstrate that high-quality relationships and autonomy-promoting practices protect children from some of the deleterious effects of social adversity.

> **High-quality relationships and autonomy-promoting practices protect children from some of the deleterious effects of social adversity.**

Still, prior work has emphasized buildingwide infrastructures that support effective practices. This book shifts that emphasis to the immediate classroom contexts where children spend much of their school day. Complex interactions between children and their classroom environments can maximize or diminish each child's success (Barth, Dunlap, Dane, Lochman, & Wells, 2004; Pianta, 2001). Thus, learning problems do not "reside" within the children but instead reflect a mismatch between the children and one or more of the features within their classrooms (Pianta & Walsh, 1996).

HOW CAN CLASSROOMS BE CHANGED?

A framework for fostering classroom change can be found in the ecological systems perspective on human development. This perspective describes each child as part of an integrated ecological system—the "child-in-classroom" (Bronfenbrenner, 1979). Obvious features of the ecosystem of any classroom include the teacher, students, and physical setting. In this book, we also include less apparent features of the ecosystem such as the families that students come from each morning and return to at the end of each school day; the surrounding school with its policies, routines, and practices; and the community within which the school resides.

Systems perspectives explain that classroom systems change through coordinated efforts of the teacher, students, parents, and others who are part of the classroom or visit it regularly. Neither the child nor the classroom can change without changing the other. When the changes made by the teachers, parents, and students complement and support each other, the changes can persist and have an enduring impact on the routines and practices of the classroom (NRC/IOM, 2004; Pianta & Walsh, 1996). Uncoordinated changes, such as those unilaterally imposed by teachers or other members of the system working in isolation, are likely to have unanticipated and unintended consequences for other aspects of the system. When this occurs, tension within the system draws it back into its former state and the change effort will have failed.

Consider the example of Lewis, a fourth grader with life-threatening asthma whose class was located in an open classroom "suite" alongside three other classrooms. Lewis's potent asthma medication left him distractible, inattentive, and disorganized. His daily seatwork was rarely completed and, despite his high intelligence, he was assigned to the slower-paced groups for work in reading and mathematics. Lewis's teacher sat him near her desk, apart from his classmates, so that he wouldn't interrupt their work. In response, Lewis spent more time daydreaming and forgot even more of his work. The school nurse decided that his inattention was asthma related and established a reinforcement program so he would remember to come to the office twice a day for his medication and treatments. The program worked for 3 weeks, and then Lewis slipped back into forgetting. By the end of the year, Lewis had a reputation for being an intractable student who wouldn't cooperate with staff efforts to help him.

Then, in his fifth-grade year, Lewis was assigned to a very different classroom. The class was organized around precise management routines. At predictable times each day, students would write assignments into their notebooks and take note of those that they had not yet completed. Seatwork instructions were always written in a standard location on one of the class chalkboards. Students were taught standard routines for frequent class activities such as taking a quiz, writing an essay, or checking a math paper. Class problem-solving meetings were used to develop planned activities during class recess periods, and problems were debriefed afterward. Desks were arranged in groups of four with ample space between every group. Students described their classroom teachers as "tough but cool." By October, it was clear that Lewis was no longer a problem student. His work was usually complete and on time, he remembered to go to the office for his medicine, and class visitors noted that he was usually engaged and on task. School lounge talk suggested that Lewis had finally matured—the extra growth over the summer months had "fixed" his distractibility and inattention. We pose another alternative: that the new class routines and relationships created a context that allowed Lewis to express his competence.

How can classrooms provide effective contexts for learning? Educators need to become a catalyst for coordinated change that advances the learning goals of classrooms. This requires that they (1) understand what makes a classroom a healthy place to learn, (2) recognize when essential supports are missing in a classroom, (3) intervene to strengthen those supports when necessary, and (4) demonstrate that their interventions have enhanced the learning and development of children in the classrooms. Strengthening supports requires knowing how to engage all essential members of the classroom in coordinated efforts to change the classroom ecology.

In this book, we apply a tested model for data-based problem solving to the task of ecological classroom change. Research has shown that effective behavior change occurs when there is a clear description of the problem; an identified goal for change; the collection of data before, during, and after the intervention; and a written plan for intervention (Burns & Symington, 2002; Gutkin & Curtis, 2009). The National Association of School Psychologists (NASP) recognizes the central importance of this framework for data-based decision making in its Standards for Professional Practice (NASP, 2006, 2010). As this model is applied to classroom change, ecological classroom interventions will be more effective when there are:

- Precise descriptions of necessary classroom supports that are specific and measurable.
- Data-based needs assessments that describe classroom environments before intervention and after improvement.
- Ecosystemic planning activities that involve teachers, students, and other classroom participants in hypothesizing why some resilience characteristics are deficient in the classroom, and articulating a step-by-step plan for change describing what will be done, when, and by whom.
- Interventions accompanied by evidence that the changes follow the plan and by data describing the classroom changes that occur in response to the intervention.
- Thoughtful and comprehensive comparisons of pre- and postintervention data that describe the classroom changes that were made and their impact on student success.

In many ways, this cycle of change resembles response-to-intervention (RTI) frameworks that schools use to systematically examine the impact of individual student interventions on students' academic or behavioral deficits (Brown-Chidsey & Steege, 2005; Burns & Gibbons, 2008). Resilient classrooms' data-based decision making targets improvements at the level of classrooms while most RTI decision making targets individual students. Still, the two frameworks are highly compatible. Many students' disturbances in learning, behavior, or academic engagement could be minimized if resilient classrooms strategies were used at universal levels in schools, reducing the total number of students who need RTI programs or raising the likelihood that these programs will succeed. At the same time, the need for individual programs will never totally disappear. Some students will continue to struggle with learning, behavior, or academic engagement even in highly resilient classroom learning environments, and individualized RTI programs will still be required for those students. Combined, resilient classrooms and RTI strategies respect the systemic character of school classrooms with their multiple participants (adults and children) and interlocking responsibilities for students' academic, behavioral, social, and personal success.

This model for change also borrows heavily from universal prevention programs that have emerged within the past two decades to promote the social, emotional, and psychological wellness of students (Doll, Pfohl, & Yoon, 2010). In schools, these programs are frequently represented by variations on the prevention "triangle" or "pyramid." At the universal level, all classrooms in a school could be screened to describe the supports that they provide for students' school success. At the second level, classrooms with one or more missing or deficient support would participate in the resilient classrooms change activities. If significant impairments in classroom supports continued after two or more cycles of classroom change, teachers could decide to implement a manualized, evidence-based intervention or secure additional resources. At each level, decisions to engage in more ambitious classroom change procedures would be supported by local data describing ongoing classroom needs.

HOW WILL THIS BOOK HELP?

This book prepares school psychologists, teachers, administrators, school counselors, school social workers, and other educators to be catalysts for creating resilient classrooms that support academic success for all students. Toward this goal, Chapters 2, 3, and 4 draw upon existing developmental and educational research to describe resilient classrooms including classroom characteristics that support optimal conditions for learning and the classroom practices and activities that support the features in classrooms. Chapter 5 describes ways to assess these elements of resilient classrooms. We emphasize assessment strategies that are brief, are practical, and can be used repeatedly in order to track changes over time. Chapters 6 and 7 explain how to use the assessment data to engage all of the classroom's participants in understanding its strengths and limitations and contributing to a promising plan for classroom change. Chapter 8 describes intervention strategies for strengthening classroom relationships and supports for autonomy, as well as identifying and evaluating intervention strategies that emerge from other research. Chapter 9 explains how to evaluate the impact of classroom changes on students' school success and how to keep other stakeholders informed about the classroom's resilient classrooms activities. Finally, Chapter 10 describes the integration of these change-the-classroom strategies into existing school mental health services that emphasize change-the-kid strategies. Case studies distributed throughout the book show how these strategies have been used by actual educators in their daily work. Copies of the ClassMaps Survey and resilient classroom worksheets are available in the appendices.

CHAPTER 2

What Are Resilient Classrooms?

Resilient classrooms are places where all children can be successful emotionally, academically, and socially. The essential environmental supports that promote children's success have already been isolated and described in three important lines of research: developmental research that examines risk and resilience in vulnerable children, educational research that identifies the underpinnings of academic success in vulnerable children, and special education research that describes conditions for the successful inclusion of children with disabilities in general education classrooms. Although all three lines of research grew from different purposes, their findings converge to identify very similar characteristics as predicting the developmental competence of children.

Our working definition of resilient classrooms borrows heavily from the major studies of developmental risk that were initiated in the 1940s and 1950s and reached maturity in the 1980s and 1990s (Werner, 2013). These longitudinal studies were carefully designed, methodologically sound, and were replicated across six or more independent research groups, so their cumulative results are very convincing. In each study, a community's children were tracked across the decades to identify the family, community, and child characteristics that predicted important life successes such as the children's educational achievement, employment, financial independence, and social adjustment. Results of these studies were highly consistent in identifying a small list of risk and resilience factors that ultimately predicted life outcomes (Doll & Lyon, 1998; Masten, 2001; Werner, 2013). A striking finding of the studies is that many of the most powerful predictors were not characteristics of the children but instead described the families and communities in which the children were raised. This very important finding led us to suggest that resilience should be conceptualized as a property of caretaking settings rather than of individual children (Doll & Lyon, 1998).

Children living in impoverished urban communities present a special challenge to schools because they exist within niches of high risk (Pianta & Walsh, 1996). In addition to poverty, these children struggle to grow up while experiencing high rates of community violence, family discord, and diminished health care—many of the factors that predict poor life outcomes. Several prominent programs have emerged to address the extensive needs of these children. Inevitably, the successful programs have emphasized strengthening personal relationships among members of the community, families, and the school. The cornerstone of the School Development Program (Comer et al., 1996) is a community–school team that strengthens the relationships between students and staff and between staff and parents. Its ultimate purpose is to give adults in the school a predictable and caring presence with the children. Similarly, the Primary Mental Health Project (Cowen et al., 1996) assigns nonprofessional child associates to establish a caring, trusting, and predictable relationship with young children who are at risk for school failure. The "Success for All" schools (Slavin & Madden, 2001) implement an enriched reading curriculum accompanied by family support teams to significantly increase family involvement in their children's education. All three programs monitor the progress of the schools by continuously collecting data that are reviewed regularly by school staff. When carefully planned and collected, data dissemination can be a powerful incentive for change. In a recent initiative, the American Institutes for Research partnered with CASEL to systematically assess the social–emotional conditions for learning in the Chicago Public Schools (Osher & Kendziora, 2010). Then they summarized and published the data so that they were widely available to parents, community members, and school leaders. The data quickly became the basis for planning and decisions made to strengthen the schools' success.

One out of every 11 children attending public school in this country has been identified with a disability (U.S. Department of Education, 2010). Sadly, the education of children with disabilities has not been as successful as that of their nondisabled peers. They drop out of schools twice as often as their peers, enter into higher education at half the rate, and are far less likely to be employed after graduation (President's Commission on Excellence in Special Education, 2002; Reschly & Christenson, 2006). However, progress is being made. Between 1995 and 2005, the proportion of students with disabilities who graduated with a regular high school diploma increased from 42.4% to 54.4%, and the proportion who dropped out of school declined from 46.8% to 28.3% (U.S. Department of Education, 2010). Efforts to strengthen results for children with disabilities have emphasized learning conditions in the general education classrooms, since the majority of children with disabilities spend 80% of their school day in such regular education classrooms (U.S. Department of Education, 1999). Special education research has sought to identify the general education conditions that raise the educational achievements of children with disabilities. For example, the social integration of children with disabilities is stronger when peers are academically and personally supportive of each other and when the social environment supports frequent peer interactions (NRC/IOM, 2004; Salisbury, Gallucci, Palombaro, & Peck, 1995). Learning is enhanced when classmates support, help, and befriend the students with disabilities (Johnson, Johnson, & Anderson, 1983). Students are more engaged in the classroom's learning activities when they are provided with instruction in a setting that empowers their learning and apply the content knowledge in meaningful ways (Pullin, 2008) with teachers who students describe as warm and caring (Reschly & Christenson, 2006).

From these three bodies of research, we have identified six characteristics that describe the classrooms where children can be most successful academically and interpersonally. These characteristics describe classrooms where (1) students believe that they are competent and effective learners (academic efficacy), (2) students set and work toward self-selected learning goals (academic self-determination), (3) students behave appropriately and adaptively with a minimum of adult supervision (behavioral self-control), (4) there are caring and authentic relationships between teachers and the students (teacher–student relationships), (5) students have ongoing and rewarding friendships with their classmates (peer relationships), and (6) families know about and strengthen the learning that occurs in the classroom (home–school relationships). One prominent hypothesis is that these aspects of classrooms contribute to students' academic engagement—their conscious and purposeful efforts to learn—and these enhanced efforts increase the amount and quality of students' learning (NRC/IOM, 2004). Indeed, the seminal report of the NRC argues that such learning environments are important for all students but hold particular importance for students from disadvantaged backgrounds. Their logic is that advantaged students may falter in their learning but are likely to have multiple new chances to overcome their initial struggles, whereas disadvantaged students may have very limited new chances to succeed.

> **The six characteristics of resilient classrooms are academic efficacy, academic self-determination, behavioral self-control, strong teacher–student relationships, effective peer relationships, and close home–school relationships.**

Throughout the remainder of this book, we use these six characteristics as a working definition of resilient classrooms. In traditional models of academic success, these are frequently understood to be characteristics of individual children. For example, Martha might be seen as having great academic efficacy because of the confidence she shows in her schoolwork, while Melita is seen as having a problem with academic efficacy because she gives up too soon and will not attempt difficult work. From our ecological review of the research, we find evidence that classwide routines and practices hold great influence over the emergence of these characteristics in a classroom's students. For example, encouraging words, sensitively delivered help, and celebrations of success can enhance the academic efficacy of Melita, Martha, and all of their classmates. Moreover, systemic classroom characteristics are amenable to change and can do much to enhance the learning of all students who spend 30 hours each week learning together.

This chapter clearly defines each characteristic of resilient classrooms and will describe an empirical knowledge base that links each characteristic to enhanced academic engagement, improved academic performance, lower student dropout rates, and more successful inclusion of students with disabilities in regular education classrooms. Chapters 3 and 4 provide expanded explanations of each characteristic, including the classroom practices and routines that comprise the characteristic, how and why each characteristic fosters children's competence, and an explanation of what strengthens each characteristic of classroom environments.

ACADEMIC EFFICACY

Academic efficacy describes the beliefs that students hold about their ability to learn and be successful in the classroom. It is a construct of self-fulfilling prophecies: Children who expect to be successful take steps that make their success likely, whereas those who expect to fail behave in ways that almost ensure their failure (Bandura, 1997). Students' academic efficacy beliefs influence such critical achievement behaviors as their persistence, the amount of effort they spend on learning, their efforts to organize academic learning tasks, their willingness to attempt difficult tasks, whether they ask for help when they need it, and whether or not they act in ways necessary to be successful (Ryan, Patrick, & Shim, 2005; Schunk & Pajares, 2005). These achievement behaviors are the first step in a cycle of beliefs, feelings, and actions in which children with high academic efficacy complete more of their work, are more strategic in their learning, and take more pride in their work than children with low academic efficacy. These actions contribute to learning success and the success experiences, in turn, strengthen students' efficacy for similar tasks in the future. Empirical research has made it very clear that efficacy beliefs are specific to a task (Bandura, 1997). For example, some students might expect to be successful in mathematics but expect to fail in reading or writing. Still, efficacy in one subject contributes to students' general sense of efficacy and so can generalize to other tasks (Lorsbach & Jinks, 1999). In our own work in elementary and middle schools, most students described a healthy confidence in their own ability to be successful, noting that they "often" or "almost always" expected to do well on their work and learn what is taught (Doll, Spies, Champion, et al., 2010; Doll, Spies, LeClair, Kurien, & Foley, 2010).

> **Children who expect to be successful take steps that make their success likely, whereas those who expect to fail behave in ways that almost ensure their failure.**

In a classroom, academic efficacy emerges out of opportunities to tackle challenging learning tasks with the instructional supports that make success likely (Bandura, 1997). It is also enhanced when students see that their classmates are successful in learning similar tasks. Efficacy is diminished when students are emotionally distressed or discouraged (Schunk & Pajares, 2005). Perhaps most important, it is strengthened by early, persuasive feedback from the teacher and classmates that all students can be successful. In resilient classrooms, students receive regular and prompt feedback on their work and are encouraged to monitor their own successes (Pastorelli et al., 2001). Their successes are immediately apparent and provide occasions for mutual celebration and congratulations. Thus, within classrooms, efficacy is contagious: Students develop collective efficacy beliefs about their shared ability to learn and be successful (Bandura, Caprara, Barbaranelli, Gerbino, & Pastorelli, 2003; Schunk & Pajares, 2005).

For example, in a second-grade classroom, students struggled mightily with timed mathematics computation tests that were administered twice a week to satisfy a district mandate. Their teacher noted that the students' math skills were stronger than their test performance suggested. Through a classwide student survey and a classroom meeting, the students explained that they could not do well on the tests, were nervous, expected to fail, and many suspected that their classmates were more capable than they were. To raise their likelihood of success, the teacher led the students through brief relaxation exercises before each of the timed tests. Next, the class helped her identify test-taking tricks that they could use to improve their performance. Finally, so that they noticed their own success, she graphed the classroom's overall performance and led celebrations of their successful progress.

What is the impact of academic efficacy on learning? Efficacious students are more likely to be self-regulated students; they set goals for their learning, are strategic in their approaches to learn, and self-evaluate their own performance (Schunk & Pajares, 2005). Thus, it is not surprising that research has repeatedly shown that children with higher academic efficacy earn higher grades, perform better on tests and other assignments, and progress more successfully through school (Pajares & Schunk, 2002; Pintrich, 2003). More important, Schunk and Pajares (2009) explain that students can be helped to be more efficacious and their achievement improves as a result.

BEHAVIORAL SELF-CONTROL

Behavioral self-control is the degree to which students' classroom conduct is appropriate and self-regulated. Classroom behaviors that are essential for learning include being responsive to the teacher and the lesson, paying active attention to academic work, interacting effectively with peers, and moving efficiently through transitions from one learning activity to the next (Reynolds & Kamphaus, 2004). Disturbing and disruptive behaviors that preclude learning include fidgeting or moving about, being inattentive to the teacher or the lesson, making noises out of turn, or being aggressive or disruptive toward classmates. Innumerable studies have shown that teachers can control students' classroom behaviors by carefully managing classroom routines, supervising carefully, and systematically manipulating antecedents and consequences (Bear, 2010; Bear, Cavalier, & Manning, 2005). Still, when strict behavioral contingencies are teacher-imposed and teacher-enforced, students may not control their own behavior outside the presence of the adults who notice and cue it (Bear et al., 2005; Osher, Bear, Sprague, & Doyle, 2010). A classroom demonstrates behavioral self-control when its students' behavior is appropriate for learning regardless of the presence of an authority in the room.

> A classroom demonstrates behavioral self-control when its students' behavior is appropriate for learning regardless of the presence of an authority in the room.

When framing self-control within individual students, Zimmerman (2000) describes three phases: thinking about the action in advance (thinking ahead), acting as planned (in the moment), and reflecting on the impact of the behavior after the fact (thinking back). Within classrooms, complex ecological systems may predispose students to be well controlled or disruptive. For example, a single disturbing student may disrupt the class with loud comments or noises, by fidgeting or roaming around the classroom, or by arguing or fighting with classmates. Difficult students who demand an extraordinary amount of teacher attention can limit teacher time for positive interactions in the classroom. Alternatively, classrooms may have difficult learning environments due to confusing standards for classroom behavior, a lack of routines to guide orderly transitions, or uncomfortable or crowded facilities. Even more important, frustrating and negative interactions between the teacher and students detract significantly from learning that can occur in the class (Lane, Pierson, & Givner, 2003). Consequently, it is concerning that both elementary and middle school students' ratings of their classmates' rule following are generally among the lowest ratings given on the ClassMaps Survey (CMS; Doll, 2005; Doll, Spies, Champion, et al., 2010; Doll, Spies, LeClair, et al., 2010).

Problems with behavioral self-control were exemplified by a second-grade classroom, where the morning reading instruction was interrupted constantly by loud arguments among students who were completing seatwork at their desks. The arguments erupted several times a morning and often became so disruptive that the teacher had to leave his reading group to resolve the conflicts. The interruptions were frustrating for the teacher, and the students worried about the hurtful arguments and were hesitant to play together at recess. To resolve the problem, the teacher and his class agreed on a few simple rules for resolving arguments without the teacher's help. Next, the class practiced the rules during several class role plays. Finally, the class tracked their progress in resolving arguments without the teacher's help and awarded themselves "Friday popcorn parties" for reduced interruptions. This guided practice in self-control was sufficient to reduce the classroom interruptions from 21 per day to an average of three per day.

Adaptive classroom conduct is both caused by and causes academic success (Hawkins et al., 2003; NRC/IOM, 2004; Osher et al., 2010): Problem behavior undermines academic achievement, while academic failures contribute to students' disengagement and increased rule breaking. In part, this is because improved behavior in a classroom increases the time allocated for instruction and when academic engaged time increases, learning improves (Mitchem, Young, West, & Benyo, 2001; NRC/IOM, 2004). When students are helped to monitor their own behavior and to make decisions about whether and how to behave appropriately, their academic progress can significantly increase (Bear, 2010; Bear et al., 2005; McDermott, Mordell, & Stoltzfus, 2001).

ACADEMIC SELF-DETERMINATION

Self-determination lies at the heart of students' emerging autonomy. Autonomous students have personal goals for their own learning, can identify and solve problems that might block their achievement of those goals, and systematically select and implement actions that allow them to progress toward their goals (Black & Deci, 2000; Deci & Ryan, 2008a). They identify with the importance of academic learning and self-govern the ways that they spend their time and the effort given to learning (Brophy, 2004: Masten, 2001; Masten et al., 1999). Because they assume personal responsibility for their own learning, they take credit for their successes and react to temporary failures with revised goals, new action plans, or strengthened strategies for improvement. When asked the degree to which they take charge of their learning, most students in our prior work described a modest level of autonomy: typical elementary and middle school students reported that they "sometimes" or "often" work as hard as they can or work because they want to and not because they have to (Doll, Spies, Champion, et al., 2010; Doll, Spies, LeClair, et al., 2010).

Students are helped to be more self-determined learners in classrooms that set mastery goals for learning—goals that challenge students to master new skills or understanding rather than competitive goals—goals that promote competition among students to perform better than their classmates. In addition, resilient classrooms provide students with practice, feedback, and direct instruction in academic goal setting, decision making, problem solving, and self-evaluation of academic skills (Brophy, 2004). These key skills make it possible for students to self-direct their own learning.

As an example, an eighth-grade math teacher was concerned that his students lacked the self-determination that they needed to meet the state's standards for eighth-grade math. Although they seemed unaware of the fact, if the students failed one or more of the standards at the end of the year, they would not be allowed to graduate into high school math classes. To increase his students' commitment to achieving the state standards, the teacher posted a large graph on the front bulletin board and marked successes for each student as each standard was passed. Next, he delivered an instructional unit on goal setting and decision making to the class, emphasizing the overall class goal for all students to pass every standard by year's end. Students set individual goals for personal activities they would carry out in order to increase their success on the math standards tests. The class conducted weekly updates when students would mark their progress in meeting their personal goals and when the class would assess its progress toward meeting the class goal. With this kind of support for goal-directed behaviors, the students' performance on state standards tests improved markedly.

Research has consistently shown that self-determined learners are more curious, prefer more challenging tasks, independently seek to master new skills, see themselves as more competent, and have higher self-efficacy (Black & Deci, 2000; Deci & Ryan, 2008a). Moreover, students perform better and show more academic persistence when they are working toward instructional goals that they value (Assor, Kaplan, & Roth, 2002; Brophy, 2004; Pajares & Schunk, 2001, 2002). Ultimately, increased student self-determination is positively related to quality engagement in learning activities, higher levels of conceptual learning, and increased retention of learned knowledge (Hughes, Wu, & West, 2011; Lau & Nie, 2008; Linnenbrink, 2005; Pajares & Schunk, 2001).

> **Self-determined learners are more curious, prefer more challenging tasks, and independently seek to master new skills.**

EFFECTIVE TEACHER–STUDENT RELATIONSHIPS

Teacher–student relationships are most effective when they are warm, engaged, authentic, responsive, characterized by high expectations, and provide the class with structure and clear limits (Pianta, 1999; Rudasill, Reio, Stipanovic, & Taylor, 2010; Wentzel, 2002). Still, the complexity of effective teacher–student relationships is difficult to capture in lists like these. Teacher–student relationships are also emotion-based experiences that emerge out of the teachers' ongoing interactions with their students. In many cases, students' attachment to their teachers is similar to but less intense than their attachment to parents (Kesner, 2000). Contemporary teachers are simultaneously interacting with all the children in their class, limiting the interpersonal intimacy they can achieve with any one student and imposing some distance and stereotypy into teacher–student relationships. Pianta (1999) has shown that larger class sizes lead to fewer and less positive teacher responses to each student. Moreover, the number of students makes it more challenging for teachers to accommodate to children who are exceptional in any important respect. Teachers exert control over their relationships with students by maximizing the attention and praise that they provide to them. Effective teachers praise their students three to four times as often as they reprimand them (Sutherland & Wehby, 2001; Walker, Colvin, & Ramsey, 1995). Most teachers are quite successful in establishing useful relationships with their students; consistently and across several independent studies, students' ratings on the My Teacher subscale of the CMS has been the strongest of the eight subscales (Doll, 2005; Doll, Spies, Champion, et al., 2010; Doll, Spies, LeClair, et al., 2010).

In a classroom, effective teacher–student relationships contribute to learning by raising students' expectations of success, reassuring them in the face of failure, and engaging them in active interaction with new knowledge. Teachers hold the larger responsibility but not the sole responsibility for forging instructional relationships that enhance the learning of their students. Students also share some power over the quality of the relationship and its expression. Indeed, while any one student's relational power is small relative to that of the teacher, the cumulative relational power of all students in a classroom can be overwhelming, especially for beginning teachers.

Consider the example of an elementary choir teacher. One group of fifth graders thought that he was arrogant and condescending and thought that his class activities were boring. Consequently, whenever they were required to assemble on the classroom's risers to sing, several of the boys surreptitiously used their watch crystals to dance sunbeams across the teacher's balding head. The rest of the class had trouble controlling their giggles, and the teacher frequently complained that for some reason this fifth grade was his most frustrating class to teach. Once the class became caught in this routine, the teacher could not single-handedly repair his relationship with the fifth graders.

Caring relationships among students, teachers, and other adults in a school are consistently associated with increased academic engagement, stronger achievement, and higher student satisfaction with school (Baker 2006; Hamre & Pianta, 2001; NRC/IOM, 2004; Rudasill et al., 2010). The relation may be even more pronounced for students living with demographic adversities (Hamre & Pianta, 2005) or struggling with learning and behavior problems (Brooks & Goldstein, 2007). Caring teachers raise academic efficacy even in classrooms where students work in active competition with one another (Ryan, Gheen, & Midgley, 1998). Conversely, isolation and the lack of personally meaningful relationships with teachers contribute to school failure (Ang, 2005; Murray & Malmgren, 2005; Murray & Murray, 2004; Rudasill et al., 2010). Indeed, school dropouts repeatedly say that the main reason they leave school is that no one there really cares about them (Kortering & Braziel, 2002). Comer (1993) emphasizes the particular importance of teacher–student relationships in schools serving impoverished or minority youth, saying that schools are unlikely to touch the lives of inner-city poor children in any meaningful way unless they re-create a sense of community.

EFFECTIVE PEER RELATIONSHIPS

The peer relationships that exist within school classrooms are frequently the first opportunities that children have to form relationships independent of their parents' oversight. Classroom peer relationships are effective when all children have supportive friends in a class and when classmates know how to resolve conflicts with each other quickly to the satisfaction of both children and without disrupting their friendship (Doll & Brehm, 2010; Doll, Murphy, & Song, 2003). Of these two, conflict resolution has received greater attention because unresolved conflicts may deteriorate into aggressive physical or verbal confrontations that are highly disruptive to the ongoing activities of the class. These may, in extreme cases, represent a safety hazard. While conflict is present in all normal peer relationships (Cairns & Cairns, 2000), in healthy interactions most students can overlook or resolve minor conflicts so that friendships are maintained and the interaction can continue. The promotion of peer friendships also plays an important role in shaping classrooms' social climate. Students with friends enjoy school more because they have someone to sit with on the bus, someone to play with at recess, someone to eat with at lunch, someone who chooses them for his or her team, and someone to talk with during free moments in a classroom. Finally, having friends is a protective factor that insulates children from the inevitable peer bullying that occurs in schools (Song & Sogo, 2010; Song & Stoiber, 2008).

Early research tended to focus on the deficits of the individual students when describing problems with peer conflicts and attributed student isolation to deficits in a student's social skills, social acceptance, or social cognition. However, classroom contexts can also be reshaped so that more students in a class are included by peers and conflicts are reduced (Doll, 2006). Classroom peer relationships are particularly rewarding when peers experience mutual acceptance, enjoyable opportunities to play, and routines to resolve conflicts when these occur. In the typical classroom, almost all of the students have rewarding friendships; an average of 4% of students are not identified by any classmate as a friend, and only 8% of students are actively disliked by their classmates (Doll & Brehm, 2010; Doll et al., 2003). Still, disturbing levels of peer conflict characterize many classrooms, and students' ratings on the Kids in This Class subscale of the CMS are often among the lowest of the eight subscales (Doll, 2005; Doll, Spies, Champion, et al., 2010; Doll, Spies, LeClair, et al., 2010). It may be difficult to reconcile this pattern of high conflict with the similarly high student ratings of peer friendships. However, most conflict occurs within friendships, and students with more peer interactions also have more opportunities for conflicts (Doll & Brehm, 2010; Gropeter & Crick, 1996). As one very lonely seventh grader once explained, "I've never had a problem with a friend because I've never had a friend." Still, classroom routines and practices can promote positive conflict management strategies that soften or even eliminate the deleterious impacts of many classroom conflicts (Doll & Brehm, 2010; Smith, Daunic, & Miller, 2002).

For example, an inner-city eighth-grade classroom struggled with high rates of recess conflicts and, because many of the disagreements escalated into physical fights, students were frequently suspended for one or more days. The teacher believed that students were stressed and frightened by the many noontime fights and wanted stricter enforcement of the school rules. However, a classroom meeting revealed that the students' biggest complaint was that recess was boring because there was so little to do. Recess was held on a large, concrete slab with four basketball hoops and little else. In response, the teachers purchased a few simple games that the students could take out with them—foot bags, sponge rubber Frisbees, checkers, and some jump ropes. The classroom's suspension rate fell noticeably as a result.

The importance of peer relationships to the development of social competence is well established in the research. Having a friend in class makes it easier for students to enjoy daily activities in the classroom, ask for assistance in times of stress, and receive help when they ask for it (Malecki & Elliott, 2002; Wentzel & Watkins, 2002). Alternatively, having persistent and marked difficulties with peers is one of the most common reasons why staffing teams move students with disabilities out of general education classrooms and into self-contained programs (Schonert-Reichl, 1993). Research has shown the pivotal role that friendships play in promoting academic success. Friends help each other with academic tasks (Zajac & Hartup, 1997), shape each other's enjoyment of school and learning (Wentzel & Watkins, 2002), and reinforce each other's commitment to being in school and doing well there (NRC/IOM, 2004). Perhaps most important, students who are unliked in elementary school drop out of middle school at five times the rate of popular students (Barclay, 1966; Ladd, 2005; Pellegrini & Bartini, 2000).

EFFECTIVE HOME–SCHOOL RELATIONSHIPS

Many parents are not a striking presence in their child's school, and secondary parents are the least involved in their children's school experiences (Adams & Christenson, 2000; Christenson, 2004). As a result, home–school relationships are too-often awkward and forced, and teachers struggle to work cooperatively with their students' families. Teachers informally define parent involvement as family attendance at parent–teacher conferences, school assemblies, or classroom events (Anderson & Minke, 2007; Fan & Chen, 2001). However, systematic studies have shown that the actions that parents take within their home may be more important for their children's success than anything that parents do in the school building (Grolnick, Friendly, & Bellas, 2009). Important home actions include such things as monitoring television, providing a quiet place to study, checking homework completion, and reinforcing teacher discipline. The impact of meaningful parental involvement is especially marked when teachers tell parents what specific home activities are most likely to help their children do better in school (Hoover-Dempsey et al., 2005).

> Actions that parents take within their home may be more important for their children's success than anything parents do in the school building.

Miscommunication between home and school was seriously limiting homework completion in a second-grade classroom. Although math homework was assigned twice each week, a third of the class failed to complete it. Most students reported that they did not talk with their parents about the homework and were not sure their parents knew what they were doing at school. Together with the teacher, they set a goal to complete all of their homework all of the time and made a new rule that their parents would sign their homework. The teacher sent a note home to their parents explaining when homework would be assigned and asking them to sign the homework checkoff sheet attached to each assignment. Next, the class created a homework chart that recorded all completed homework. Finally, a classwide reinforcement was used when the class met its goal. Homework completion rates rose from an average of 70% to 89%, and students reported speaking daily with their parents about their schoolwork.

When parents stay involved in their children's education, their children earn higher grades and test scores, stay in school longer, and participate more actively in learning (Buerkle, Whitehouse, & Christenson, 2009; Grolnick et al., 2009; NRC/IOM, 2004). Students of involved parents have higher attendance rates and lower suspension and dropout rates (Christenson, Whitehouse, & VanGetson, 2008; Grolnick et al., 2009). Alternatively, when parents are disengaged, their children's attendance is poorer, they drop out more frequently, they are more likely to become teenage parents, and they are more likely to be adjudicated by the courts.

SUMMARY

These six characteristics form a two-stranded tether that binds students to their classroom community. One strand emphasizes the self-agency of the classroom's students—their autonomy, self-regulation, and self-efficacy. The second strand emphasizes the caring and connected relationships among members of the classroom community. Both strands are important for creating resilient classrooms that promote student success. Their importance is not only evident in educational research but has been reinforced by the many teachers and principals who have worked with us over the past 15 years. The contribution of this book is to build upon existing research by creating precise operational definitions that organize the knowledge base and make it available for practical use in schools.

INTRODUCTION TO A CASE STUDY OF RESILIENT CLASSROOMS

Immediately following this chapter you will find Stefanie Weitzenkamp's case study illustrating a practical use for these operational definitions. Her resource students were clearly discontented with recess, and she was able to use the definition of peer relations to examine practices that contributed to the problem. The attention that she paid to the playground environment strengthened the quality of her students' relationships with their peers. This made it possible for the recess break to contribute to, rather than detract from, the students' commitment to school.

CASE STUDY

A Teacher's Journey during Recess

Stefanie Weitzenkamp
Wayne State College

The Problem

I became concerned about recess when day after day my resource students would come into class after lunch angry and crying. They were upset, frustrated, and hurt because other kids would not let them join games. They were ignored, rejected, and left out of recess play, and no matter what suggestions I made or how many situations and social skills we would discuss and role-play, the recess result was the same. I realized I needed to do something different. When school started in the fall of 2010, I scheduled recess into my teaching day knowing my time with them on the playground was as valuable to our students as time in the classroom. Every day we would play kickball or a game of tag. Still, recess was complicated because the playground equipment and swing sets had been dismantled over the summer and couldn't be replaced until the workers finished installing a handicapped accessible surface. It was the first full week of October before the students could play on the equipment.

Using Student Journals and Meetings as Assessment

In February 2010, I began to assess the problem with a student meeting in which children in grades 3–6 got together to discuss recess. Many students, not only those in my resource classroom, shared that they were tired of being left out because they were too short, too slow, the teams were already full, or other ridiculous excuses that meant classmates did not want them to play. Then, in September, I asked students and teachers to complete a 3-minute journal to the prompt, "Recess is. . . ." Students completed the journal with comments like "not fun because there is no playground equipment"; "sometimes fun but I want to play on the playground equipment"; and "sad we can't play on the playground."

Putting the Plan Together

In the original recess meeting, I explained the idea of game clinics where each week I would introduce a game that anyone of any ability could play. I would always let anyone play no matter what, and I would play too. It took about a week to get game clinics really going and we tried a few tag games outdoors at first. We played games like "Race Track Tag," which was a hot, sweaty, nonstop running game. Rosy cheeks, time-outs, and the August sun wore us all out.

About 2 weeks into school we decided to play kickball. All were welcome, all ages wanted to play, teams were easy to pick, we could run hard, and play could continue the entire hour. Instantly, I had from 25 to 50 players with me at any given time.

How Well Did It Work?

It didn't take long for game clinics to be a positive thing for many students. The kids were very responsive to game clinics and, when I repeated the 3-minute journal in November, they mostly responded to my "Recess is . . . " prompt with comments like "fun," "awesome," "cool." Seventy-three percent of kids felt like they "almost always" have fun with their friends at recess. They enjoyed having something to do.

Kids appreciated having someone there and because of the adult participation, there was no fighting or people playing unfairly. Interestingly, one survey I conducted found that 65% of kids admitted that they only follow the game rules when they are being watched.

The other recess supervisors felt the game clinics made recess better because students had a safe place to play without worrying about being excluded or if the game was being played fairly. It also made their jobs easier because a few game clinics participants were students they tried to keep their eyes on.

Summary

Game clinics are a very positive thing for students' recesses. More work is needed to plan and prepare for the recess classroom, and more responsibility is needed on the part of the students to stand up and make sure that recess is a fun experience for everyone. Recess supervision needs to increase as well as adult participation in the activity. So many behaviors, so little time.

CHAPTER 3

Relationship Characteristics of Resilient Classrooms

The relationships that characterize resilient classrooms include teacher–student relationships, or the degree to which students feel supported, respected, and valued by their teacher; peer relationships, or the degree to which students have effective and mutually satisfying relationships with classmates; and home–school relationships, or the degree to which parents and children communicate about and reinforce the work of the classroom. Caring relationships with teachers, family engagement with schooling, and the availability of socially competent peers can serve as protective influences when these factors are embedded within schools and classrooms (Baker, 2006; NRC/IOM, 2004). This chapter describes the mechanisms by which these relationships support learning and mental health, the classroom practices and activities that foster effective relationships in classrooms, and classroom examples of the relationships' positive impact. Additional information about strategies to strengthen the relationship characteristics of classrooms are described in Chapter 8 together with a strategy sheet for each characteristic that lists brief strategies and evidence-based interventions.

TEACHER–STUDENT RELATIONSHIPS

Watch a 13-month-old boy putting blocks atop one another. His enthusiasm will grow stronger with every attempt, successful or not. His glee and determination to master block stacking will be almost palpable. In some homes, his parents will warmly praise each of his attempts while giving him repeated congratulatory "high fives." Such parental encouragement is supporting the development of a competent child. If this child is raised in a family in which parental support is absent, the child may be on a very different life path toward self-doubt, underachievement, and discouragement. Likewise, teachers encourage their students along the path to academic and social competence by providing strong emotional support, especially in the early school years (Bergin & Bergin, 2009; Curby, Rimm-Kaufman, & Ponitz, 2009; Wentzel, 2009). When teacher support and caring is less frequent, or not clearly evident to students, it is easier for children to falter. "Of all the various school relationships that students are part of, teacher–student relationships are the most influential for students' academic success" (Doll et al., 2009, p. 216).

How Do Effective Teacher–Student Relationships Support Student Success?

Just as sensitive parenting promotes a child's sense of security and competence, effective teacher–student relationships, and children's attachment to the classroom, promote engagement, confidence, and school success (Bergin & Bergin, 2009; Pianta, 1999; Rudasill et al., 2010). Children who have secure attachments to their parents arrive at school prepared to interact comfortably with teachers. They have internalized the values and beliefs that their parents hold about the world and about them, and these beliefs, in turn, influence the students' school adaptation and their cognitive and emotional capacity to learn in the classroom. Multiple studies have shown that, regardless of ethnicity, gender, socioeconomic status, and intellectual level, the quality of parent–child interactions in kindergarten was positively associated with high school graduation and, in some instances, grade point average (Gregory & Rimm-Kaufman, 2008; Jimerson, Egeland, Sroufe, & Carlson, 2000).

Students who feel valued by their teachers similarly internalize the values and goals that the teachers hold for them (Bergin & Bergin, 2009; Wentzel, 2009). Learning is more important to students when their learning is important to a teacher they care about, and they will participate more and work harder when they feel supported and trusted by their teacher (Frisby & Martin, 2010; NRC/IOM, 2004; Werner, 2013). Once students' engagement and motivation are enhanced, they can benefit from the carefully constructed curriculum that teachers provide. In the same way that parental applause can be reason enough for a child to persist at stacking blocks, a teacher's sensitive responses can motivate students to plug away at a challenging assignment. Students' attachment in the classroom, fostered by high-quality teacher–student interactions, is associated with higher achievement, emotional competence, and persistence to tasks. This is especially true for alienated, isolated, and at-risk students (Bergin & Bergin; 2009; NRC/IOM, 2004).

> **Learning is more important to students when their learning is important to a teacher they care about.**

Although the bulk of research on the significance of teacher–student relationships has focused on the elementary grades, supportive relationships are also critical when students transition to middle school (Juvonen, 2007; Suldo et al., 2009; Wentzel, 2009). Consistency, predictability, clarity of communication, and structure are important underpinnings of students' sense of security in the classroom; alternatively, the transition to middle school and later to high school, introduces uncertainty and some anxiety for many students. This uncertainty can undermine, at least temporarily, the students' sense of connectedness to the school and classroom—especially in very large schools. While teacher–student relationships grow tenuous during adolescence, their decline in quality during the middle school years is not inevitable (Wentzel, 2009). Middle school students perceive teachers to be supportive when they demonstrate fairness, connect with students on an emotional level, and foster a safe classroom environment in which questions and discussion are encouraged (Suldo et al., 2009). Subsequently, high school students who report feeling connected to their school and their teachers are more likely to achieve better grades and to complete high school (NRC/ IOM, 2004). Sadly, in one report on a very diverse sample of high school dropouts, only 56% of the students said they could talk with a school staff member about school problems and just 41% had someone in school to talk to about personal problems (Bridgeland, DiIulio, & Morison, 2006). Many of these students reported that their best days in school were when teachers paid attention to them. By strengthening the quality and frequency of their interactions with students, middle and high school teachers and support staff can help students transition successfully into secondary schools while retaining their sense of security and connectedness.

What Are Classroom Routines and Practices That Strengthen Teacher–Student Relationships?

A very simple rule of thumb is that strong and supportive relationships emerge out of time spent together in enjoyable activities. Thus, teacher–student relationships are strengthened by activities that increase the amount and enjoyability of time that teachers spend with their students (Hamre & Pianta, 2005; Pianta, 1999). Consistent with this very pragmatic rule, teachers can create an ethos of caring in the classroom by engaging in ongoing, frequent conversations with their students. Students report that caring teachers are those who talk with them, listen to their concerns, help them with their work, and communicate fairness and nurturance. These teachers share their own experiences, and their stories instill a sense of confidence in their students. They show interest in the students' daily lives and know about their achievements and disappointments. They create a classroom environment "in which students can see that their learning, their opinions, and their concerns are taken seriously" (Developmental Studies Center, 1996, p. 3). Caring is conveyed through comments that are encouraging, provide constructive feedback, and describe the teacher's high expectations for students (Wentzel, 2009). For a large number of children, a caring, reliable teacher may provide an essential experience with an adult who thinks about them, helps them make sense of confusing thoughts and feelings, and provides them a sense of being understood. For some children, this may become the building block of learning to trust another person—and themselves (Riley, 2011). Students become attached to teachers who remind them of the collective experiences that they have shared and who tell students that they think of them often. In effective classroom communities, students' talking with supportive teachers becomes the "currency of caring" (Noblit, Dwight, & McCadden, 1995). Through a process of frequent, reflective discussions (rather than nonreflective discipline) the classroom can become a place of comfort and security (Developmental Studies Center, 1996).

Teachers' sensitive responses to student-initiated conversations are also influential in determining classroom adjustment (Brooks & Goldstein, 2007; Pianta & Walsh, 1996). It is not always possible for teachers to set aside their other responsibilities when students come to them with important comments or questions, but it is possible for teachers to reliably respond even if that response is sometimes postponed. Faber and Mazlish (1995) suggest alternative ways to respond to students' comments so that they leave the conversation knowing that the teacher has understood their concerns and has appreciated their competence. Applying basic lessons of active listening to teaching, they recommend reflecting the students' comments, validating the students' experience, avoiding blame or criticism, and helping the students make a plan rather than suggesting solutions. The pragmatics of these conversations are also important. Students will be more open in conversations where there is comfortable eye contact and they are sitting on a level with the teacher. Some teachers use a personal moment board on which students can sign up for a 5-minute chat with the teacher. Students may discuss whatever they choose during this private time and may be more likely to share personal information in these one-on-one conversations. These opportunities show students that the things they say and experience are important to their teacher.

The most essential ingredient in forging a safe, supportive classroom environment will always be the quality and consistency of the teacher's sensitive rapport with students (Wentzel, 2009). For children who have experienced earlier rejection from other adults, it is especially important that teachers avoid repeating these rejection experiences—a difficult task for teachers who are simultaneously struggling with ever-increasing achievement standards or with challenging or disruptive behaviors from other students in the class. Important first steps in establishing rapport are knowing the students and helping the students know one another. Familiarity can be strengthened through opportunities for students to bring in pictures, trophies, or other personal possessions and talk about the importance these personally hold for them. These kinds of activities will be especially important in helping many students feel safe enough to take risks with subsequent classroom work or with classmates on the playground.

Weekly classroom meetings are another way of helping students and teachers get to know each other and contribute to the environment of the classroom. Classroom meetings are highly versatile and can be adapted to classroom planning or decision making, problem solving of social or academic difficulties, or simply checking in with the class about what the students are learning or how they are behaving. Frequent classroom meetings can foster connections between the students and the teacher and create the expectation that the class will routinely solve its problems in cooperative and mutually satisfying ways.

Cultural differences between teachers and students can also affect their relationship with one another, and attention must be paid to cultural values and expectations when strengthening the quality of teacher–student interactions. Latino students, for example, are an ever-increasing presence in our educational system and are the fastest growing ethnic group in the United States (U.S. Bureau of the Census, 2004), while teachers of underrepresented minority groups comprise only 16.5% of public school teachers (Ingersoll & May, 2011). Fortunately, the deleterious effects of cultural differences between teachers and students appear to diminish over the course of one or more school

Attention must be paid to cultural values and expectations when strengthening the quality of teacher–student interactions.

years, suggesting that teachers may be wise to withhold early judgment regarding these students' social competence until a period of adaptation has occurred and the teachers become more familiar with the student. The gaps in student achievement become much smaller when minority students perceive that their teachers care about them, trust them, want to help them, and expect and encourage them to meet high academic standards (Hughes & Kwok, 2007).

Not surprisingly, the microstrategies for improving teacher–student relationships (displayed in Figure 8.2, Chapter 8, p. 101) emphasize the creation of moments or opportunities for interaction that are both meaningful and enjoyable. Then, the evidence-based interventions described in Figure 8.2 build on this principle in more systematic ways.

A Classroom Illustration

Mr. G was a seventh-grade teacher in a rural school district. His students were primarily Latino, and the majority came from families that were struggling financially. The standardized test scores in the school were well below the state norm, and the school had been placed on notice that test scores needed to improve. While this might cause some teachers to restrict their focus to academic content, Mr. G believed that the quality of his relationships with students needed to be his top priority. He held regular classroom meetings to discuss the quality of daily life in the classroom. He collected anonymous classroom surveys from his students to describe their collective views on the classroom relationships. The surveys suggested that Mr. G's rapport with his students was exceptionally strong. Students believed that Mr. G would always find a way to help them learn even the most difficult material. When asked what made Mr. G's class their favorite, they explained, "It's the teacher who makes the class, not the material he presents"; "The teacher sets the tone for the class and how the kids behave—that's why we work quietly in here but not in other classes"; "With teachers who have no control, we wind up teasing and not sticking up for each other"; "The kids' level of excitement is based on the level of excitement of the teacher"; "He checks in with each group individually—he doesn't just give us answers, he helps us figure it out"; "Mr. G listens to us—if we don't get it, we have a class discussion about it"; "He doesn't treat us like kids—he doesn't insult us—he listens to us"; "This is not a class, it's a democracy!" For these students, the influence of the classroom relationships on behavior was pronounced. Their social behavior and their academic engagement were far more positive in this favorite class than in their other classes.

PEER RELATIONSHIPS

Students' relationships with classroom peers are highly predictive of their academic and social engagement in the classroom and academic achievement (Doll & Brehm, 2010; Ladd, Herald-Brown, & Kochel, 2009; Pellegrini, 2005). Effective peer relationships create a social context in the classroom that prompts students to actively participate in learning activities, maintain interest in academic tasks, develop social competence, and be successful in learning (Malecki & Elliott, 2002; Wentzel, 2009; Wentzel, Barry, & Caldwell, 2007).

How Do Effective Peer Relationships Support Student Success?

In resilient classrooms, there are norms and rules for how students interact with one another so that they have comfortable friendships and resolve conflicts efficiently and satisfactorily. These norms and rules emerge out of the shared expectations of all students and adults who work in the classroom. This creates a social context in which students value and pursue the classroom's shared social and academic goals (Doll & Brehm, 2010; Juvonen, 2007; Wentzel et al., 2007). When students feel like important members of their classes, they become more thoroughly engaged in the classroom's social and academic activities and learning is enhanced. It is not always possible to measure the quality of these relationships through objective observations or assessments. However, student ratings are powerful measures of peer relationships because it is relationships' perceived quality, from the students' perspective, that fosters an important sense of well-being and social relatedness (Doll & Brehm, 2010).

> **In resilient classrooms, there are norms and rules for how students interact with one another so that they have comfortable friendships and resolve conflicts efficiently and satisfactorily.**

Prosocial behaviors such as sharing, helping, and cooperating are essential to these norms because they provide the foundation for such crucial academic processes as problem solving and academic motivation (Wentzel & Watkins, 2002). Whereas interventions that foster prosocial behaviors in the classroom frequently lead to improvements in academic performance, interventions designed to improve academic achievement have not always shown corresponding increases in prosocial classroom behaviors. The relationship is bidirectional, but some early evidence suggests that the influence of prosocial behavior on achievement is far stronger than the influence of achievement on peer relationships (Wentzel, 1993, 2009).

Still, effective peer relationships are much more than a collection of prosocial behaviors. In resilient classrooms, all students are included in multiple peer friendships with their classmates, and these students eat lunch together, go to recess together, and spend time together during any unstructured classroom moments (Buhs & Ladd, 2001; Doll & Brehm, 2010). These mutual peer friendships emerge from having fun doing things together and are maintained when students have frequent enjoyable interactions with their friends. In addition to caring for and sharing with one another, friends routinely joke around, tease each other, call each other names, play fight, and push and shove—jostling behaviors that mimic peer aggression but have very different intentions within the trust and intimacy of friendships (Pellegrini, 2005).

Having friends gives students many social, academic, and cognitive advantages, such as increasing students' social standing in a group, reducing their vulnerability to social aggression, and providing a buffer against minor social stresses (Pellegrini & Blatchford, 2000). When they are accompanied by friends, students are better prepared to cope with challenging circumstances, like moving to a new class or school. Academically, friends can serve as tutors for one another and can solve difficult problems together (Wentzel, 2009). Cognitively, they can extend one another's understanding through conversations and shared attempts to master new information. Perhaps most important, friends are the tether that binds students to schools: the opportunity to make friends and be with friends is the aspect of school that students value most highly (NRC/IOM, 2004). Friendships can also compensate when adolescents have low levels of family cohesion (Juvonen, 2007). In this case, close and supportive friendships strengthen the adolescent's self-worth and social competence equal to their peers who come from cohesive families. Peer relationships can also be a source of distress and distraction for students. When conflicts occur within the classroom, these can interrupt friendships and interfere with learning activities and classroom routines (Pellegrini, 2005). It is quite common for students to experience normal peer conflict with classmates and friends—such as arguing and teasing. When such conflict goes unresolved, this can lead to disengagement in classroom activities and (when conflict is chronic and sustained) dropping out of school altogether (Doll & Brehm, 2010).

Bullying is a special case of peer aggression that occurs repeatedly, that is intended to hurt or coerce, and and that targets students who are weaker than the bullying students and less able to defend themselves against the aggression (Swearer & Espelage, 2011). Adults' consciousness about childhood bullying has been raised dramatically in the past few decades in the aftermath of tragic childhood injuries or deaths. Thirty-five states have passed laws that require schools to put anti-bullying programs in place (High, 2008). Reported rates of student involvement in bullying in school range from 30 to 60%, and rates differ dramatically depending on how these are assessed (Sharkey, Furlong, & Yetter, 2006). There is some evidence that bullying is worst in middle school, with 42.9% of students in sixth grade reporting being bullied (Pellegrini, 2002). Recent research suggests that African American and Latino students feel safer from bullying when their schools and classrooms are ethnically diverse than in settings in which they are striking ethnic minorities (Juvonen, Nishina, & Graham, 2006).

What Are Classroom Routines and Practices That Strengthen Peer Relationships?

Teachers can organize students' social interactions in classrooms so that social–developmental tasks are within the students' zone of proximal development (Pianta, 1999). For example, early elementary students are usually able to work in pairs but late elementary students can often work in slightly larger groups of four. Older students are better able to work together despite widely disparate skill levels, whereas younger students can struggle when asked to work cooperatively with students who are too different in ability from themselves. Groups can be carefully composed so that they include some students with strong leadership abilities, others with effective conflict resolution skills, and still others capable of explaining the assigned task. In most cases, students will need explicit training in how to work collaboratively as a group, help their partners, explain their work to each other, and engage all group members in the task (Wentzel & Watkins, 2002).

Classroom practices can also promote prosocial behaviors by encouraging students to share resources, work constructively together, and solve problems in a positive and productive manner (Koplow, 2002). For example, in a fourth-grade classroom, a classroom meeting to discuss frequent playground arguments prompted the students to write a comprehensive set of soccer rules for their noontime game. Chapter 5 describes a classroom where students reduced the intimidation on their playground through a program to welcome new students into their class. In both cases, classroom conflicts were significantly reduced once students proposed and implemented solutions that their teacher had not anticipated. Prosocial behaviors emerge and conflicts are diminished in classrooms where there are open discussions of students' ongoing activities, problems, and celebrations (Doll, 1996; Doll & Brehm, 2010). In addition to providing valuable practice in social problem solving, classroom meetings about peer conflicts also make the varying viewpoints of classmates explicit and so provide students with direct instruction in perspective taking and empathy.

Classroom routines can also facilitate peer friendships, but it is not necessary to directly manage classmates' personal relationships with each other. Instead, practices can be embedded into the daily routines and rituals of classrooms that will support students' peer relationships without being overly prescriptive (Doll & Brehm, 2010). Simply put, friendships emerge from frequent opportunities to have fun working and playing together. Incidental activities are as effective or more effective in fostering friendships as are activities with the immediate purpose of teaching social skills. For example, a fifth grader who was new to her school volunteered for cafeteria cleanup because students were always assigned in pairs, and it gave her an opportunity to work with a potential friend. Children's opportunities for classroom friendships expand geometrically if their working groups are periodically rearranged so that they have a chance to work with less familiar classmates as well as those whom they know well.

Friendships emerge from frequent opportunities to have fun working and playing together.

Strengthening playground settings can be another important first step toward fostering students' social success and ultimately their social competence (Doll & Brehm, 2010). Effective playgrounds are those on which all students have friends to play with, can cope successfully with the occasional fight or argument, and feel safe from bullying or intimidation. Playgrounds are unique settings in many respects. They are almost always large settings, larger than most students' yards or indoor classrooms or gymnasiums, and their size allows students to run, tumble, and jump faster, farther, and for longer periods than in most other play settings. On most playgrounds, adult supervisors are fewer and farther away and supervision is less constant than in classrooms, youth clubs, or after-school day care centers (Pellegrini & Blatchford, 2000). As a result, the playground at recess is "one of the very few places in school where there is minimal adult direction, where students can interact with each other on their own terms" (Pellegrini & Blatchford, 2000, p. 21). Students' interactions will be more competent when the playground is carefully designed for safety and enjoyability, there are ample developmentally appropriate games, and the adult supervisors promote positive play as well as monitor peer aggression (Doll & Brehm, 2010). Boring playgrounds can perpetuate conflicts within peer groups. A sixth grader explained, "If there's not enough to do, fighting is a lot more fun than doing nothing."

Interventions to promote positive peer relationships will be most effective when applied within the classroom and playground environment where students live and learn rather than through traditional pullout services to promote social competence (Doll & Brehm, 2010). Children's empathy, their orientation toward interpersonal relationships, and their ability to regulate behavior are processes that develop over time in the context of frequent and satisfying interactions with peers. Within natural classroom groups, higher achieving or more socially competent classmates can be taught to coach less skilled classmates and engage them in strategic problem-solving behavior (Wentzel & Watkins, 2002).

Students who are less socially adept can also benefit from opportunities to work or play together in pairs or very small groups with their more competent classmates. Many students have a difficult time negotiating work or play within large groups of students. Mixing in large groups is especially difficult when there are unfamiliar students from other classes, as occurs in the lunchroom and on the playground. Large groups prompt greater anxiety in students who are prone to self-isolate, making it more difficult for them to initiate interactions with classmates or secure invitations to play. Timid students are easily overlooked within the chaos and disorganization of larger peer groups. Teachers who acknowledge and discuss these challenges with students can normalize the feelings of withdrawn students, raise their classmates' awareness of their feelings, and prompt their classmates to take the first step to include them more often. "Schools need to examine ways to reengineer the social opportunities available to students so that the task of adjusting to peers is less onerous and more possible for a broader group of students" (Doll, 1996, p. 177).

The complexity of interventions in peer relationships is captured in the lengthy, categorized list of mini-strategies presented in Figure 8.3 (Chapter 8, p. 103). While strategies promoting peer friendships emphasize multiple opportunities for students to interact and play together, those related to peer conflict emphasize engineering settings to remove common frustrations or coaching students in advance (or just in time) in resolving peer conflicts. Because peer relationships are a prominent concern of adults in schools, there are multiple evidence-based curricula that prepare students to manage conflict in their relationships. Uniform across all of these curricula, emphasis is placed on promoting positive interactions together with reducing negative interactions.

A Classroom Illustration

A fifth-grade teacher was worried about her students' verbal aggression in the classroom and physical aggression on the playground. Through anonymous student surveys, she learned that the students thought the disagreements were caused by the very competitive soccer game played during each lunchtime recess. They explained that if they didn't play soccer, there would be nothing else to do. As an alternative, the school psychologist offered to teach the students noncompetitive games that they could play at recess. The class planned a Frisbee course using existing playground equipment and "soft" Frisbees. They tackled group problem-solving skills using hula hoop games. In the classroom, similar games were used as an appropriate reward for productive academic work. The teacher also held postrecess classroom meetings to discuss that day's play and students' efforts to be more cooperative. Six weeks later, the surveys were readministered and showed that the number of arguments and fights had decreased considerably.

HOME–SCHOOL RELATIONSHIPS

Contextual influences on students' learning and behavior extend beyond the classroom to include the home–school relationship. In the same way that the classroom context can influence the quality of communication that occurs among students and teachers, the classroom context can influence effective partnerships with families that support their attachment to their children's school, classroom, and teachers. Ongoing, reciprocal school–family communication and collaboration will ensure adequate learning and behavioral supports for students' academic and social success. While families and educators may have differing goals for, expectations of, and patterns of communication with their students, these differences do not necessarily disrupt family–school partnerships. Instead, when both families and schools recognize and address these differences while still engaging in ongoing and respectful communication, students' two most critical support systems operate in symmetry with each other (Christenson et al., 2008; NASP, 2012).

How Do Effective Home–School Relationships Support Student Success?

Families' academic orientation and instructional practices exert substantial influence on students' academic, social, and behavioral competence—especially when students' learning is supported by high-quality home–school interactions over a sustained period of time (Christenson et al., 2008; Grolnick et al., 2009; Pianta & Walsh, 1996). When these interactions are sufficiently frequent and relevant, families and schools develop shared understanding of students' needs that allows them to convey congruent messages to children about learning and school. Families can dramatically influence the degree to which children become engaged in school and can facilitate their identification of themselves as learners. Substantial evidence suggests that strong family–school partnerships will improve both academic and behavioral outcomes for children (Buerkle et al., 2009). Indeed, "academic and motivational home support for learning has a stronger impact on students' development and school success than demographic characteristics such as income level" (Christenson et al., 2008, p. 71).

> **Families can dramatically influence the degree to which children become engaged in school and can facilitate their identification of themselves as learners.**

Students' beliefs and expectations about academic achievement are highly influenced by parental and teacher beliefs about the value of education and their expectations for the child's success (Grolnick et al., 2009). Children from different families show enormous variability in the skills, attitudes, values, and resources that they bring to school. Some students come to school from families in which the educational values and expectations are quite consistent with the school. Others do not. Some students come from families that have many rich and varied resources to support learning. Others do not. While this variability presents unique challenges for schools, it is important to disentangle what parents do from what parents have. It is what parents and schools do that matters most for students' learning and social competence (NASP, 2012; NRC/IOM, 2004). Resilient schools take the lead role in providing opportunities for collaboration between parents and the school and in sustaining these collaborative efforts over time. They allocate sufficient resources for families and educators to fulfill and maintain their collaborative partnerships (NASP, 2012). Sustained collaboration has multiple benefits for students. When effective partnerships exist between schools and families, students hold more positive attitudes about school and learning, are more likely to behave well and complete their homework, show higher achievement levels, and are less likely to be identified for special education placement (Doll et al., 2009; NASP, 2012). The converse is also true. Students who experience significant discontinuity among their home, peer, and school worlds are most at risk for poor school performance and emotional problems (Pianta & Walsh, 1996). One key to effective home–school partnerships is keeping parents informed. Surveys have shown that parents want and need more information from their children's schools than is typically sent home (Christenson et al., 2008). Therefore, effective home–school partnerships are more likely when schools keep parents informed of policies, practices, expectations, and their shared responsibility for students' school success (NASP, 2012).

Students learn best when families and classrooms hold high expectations for effort, behavior, and desired performance; clearly describe the rules and guidelines for school-related tasks; demonstrate their support for and interest in the student; and model consistency in directions, problem solving, and goal setting (Grolnick et al., 2009; NASP, 2012). When these practices are present in both home and school, students internalize the education-enhancing values held by parents and teachers and their achievement rises (Bergin & Bergin, 2009; Wentzel, 2009). As home and school efforts become more connected, their influence on a student's success is enhanced. Students gain a sense of belongingness or membership in a learning community that, in turn, is associated with positive attitudes toward school and active participation in the learning activities of the classroom (Osterman, 2000).

What Are Classroom Routines and Practices That Strengthen Home–School Relationships?

Strategies for promoting effective home–school relationships often go beyond the scope of an individual classroom to include schoolwide or districtwide programs (e.g., Christenson & Godber, 2001; Christenson & Sheridan, 2001; Christenson et al., 2008). While these should be a top priority, our goal in this section is to detail practices that teachers can use to raise parental involvement in their own classrooms.

Parental involvement at home and parental involvement at school are not equally important to children's learning. Student achievement is influenced more by what parents do to support their children's schooling in the home than by what they do inside the school building (Grolnick et al., 2009). Frequent student–parent conversations about school provide an indirect gauge of parents' engagement in their children's education and suggest that education is integrated into the life of the family. Teachers can facilitate this integration by initiating and maintaining open lines of communication with the family. Parents are more highly and consistently involved when they believe that their participation is directly related to the achievement of their students (Finn, 1998).

A good place to start is informing parents about effective, complementary home-based practices that support their children's work in the classroom. Research reports about parental practices that raise achievement can be reframed as classroom tips in newsletters, phone calls, or personal notes sent to parents in students' homework folders. These can let parents know how important it is for them to convey high expectations, set firm but reasonable standards around effort and performance, and enforce rules around homework routines. In bilingual or low-income communities, parents do not always understand how to do the work that their children bring home from the classroom, and sometimes they believe that they cannot help their children with homework. However, parents can advocate for their students by reassuring and encouraging them, and by cultivating their children's diligence and persistence in the face of challenges (Bempechat, Graham, & Jimenez, 1999). Since families come in many shapes and sizes, and have varying beliefs, expectations, and communication styles, schools need to provide training and support for teachers who are working to partner with families from diverse cultural backgrounds. Students from diverse families will experience the most success when their teachers encourage understanding among various cultures and celebrate many different family forms, cultures, ethnicities, and linguistic backgrounds (NASP, 2012). In one recent study (Kyriakides, 2005), almost 86% of parents felt that being more involved in their child's school helped them learn more about their child. The involved parents were more confident in assisting their children at home while using teaching methods they observed in the classroom.

Students can share responsibility for fostering more communication with their parents about school. For example, students can be assigned to interview their parents and report back on their parents' knowledge of the daily routines and practices of the classroom. They can use their parents as "experts" who they consult when researching classroom topics. In a unit on relationships between the United States and the Middle East, some students could interview their parents who served in the military in the Middle East, while others could interview family members who were displaced into refugee camps. Students might gather their parents' suggestions for modifying classroom practices so that they are more family friendly or better support student learning. Parents might have ideas about the schedule of classroom assignments, the amount of homework support that parents should provide, or what the classroom can do to help parents help from home.

Classroom teachers' efforts to involve parents will not be successful unless such efforts are mutual. In the same way that schools recommend that parents do certain things with their children, parents should have opportunities to make recommendations to the classroom (NASP, 2012). Traditionally, teachers have asked parents to help by supervising field trips, holding bake sales, copying classroom materials, or filing library cards. Instead, the Parent–Teacher Association (PTA) Quality Indicators suggest that parents be asked for recommendations about course offerings, student course schedules and class placement, optional enrichment programs that the school may develop, or the quality of their children's schoolwork (National Parent–Teacher Association, 1997). The contrast between these lists is striking. The first list incorporates a number of menial tasks that do not respect or use the talents that parents frequently have. The second list includes the parents as full partners in planning, delivering, and evaluating their child's education. Most parents are not accustomed to being asked for these kinds of recommendations, and so teachers will need to actively solicit meaningful parental inputs (Christenson & Sheridan, 2001). This will require that classrooms be welcoming, use a variety of communication strategies to reach all parents, adjust communications to different languages and cultural expectations, and—above all—be responsive to parental recommendations once they are made.

The most successful efforts to encourage parental involvement in the classroom are convenient for families, clearly relevant to school success, and emphasize honest, respectful, collaborative interactions with families (Buerkle et al., 2009; Grolnick et al., 2009; Machen, Wilson, & Notar, 2005; NASP, 2012). Classroom efforts to initiate these interactions are especially critical among low-income families in which students' academic achievement is highly dependent upon parental interest, support, and encouragement (Patrikakou & Weissberg, 2000; NRC/IOM, 2004; Peña, 2000).

Communication underlies every microstrategy in Figure 8.4 (Chapter 8, p. 108) to enhance home-school relationships. Effective communication is two-way communication, requiring that classrooms both communicate with and listen to families. The evidence-based interventions listed in Figure 8.4 take this communication a step further by engaging schools and families in shared problem solving or training that addresses the students' needs.

A Classroom Illustration

In a third-grade classroom, most students were from Spanish-speaking families, and their parents' limited English made it difficult for them to help with schoolwork. The teacher, the school psychologist, and the students brainstormed solutions to this dilemma and decided to show the parents how they could help. The teacher sent a letter home to parents in English and Spanish asking for permission to videotape the teacher and their child working together on typical homework problems. This solution alone generated more parent communication than before. The videotape was crafted so that every student in the classroom was shown for a brief segment being helped by the teacher. In this way, parents had an opportunity to "meet" their child's classmates and gain a mental picture of the classroom. The parents also had a chance to see an effective teacher in action and to gain more confidence about what they could do to help their child. Students reported that they had to translate much of the dialogue on the videotape and that this task prompted additional discussions about classroom practices and the nature of assignments.

SUMMARY

In this chapter we have provided a more complete description of the mechanisms by which effective classroom relationships promote students' academic and social success. For purposes of clarity, we have described the three relational characteristics of resilient classrooms in separate sections, but this separation does not sufficiently acknowledge the potentiating influences that occur when these relationships are considered in unison. For example, the quality of teacher–student relationships can influence students' social competencies and so contribute to the peer relations in a classroom and to students' academic and social risk taking. Alternatively, when parents respect their students' teachers and reinforce the teachers' rules and recommendations, students are likely to form more comfortable teacher–student relationships. All three kinds of relationships contribute to the classroom's social context for learning, fostering an environment that is emotionally comfortable, encourages risk taking, and provides the student with a sense of being valued and respected. Relational factors can also impact students' academic success by setting the stage for the autonomy-promoting characteristics. These are discussed more fully in Chapter 4. More extensive discussion of relationship-enhancing strategies are described in Chapter 8.

INTRODUCTION TO A CASE STUDY OF CLASSROOM RELATIONSHIPS

In the case study immediately following this chapter, Laura Monahon describes an art teacher's work to create a meaningful relationship with her students. By gathering students' perceptions, paying attention to students' insights, and altering classroom routines, the teacher was able to create a learning environment that strengthened students' success in the classroom. Notice how important it was that the teacher had "post" data that made the changes in the classroom clearly evident.

CASE STUDY

The New Art Teacher

Laura Monahon
Philadelphia College of Osteopathic Medicine

The Problem

Ms. P was a first-year teacher assigned to teach Basic Art to seventh- and eighth-grade students in a middle school setting. Her class sizes were large by the standards of the school district; some classes had as many as 35 students enrolled. Ms. P was especially concerned with her fourth-period Basic Art class. The class comprised 35 seventh graders and, as Ms. P described, "things have been headed downhill [since the beginning of the school year]" in terms of student behavior and productivity levels. Ms. P also indicated that she felt that she was "just not reaching" the students in a meaningful way. Ms. P and the school psychologist talked about the problem with the students during one 42-minute Basic Art class. They asked the students to help them gather data about their perceptions of the teacher–student relationships in fourth-period Basic Art. Once the responses were gathered,

Ms. P and the school psychologist teamed up with the music teacher (a seasoned teacher who was mentoring Ms. P and who also taught the same group of students during another class period) and studied the data to determine ways to enhance the teacher–student relationships in the class.

The ClassMaps Results

Students began by completing the anonymous ClassMaps Survey. An overhead projector was used to read each item to the students. Results from the My Teacher subscale showed that 46% of students in Ms. P's fourth-period Basic Art class felt that they were not listened to carefully in class.

The Teacher's Sense

Looking carefully at the data shown in Figure 3.1, the team (the two teachers and the school psychologist) noted that the area of primary significance to the students was that Ms. P was not listening carefully to them when they spoke in class. Ms. P agreed that she felt pressure to "deliver the lesson" and often asked students to "hold their questions" until the end of the lesson. However, when Ms. P checked back with students after the lesson to address their questions or concerns, students would make statements such as "Oh, I forgot" and "I figured it out already." The problem-solving team began investigating Ms. P's lesson plans to determine if there was a way to adapt the lessons to accommodate student input on an ongoing basis throughout the class period.

Results of the Classroom Meeting

Next, Ms. P and the school psychologist shared the ClassMaps Survey data with the students during a class meeting. The students were initially hesitant to agree that the data were accurate, likely

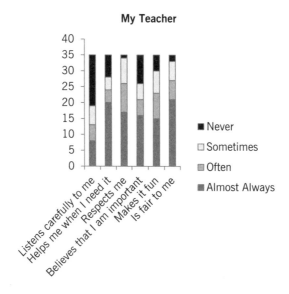

FIGURE 3.1. ClassMaps Survey preintervention graph for Ms. P's seventh-grade Basic Art class.

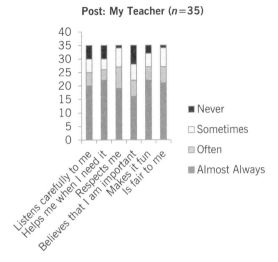

FIGURE 3.2. ClassMaps Survey postintervention graph for Ms. P's seventh-grade Basic Art class.

out of concern for Ms. P's feelings. However, once Ms. P established that she was eager to change and interested in their input, students indicated that the data regarding the Basic Art class were accurate.

Plan for Change

The students suggested that it would be helpful for Ms. P to reduce the number of projects the students were expected to complete to one project per week. This was suggested as a minimum number, and students volunteered that additional projects could be completed by those who worked at a faster pace than their classmates. The students and Ms. P determined that the entire class period each Monday would be devoted to Ms. P's direct instruction of the technique and explanation of the project for the week. The remaining four class periods of each week would be devoted to hands-on exploration of the techniques through the projects. During this time, Ms. P would be available to answer questions, provide additional insight and, if needed, review points from Monday's lesson. They decided that the My Teacher subscale would be readministered after the plan for change had been implemented for 2 full weeks.

Results

Results of the second administration of the My Teacher subscale show that there were significant increases in the number of students who felt that Ms. P was listening to them when they spoke in class (see Figure 3.2). Interestingly, the number of students who indicated that Ms. P made the Basic Art class fun also increased. Anecdotal input provided by Ms. P indicated that, once she adopted the weekly schedule, she felt less pressure to "deliver the lesson" every day. She indicated that this allowed her to "enjoy the students in their process [of creating art]" and "generally made the classroom a more pleasant place."

CHAPTER 4

Autonomy-Promoting Characteristics of Resilient Classrooms

Resilient classrooms help students feel competent to meet academic challenges (academic efficacy), take responsibility for their learning (academic self-determination), and manage their own behavior (behavioral self-control). This chapter describes the mechanisms by which academic efficacy, academic self-determination, and behavioral self-control support students' success; the classroom activities and practices that promote student autonomy; and classroom examples of each characteristic's positive impact. Additional information about strategies to strengthen the autonomy-promoting characteristics of classrooms are described in Chapter 8, together with a strategy sheet for each characteristic that lists brief strategies and evidence-based interventions.

ACADEMIC EFFICACY

Resilient classrooms improve student achievement by strengthening students' beliefs that they can succeed. Students' collective beliefs about their ability to succeed in school are called academic efficacy. Academic efficacy is a primary motivator of their efforts, interest, and aspirations for learning. It gives them the confidence to take risks needed for learning. These efficacy beliefs come both from within the student and from external sources, such as an anticipated reward or the praise of a well-liked teacher. Consequently, it is disturbing that students' perception of their academic capability declines precipitously across their school career. Kindergarten children enter school with highly positive views of their abilities. By third grade, however, students begin to significantly underestimate their abilities, and by middle school this decline is dramatic (Paris, Byrnes, & Paris, 2001).

> Academic efficacy is a primary motivator of students' efforts, interest, and aspirations for learning.

Four types of efficacy are important for learning (Schunk & Pajares, 2009). Self-efficacy for performance concerns students' expectations that they will successfully achieve their desired outcome. Self-efficacy for learning reflects students' perception that they either have or can learn the skills they need to accomplish a particular task. Classrooms have collective efficacy when a group of students believes that they are able to perform assigned tasks. Teachers also demonstrate efficacy when they individually, and collectively as a faculty, believe in their ability to be effective in their teaching. The task for educators is to create resilient classrooms that offer support for all of these forms of academic efficacy.

How Does Academic Efficacy Support Student Success?

Students' interest in an academic task and the importance they assign to it can engage them in initial attempts to learn it, somewhat like a "starter" for a car. In contrast, efficacy beliefs "steer" their actual performance by focusing their efforts and "fuel" their commitment to the task over time (Brophy, 2004). Students who expect to be successful deliberately engage in cognitive actions that foster their learning. Positive efficacy beliefs exert their strongest influence by enhancing basic cognitive skills, such as memory and attention (Multon, Brown, & Lent, 1991; Schunk & Pajares, 2009). Their performance on classwork improves once students' memory and attention become more deliberate, and eventually these improvements will be reflected in higher grades and test scores. Thus, academic efficacy contributes to classroom resilience by engaging students in using skills that they already possess, and their subsequent success reaffirms their efficacy beliefs.

Students' efficacious expectations of success also enhance their use of self-regulation strategies, including such strategies as selecting tasks on which they expect to succeed, spending more time and effort on those tasks even when distracted, and managing time wisely during periods of inactivity or while waiting for teacher instructions (DiBenedetto & Zimmerman, 2010; Zimmerman, 2000). These improvements in strategy use have been demonstrated in students of all ability levels (Bouffard-Bouchard, 1989). Also, students with stronger academic efficacy set higher goals for themselves, persevere in the face of challenge, and evaluate their performance more accurately (Schunk & Meece, 2006; Zimmerman & Schunk, 2008). Clearly, the achievement of these goal-directed, efficacious students is likely to be higher than that of students who lack persistence and use less efficient strategies (Pajares & Miller, 1994; Shim, Ryan, & Anderson, 2008; Zimmerman, Bandura, & Martinez-Pons, 1992). Unsuccessful students who nevertheless believe in their ability to succeed may attribute their lack of success to ineffective strategies and consequently will work harder, select a better strategy, or seek help in order to improve (Schunk & Ertmer, 2000).

The same academic efficacy that promotes student achievement also enhances their social and emotional adjustment. Adolescents with high self-efficacy are more likely to perceive the relevance of classroom tasks for their personal goals and to experience feelings of enjoyment and gratification as they complete homework and class assignments (Bassi, Steca, Delle Fave, & Caprara, 2007). Students with a strong sense of efficacy are less vulnerable in the face of failure, anxiety, stress, and depression (Bandura, 1993, 1997). In states with high-stakes testing, enhanced academic efficacy, together with supportive classroom environments, can be an antidote to and a protective factor against the anxiety and stress that such testing can produce. For example, older elementary students who perceived their classroom environment to be more caring, challenging, and mastery oriented had significantly higher levels of self-efficacy for math and scored higher on standardized math tests (Fast et al., 2010).

Although individuals hold efficacy beliefs, academic efficacy is also a group phenomenon (Bandura, 1997). Groups, such as teams of teachers, classrooms, schools, and districts, develop a sense of collective efficacy characterized by Bandura (1997, p. 477) as "a group's shared belief in their capabilities to realize given levels of attainment." The more positive the beliefs that groups hold about their collective capabilities, the more they achieve. Members of the group promote mutual efficacy by encouraging each other, and evidence of the success of any single group member reaffirms the other members' beliefs that they too can succeed, contributing to a positive contagion effect (Joët, Usher, & Bressoux, 2011). Research on individual and collective teacher efficacy led to the conclusion that high collective self-efficacy produces challenging classwide goals and persistence in teachers' efforts to meet those goals (Skaalvik & Skaalvik, 2007). The resulting school culture promotes student engagement and achievement, creating a positive feedback loop that enhances individual teachers' self-efficacy. Students' collective efficacy is particularly important because shared beliefs can overcome such powerful influences as low socioeconomic status and a history of poor academic achievement (Bandura, 1993).

What Are Classroom Routines and Practices That Strengthen Academic Efficacy?

Academic efficacy is strengthened when students are provided with mastery experiences in which they complete moderately challenging tasks with only occasional help from others (Bandura, 1997; Linnenbrink & Pintrich, 2003). When tasks are too easy, students' success holds little value for them and when tasks are much too difficult, students are reduced to watching someone else complete the tasks without them. Repeated failure can undermine efficacy development, especially if it occurs early in the learning process before efficacy is firmly established (Bandura, 1977a). Thus, it is a disservice to assign very easy or much-too-difficult tasks to students or assist students in completing tasks that are beyond their ability to complete independently. This is not to say that students never be given help with their work, but rather that the task difficulty should not be so high that students are entirely dependent on someone else's skill to complete the task.

> **Academic efficacy is strengthened when students are provided with mastery experiences in which they complete moderately challenging tasks with only occasional help from others.**

With individual students, curriculum-based procedures have been used to operationally define the optimal instructional match between students' abilities and the level of instruction. For example, students' comprehension of reading passages and their on-task behavior during reading was optimal when they knew between 93 and 97% of the words in the passage (Treptow, Burns, & McComas, 2007). For instruction in mathematics, fluency as assessed by the number of digits correct per minute could be used to index instructional level. For example, Burns, Codding, Boice, and Lukito (2010) identified the fourth-grade instructional level as 24 to 49 digits correct per minute on a curriculum-based probe in mathematics. When instruction was too easy (i.e., occurring at students' "independent level"), students' attention wavered and their learning was minimized. Application of instructional match to groups of students comprising a classroom is much more complicated. First, a broad range of student instructional levels will be represented within the classroom group. A key responsibility of teachers is differentiating their instruction so that all students within the class can work within their optimal instructional level. Moreover, individual students vary somewhat in their response to tasks' instructional level, as both Treptow et al. (2007) and Burns et al. (2010) demonstrated in their studies. Finally, operational definitions describing optimal instructional matches are sparse outside of the subjects of reading and mathematics. Consequently, teachers may need to monitor for instructional match by tracking student performance on their daily work, and by routinely including students in decisions about what tasks should be completed and in what order, what are appropriate homework assignments, and how learning should be evaluated (Brophy, 2004; Schunk & Pajares, 2009).

Students may attribute their success on academic tasks to their strong efforts or to their high ability, and these attributions can affect academic efficacy differently. Effort attributions prompt students to emphasize effort on future tasks, while ability attributions may reinforce students' perceptions that they can rely on their inherent competence at a task. Young students are more likely to emphasize the role of effort when explaining their successes ("I worked really hard"), but older students place more importance on their ability to complete the task ("I'm good at this"). For students at any age, teachers are more credible when they give effort feedback for early successes on tasks that students are just learning, because students must realistically apply effort when first learning a skill. However, teachers should then switch to ability feedback as the skill develops, because ability attributions are more important for sustaining task performance over time (Brophy, 2004; Schunk & Pajares, 2009).

While positive statements about competence can raise the efficacy of all students in a class, consistently failing students should never be told that they would be successful if only they tried harder (Brophy, 2004; Schunk & Pajares, 2009). Students with already low academic efficacy experience further inadequacy when given this kind of feedback about their failure. Instead, struggling students need concrete evidence of small incremental gains in achievement that are tied to their own efforts (Jinks & Lorsbach, 2003). When students track their own progress toward learning goals, they gain more powerful and positive messages about their efficacy than when their performance is compared with that of other students (Schunk, 2003). Highlighting and publicly celebrating the strategies that led to individual and group success provide "teachable moments" when efficacy-building behaviors can be modeled. In some cases, students need to be taught how to accept public recognition of success. In all cases, classmates must be discouraged from making negative comments about one another.

Peers hold strong influence over their classmates' academic efficacy beliefs. Peer models are more effective than adult models in strengthening efficacy, especially if they demonstrate coping rather than mastery. Coping models make comments like "I'm not sure I can do this, but I'll keep trying" while working on a difficult task. In contrast, mastery models complete the task quickly and apparently effortlessly without voicing their doubts or strategies (Brophy, 2004). The use of peer models is important because struggling students may doubt that they can attain an adults' level of competence but realistically expect to match the competence of their peers. Multiple peer models are even more effective than a single model and are an inherent resource of resilient classrooms (Schunk, 2003). Peer models are routinely available when classroom instruction incorporates reciprocal teaching or the use of collaborative learning groups (Fantuzzo & Rohrbeck, 1992; Menesses & Gresham, 2009).

Diversity in the classroom is the rule, and boys, girls, and students of different ethnic groups respond better to some sources of efficacy-enhancing information than other sources (Usher & Pajares, 2006). Some research has suggested that middle school girls and African American students are more likely to base their general academic efficacy primarily on mastery experiences and social persuasion in the form of encouragement from teachers, parents, and peers. Middle school boys also benefit from mastery experiences, together with the opportunity to observe the success of other boys. Honoring culturally relevant skills builds upon latent sources of self-efficacy, as when Spanish-speaking students are encouraged to demonstrate their ability in Advance Placement Spanish language courses (Kettler, Shiu, & Johnsen, 2006). Gender and cultural differences in efficacy are likely to change over time, as social attitudes and beliefs regarding diversity become less stereotypical.

Examples of microstrategies that promote academic efficacy are included in Figure 8.5 (Chapter 8, p. 110). As expected, these incorporate various feedback mechanisms (from teachers, peers, and self-monitoring). Other strategies coach students in securing the support that they need to be successful. The evidence-based interventions listed in Figure 8.5 embed academic efficacy within broader curricula-promoting autonomy.

A Classroom Illustration

In an eighth-grade elective Spanish class, anonymous student surveys revealed that students did not feel confident that they could make good grades on weekly vocabulary tests. In response, the teacher placed the students into two-person teams and gave them 20 minutes daily to teach each other five vocabulary words from the next test. Teams were then taught several alternative strategies to use when teaching each other. Each day, they calculated and recorded their efficacy scores for the teaching strategies that they had used, and then planned their study time for the following day. Once a week, they compared their daily notes to the actual score that they received on the Friday test. Over time, the teams came to prefer the teaching strategies that increased their efficacy and raised their test scores. The study teams allowed these students to see the relationship between their effort and efficacy and to benefit from peer group modeling.

ACADEMIC SELF-DETERMINATION

Students are self-determined when they have personal goals for their own learning, can recognize barriers and solve problems that stop them from reaching those goals, and systematically plan and take actions that allow them to meet their goals (Black & Deci, 2000; Deci & Ryan, 2008a). Self-determined students are every teacher's ideal students. They understand the relevance of the things they are learning in the classroom, and they spend the time and make the effort needed to be successful (Brophy, 2004).

> **Self-determined students are every teacher's ideal students. They understand the relevance of the things they are learning in the classroom.**

How Does Academic Self-Determination Support Student Success?

Students initiate self-determination through academic goal setting. Goals focus student efforts on activities that support the goals and away from goal-irrelevant activities (Locke & Latham, 2002). Academic goals energize students to participate more actively in instruction by making its relevance to their personal needs and interests more evident (Reeve & Halusic, 2009). Goals also affect persistence because students will sustain their efforts when they are allowed to choose how much time they spend on a task. By setting a goal and working toward it, students are motivated to seek out large amounts of unfamiliar information and strategies as needed to achieve their goal.

Goals can be defined according to their specificity, proximity, and difficulty level (Bandura, 1977b; Schunk, 2003), and each of these dimensions contributes to the effectiveness of a goal. Specific goals (e.g., the number of math problems to be completed) are more likely to lead to task success than nonspecific goals like "Do your best." Short-term or proximal goals ("Turn in the first 25 math problems tomorrow") lead to higher performance and quicker success than long-term goals ("I'll raise my math grade one letter by the next report card"). Finally, challenging but attainable goals increase motivation better than do goals that appear to be too easy or too difficult (Schunk & Pajares, 2009). Teachers who use such autonomy-supportive strategies during instruction develop students who are more behaviorally and emotionally engaged in their learning (Reeve, Jang, Carrell, Jeon, & Barch, 2004).

Autonomous self-determined students have also been called "intrinsically motivated" students whose work toward these relevant goals fosters their sense of pride and satisfaction (Deci & Ryan, 2008a, 2008b). Intrinsically motivated students willingly and actively engage in classroom tasks because they see the learning as rewarding in its own right. Alternatively, students can be extrinsically motivated by external rewards or punishments; by a desire for approval from others; or by a desire to avoid feeling ashamed of inadequate efforts (Deci & Ryan, 2008b). Still, students working for extrinsic rewards frequently find the work to be less satisfying. In one study, when fifth- and sixth-grade students were given task instructions emphasizing extrinsic rewards, they enjoyed tasks less, were less persistent, and performed lower than students given instructions emphasizing the intrinsic benefits of the task (Vansteenkiste, Timmermans, Lens, Soenens, & Van den Broeck, 2008). Although early discussions presumed that students were oriented to be either intrinsically or extrinsically motivated, more recent examinations suggest that these might also be situational characteristics of classrooms or learning tasks. Thus, even if students were extrinsically motivated, they learned more when a task was framed by intrinsic goals. This suggests that optimal learning may be promoted regardless of students' motivational orientation by invoking tasks' intrinsic value.

Not all classroom learning is inherently interesting to students, and teachers sometimes use external rewards to keep students engaged in learning. There is some evidence that such rewards might be counterproductive. Joussemet, Koestner, Lekes, and Houlfort (2004) found that autonomy support enhanced students' effort and satisfaction with important but uninteresting learning tasks, but rewards did not. Moreover, students' retention and their depth of processing is greater when they are intrinsically motivated in autonomy-supporting classrooms (Vansteenkiste, Simons, Lens, Sheldon, & Deci, 2004). Autonomously motivated students remember what they learn better than those who are motivated by external benefits or deadlines (Grolnick et al., 2009; Reeve et al., 2004). For example, when students were asked to learn material for a test (externally motivated), they only remembered the material for 1 week and were less interested in it than were students who learned the material with no mention of a test (autonomously motivated). In states with high-stakes testing, the challenge for resilient classrooms is to help students identify multiple, alternative incentives for their learning without undue emphasis on a test. What happens when self-determination needs are not met in a classroom? When students' needs for autonomy are unfulfilled, they become angry, anxious, or bored; begin to fake doing schoolwork; and ultimately suffer declines in their performance (Miserandino, 1996).

Classwide goals can also be divided into mastery and performance goals, and the two types of goals have different effects on achievement. Mastery goals focus students' efforts on understanding more, acquiring new knowledge, or mastering new skills. In contrast, performance goals encourage students to excel relative to their classmates, or at least to be seen by other people as excelling (Brophy, 2004; Dweck & Master, 2009). Student mastery goals and classroom supports for autonomy have been associated with cooperativeness in peer work groups (Levy, Kaplan, & Patrick, 2004), with student willingness to pursue math content outside the classroom (Ciani, Ferguson, Bergin, & Hilpert, 2010), and with homework completion (Katz, Kaplan, & Gueta, 2010). Still, recent research suggests that performance goals might not be detrimental as long as these exist alongside (rather than in the absence of) mastery goals. Students who both want to do better than others (performance goals) and want to learn and understand the material (mastery goals) show similar adaptive patterns with regard to affect, cognition, and achievement as students who have only mastery goals (Pintrich, 2000; Shih, 2005). Pintrich concludes that the competition and social comparison that typically occurs in classrooms may not be detrimental if classrooms are also structured to promote mastery.

Academic self-determination is also closely related to academic efficacy. However, performance goals, which foster competition among students in a classroom, can lower student efficacy. For example, Chan and Lam (2008) studied the effect of competitive and noncompetitive classroom situations on self-efficacy for writing. Students in the competitive classroom, observing that some students' writing was selected as "exemplary" by the teacher, showed a lower self-evaluation of their own performance (self-efficacy for performance). In the noncompetitive classroom, where exemplary writing was presented as peer performance that all could learn from, self-efficacy for performance did not change significantly. Students who lack academic efficacy may also surrender their self-determination, hiding their perceived inadequacy by not seeking help when they need it, resisting novel strategies for academic work, or simply not trying. In one study, such self-defeating behaviors were significantly less common in elementary classrooms with efficacy-promoting practices and mastery-oriented classroom goal structures that made mistakes acceptable (Shih, 2005; Turner et al., 2002). Importantly, this relation was evident regardless of the students' gender, ethnicity, or grade. In another study, adolescents with mastery goals were less threatened by the thought of asking for help because doing so gave them additional control over the task and their ultimate success (Ryan & Pintrich, 1997). Thus, it is not surprising that classroom environments that support self-determination and academic efficacy foster students' intentions to persist in high school, even when their previous academic achievement is poor (Hardre & Reeve, 2003; Otis, Grouzet, & Pelletier, 2005).

What Are Classroom Routines and Practices That Strengthen Academic Self-Determination?

Self-determination is fostered in classrooms that emphasize the process of learning rather than the products of learning. Classroom practices that support student autonomy are those that allow students to initiate goals; help students plan, self-monitor, and evaluate their goal progress; and permit students to choose the work that interests them and when and how they will learn it (Deci & Ryan, 2008a; Reeve, 2002; Sierens, Vansteenkiste, Goossens, Soenens, & Dochy, 2009). This is not to imply that students should be left to work completely on their own, but rather that they should be supported in gradually assuming more and more responsibility for decisions related to their learning. Even when rewards are given in recognition of students' accomplishment, tasks' intrinsic value is increased when these provide information about students' competence and progress (Sungur & Senler, 2010). It may be particularly important in multiethnic classrooms to help students set meaningful future goals that focus on personal growth and competence to support their motivation for tasks in the present (Andriessen, Phalet, & Lens, 2006).

> **It may be particularly important in multiethnic classrooms to help students set meaningful future goals that focus on personal growth and competence.**

Students will frequently need structured questions to formulate the goals that are meaningful to them and give direction to their efforts (Assor et al., 2002; Palmer & Wehmeyer, 2003). In some cases, this assistance may be provided within the classroom context, such as posters on the wall that guide students through task completion, bulletin board reminders of due dates, or posted schedules that describe when and how to ask for help. Because these practices can be embedded into the daily routines of the classroom, they can exert a consistent and subtle influence that grooms the students to become self-directed, responsible learners. Meaningfulness is an integral part of instruction in resilient classrooms. When students perceive that an activity is intrinsically meaningful and addresses their own learning goals, they naturally focus more strongly on understanding the content and improving their skills.

Active student learning is also prompted by instruction that requires students to understand new information at a deep level by justifying their responses to questions and by requiring effortful activity during the instruction (Middleton & Midgley, 2002). Deep processing makes students aware of instances when they do not really understand the information, and the requirements for active participation make it more difficult for students to engage in competing and unproductive behaviors when they are supposed to be learning. Other teacher practices associated with student autonomous motivation for learning include listening carefully; helping students recognize why they are doing well or helping them diagnose the cause of their poor performance and correct it; acknowledging the difficult feelings students experience when struggling with a task; showing students new strategies to use when they are working toward their goals; and paying attention to students' perspectives on their goals (Reeve, 2006; Tsai, Kunter, Lüdtke, Trautwein, & Ryan, 2008).

The microstrategies that prompt academic self-determination have been listed in Figure 8.6 (Chapter 8, p. 112); these emphasize frequent opportunities for students to self-direct their learning, set goals, make decisions, evaluate their progress, and solve problems. Practice in these skills are not routinely incorporated into many school classrooms. As was true for academic efficacy, the evidence-based interventions fostering academic self-determination are integrated into larger interventions promoting student autonomy.

A Classroom Illustration

The seventh-grade math team at an urban middle school was concerned about low homework completion and test grades in one of the classes. While the students believed they had the skills to do the work, they were having limited success on weekly exams. The teachers were concerned that the students' false sense of confidence had convinced them that they could skip the homework and still make a good grade on the test. After they were shown the class data, the students reluctantly agreed that if they wanted to make better grades in math they were going to have to do the homework, but they also wanted to make doing the homework more fun. The students put themselves into three teams, made a chart with a team name, and created spaces to keep track of how many homework problems each team member attempted per day. Rather than competing based on the number of problems completed or accurately answered, they decided to compete based on "improvement scores": the difference between the number of problems attempted on two consecutive days. Also, a class goal was set to attempt at least one more problem each day than was attempted the day before. The students reported that the competition made doing the homework fun. The emphasis on strengthening work behaviors gave the students a healthy control over their learning, and when their weekly test grades improved, the students learned that their actions made a difference in their performance.

BEHAVIORAL SELF-CONTROL

Disruptive, unproductive student behavior in classrooms reduces academic learning time for all students and limits the time available for instruction. In resilient classrooms, students are taught to manage their own behavior with the help of classroom routines that cue appropriate behavior. Self-management strategies and their supporting routines, once embedded into the daily life of the classroom, can become self-sustaining.

> **Self-management strategies, once embedded into the daily life of the classroom, can become self-sustaining.**

How Does Effective Behavioral Self-Control Support Student Success?

Behavioral self-control is often discussed as if it were a set of skills that could be taught directly to children in the same way as spelling words, throwing a baseball, or weaving a tapestry. In fact, behavioral self-control also depends very much on students' internalized preferences for behaving in specific ways, the results they hope to achieve through their behavior, and the subjective criteria that they use to assess whether their behavior meets their own standards (Bandura, 1989; Bear, 2010). These values, preferences, and standards cannot be acquired through a discrete, 8-week course in social skills. Instead, they emerge out of the experiences that children bring with them from their homes, communities, their previous years in school, and routines and practices in their current classroom.

When a classroom's students cooperate with classroom norms, their interactions with the teacher will be more satisfying. Teachers prefer students who are cooperative, conforming, cautious, and responsible. Attentive, regulated, and persistent students receive higher grades from their teacher (McDermott et al., 2001). Students who are argumentative, disruptive, or make inappropriate demands for attention are often treated negatively and receive less one-to-one instruction (Wentzel, 1991). Notably, disciplined behavior predicts grades better than measures of verbal and nonverbal ability, suggesting that good conduct can leverage students' ability (McDermott et al., 2001). Similarly, in other studies, grade retention, placement in special education classes, and dropping out are strongly predicted by behavior independent of intellectual ability (Jimerson et al., 2000; Reschley & Christenson, 2006).

Still, disruptive behaviors can sometimes be an artifact of insensitive classroom routines and practices, and a classroom's students and teacher can frequently identify cooperative solutions that eliminate the need for disruptive behaviors. For example, a fifth-grade class was housed in a temporary classroom, and the teacher complained that the students were frequently out of their seats and whispering to one another during the daily mathematics lesson. A classroom discussion revealed that there was an irritating glare on the whiteboard making it very difficult to see the board from the students' desks. The disruption was diminished substantially by changing the color of the marker and installing a window shade. In this example, by including students in a classroom's governance, the teacher enhanced students' autonomy and encouraged their behavioral self-control.

In effect, behavioral self-control serves as the conduit between social and academic self-efficacy and goal setting. Without the ability to direct their behavior consistent with their own standards, students who set ambitious goals may not be able to act in ways that make them successful. Moreover, without the successes, students' academic and social efficacy can falter. Even though we have discussed these characteristics separately, their impact is inextricably linked.

What Are Classroom Routines and Practices That Strengthen Behavioral Self-Control?

Behavioral self-control begins with expectations for behavior that are developed cooperatively with students early in the school year. These conversations focus on the rules and routines that will allow students to act in self-determined ways and experience efficacy-building successes. After the expectations and rules become integrated into the routine of the classroom, students will generally adopt them as their own and act on them independently. Proactive classroom management provides specific techniques for teaching behavioral expectations, routines, and rules to students (Sugai, Horner, & Gresham, 2002; Witt, LaFleur, Naquin, & Gilbertson, 1999). These include directly teaching students the expectation or rule using carefully sequenced positive and negative examples and role play, arranging opportunities for students to practice the routine, and monitoring student performance and providing reinforcement or corrective feedback. Individual classroom management practices are supported by consensus among the school and community about the behaviors that are desirable in students. When classrooms' disturbing behaviors are severe and persistent, classwide and schoolwide practices benefit from the availability of interventions that are relevant to school settings, means to evaluate their effectiveness, and the necessary funding and training to implement the new behavioral practices in sustainable ways (Sugai & Horner, 2006).

Instructional practices that promote active student engagement in learning also support behavioral self-control. Some of these practices include making sure that activities are interesting and paced so that there is very little wasted time, keeping students busy with responding frequently, providing students with a variety of ways to learn, and using independent and one-on-one instructional groupings (Downer, Rimm-Kaufman, & Pianta, 2007; Greenwood, Maheady, & Delquadri, 2002; Rimm-Kaufman, Curby, Grimm, Nathanson, & Brock, 2009).

Peers can also support classmates to behave appropriately. One program, called Classwide Peer-Assisted Self-Management (CWPASM; Mitchem et al., 2001), taught middle school students self-management skills, social skills, self-monitoring, and a reinforcement procedure, then assigned the students to two-person teams. Students rated themselves and their partners at regular intervals on how well they performed self-control behaviors. CWPASM led to improvements not only in the target behaviors but also in social competence for all students and for at-risk students who demonstrated high rates of disruptive behavior. The gains were maintained after the CWPASM structure was withdrawn. A similar program resulted in decreased rates of disruptive behavior when students wrote examples of classmates' positive behaviors on cards to earn a classwide reward (Cihak, Kirk, & Boon, 2009).

Other programs use peers as effective mediators of both academic and behavioral tasks. Reciprocal Peer Tutoring uses student-set academic goals, interdependent group reward contingencies, and reciprocal peer tutoring to improve elementary students' academic achievement and classroom behavior (Fantuzzo & Rohrbeck, 1992; Menesses & Gresham, 2009). Classwide Peer Tutoring (Greenwood et al., 2002; Rohrbeck, Ginsberg-Block, Fantuzzo, & Miller, 2003) uses structured tutor–tutee pairs to increase self-control behaviors such as "raising hands" and "academic talk." Middle school students in reciprocal tutoring pairs awarded themselves points for active participation during tutoring sessions and for cooperative behavior (Kamps et al., 2008). Active student participation increased and disruptive behavior decreased significantly.

Figure 8.7 (Chapter 8, p. 115) lists several microstrategies that emphasize classwide routines that coach students in self-managing their behaviors. Subsequently, the evidence-based interventions embed similar behavioral self-control skills into broad social problem-solving frameworks. These frameworks emphasize both autonomy-promoting and relational understanding: students learn strategies that they can use to making responsible behavioral decisions, and they become sensitized to a social–cognitive understanding of the social settings within which classroom behaviors occur.

A Classroom Illustration

Students in a second-grade classroom agreed that everyone had some behavior that could be improved to make the class run smoother, such as paying attention or not interrupting. Each student was able to identify one behavior that he or she thought could be improved. The teacher paired each student with a partner, called a "behavior buddy," based on the pair's complementary strengths, and taught everyone how to give feedback on behavior in ways that were positive and supportive.

The teacher also asked how he could improve the classroom. The students told him that it was hard to pay attention when the pencil sharpener was always being used and that the way they lined up to go out for recess created a lot of shoving to be the first in line to get outside and grab a ball. The pencil sharpener distraction was eliminated by placing cans of sharpened pencils at various places in the room so that students could walk a shorter distance to exchange their dull pencil for a sharp one. The class also created a sign-up sheet so that students would take turns playing with all the playground equipment, including the balls. The students stayed in their behavior buddy groups for 3 weeks. A follow-up assessment showed that more students were paying attention and fewer were interrupting, matching the teacher's observation that the classroom was running smoother.

SUMMARY

In this chapter, we provided an elaborated explanation of the ways in which students' autonomy emerges out of classroom routines and practices, and the impact that enhanced autonomy has on student learning. For purposes of clarity, this explanation discussed students' feelings about their performance (academic efficacy), the plans and intentions that guide their performance (self-determination), and their ability to act upon these plans (behavioral self-control). In reality, though, these different aspects of autonomy are mutually inter-dependent, and classroom practices that strengthen any one of the autonomy-promoting characteristics frequently strengthen the others as well. We recognize that this focus on students' autonomy and self-sufficiency can seem out of place in authoritarian classrooms that emphasize teachers as the ultimate authorities and decision makers. Ultimately, if students are to emerge from public education as self-sufficient and successful adults, the seeds of their autonomy must be planted in the earliest elementary grades and nourished carefully throughout the 13 years of their public education. More extensive discussion of autonomy-enhancing classroom strategies are found in Chapter 8.

INTRODUCTION TO A CASE STUDY OF CHANGING CLASSROOM AUTONOMY

In the case study immediately following this chapter, Jonathon Sikorski used student survey data to help a teacher improve students' behavioral self-control during their specials classes. Students had previously relied on the paraprofessional to stop arguments and enforce fairness. By including students in the intervention, the teacher was able to reinforce their self-management of specials behavior. Ultimately, self-managing students will become more autonomous and self-determined.

CASE STUDY

Back to the Basics

Jonathon Sikorski
University of Wisconsin–River Falls

The Problem

A teacher and paraprofessional of a fourth/sixth-grade Montessori classroom became concerned with the frequency of students' off-task behavior during special programs (i.e., music and physical education). Students would often become disruptive during these activities, which resulted in the loss of instructional time. The teacher and paraprofessional addressed the issue of disruptive behavior with the classroom of 21 students during their morning meeting, and they invited the students to help solve the problem.

The ClassMaps Results

The classroom collectively completed the anonymous, computerized ClassMaps Survey midspring. The results from the Following the Class Rules subscale indicated that over 25% of students reported struggling with following directions, paying attention, behaving well, and working quietly (see Figure 4.1).

The Teacher's Sense

Prior to the implementation of ClassMaps, baseline data were collected. After reviewing the baseline data and ClassMaps results, it was apparent to the teachers that students needed to have the expectations and rules for music and physical education classes clearly established. The teachers suspected the off-task behavior in physical education class stemmed from students not playing by the same rules, which resulted in arguments and poor sportspersonship. During music, the teachers suspected the disruptive behavior was influenced by two students trying to upstage each other to be funny.

Results of the Classroom Meeting

The teachers facilitated a classroom meeting with the students to discuss the ClassMaps Survey results, as well as to gauge their willingness to brainstorm possible solutions with the teachers. The students identified the Following the Class Rules subscale as the most important domain to address. After brainstorming with a partner, students indicated they did not have a clear understanding of the rules and expectations of music and physical education, which resulted in conflict with their peers and teachers. Further, students stated they were unsure of the rules and expectations for specials because they had not been reviewed since the fall.

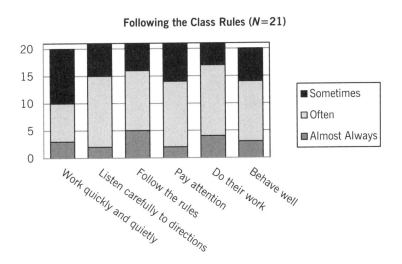

FIGURE 4.1. ClassMaps Survey preintervention graph for the Following the Class Rules subscale.

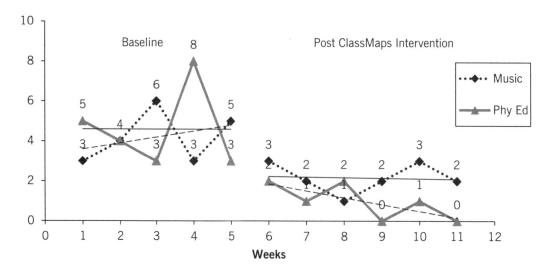

FIGURE 4.2. Number of interruptions during music and physical education pre- and postintervention.

Plan for Change

The students then requested that the classroom rules and expectations be reviewed routinely before each music and physical education class. Together, the teachers and students participated in a look, sound, and feel activity that assisted them in drafting new classroom expectations. After everyone agreed on the expectations for the classroom, the students made a poster with the expectations that was hung on the wall.

To ensure the new expectations were followed, the teachers implemented a Sit and Watch intervention (Rathvon, 2003), which required students to sit out of an activity for a pre-specified amount of time (i.e., 1 minute for first offense, 2 minutes for the second, 4 minutes for the third, etc.) and then talk with the teacher about what they learned from watching other students playing fairly. Further, students participated in conflict-resolution exercises to lessen the intensity of disagreements during specials classes and to minimize the need for teacher intervention.

Results

Figure 4.2 shows the number of conflicts or distractions during music and physical education before and after the CMS and intervention. As illustrated by the figure, the number of interruptions declined significantly after the implementation of the ClassMaps survey and intervention. The number of interruptions during music dropped from an average of 4.2 to 2.2 each week, and the number of conflicts during physical education dropped from an average of 4.6 to 1.0 each week. With the intervention, students began to self-monitor each other's behavior effectively and they had much less conflict with one another and the teacher.

CHAPTER 5

Assessing the Resilience of Classrooms

Assessment is essential to the formation of resilient classrooms. Through assessment, the characteristics of classroom resilience are measured, counted, and quantified so that they become visible to the classroom's teachers and students. Once they are visible, the characteristics can then be strengthened, extended, and infused into daily classroom routines and practices. Without assessment, the characteristics of resilience can only be discussed as abstract principles that are important for student learning but have little practical impact on daily classroom activities. Thus, a critical first step in enhancing classroom resilience is to assess existing classroom characteristics in order to define the goals of intervention and create a baseline against which progress can be measured.

Strategies for assessing classroom resilience must be practical so that teachers can readily adopt them as useful teaching tools. That is, measures of the six classroom characteristics must be brief so that the assessment does not disrupt essential learning activities in the classroom. They must be simple to code and analyze so that the assessment is time efficient. They must be easily graphed, because graphs of classroom assessment data make it easier for teachers and students to understand and plan on the basis of the information. Finally, the measures must have good face validity so that the relevance of their results is immediately obvious to the teachers and students.

Classroom assessment strategies must also have strong technical properties so that their results are convincing to external audiences for classroom data such as administrators, school boards, or community leaders. As evidence that they are reliable indices of the classroom characteristics, they need to demonstrate strong internal consistency and good test–retest reliability over brief intervals of time. Moreover, when the elements of resilience are altered within a classroom, the measures must be sensitive to these changes so that they can detect intervention effects. In order to capture successive changes in a classroom over time, the measures must be capable of repeated administrations without practice effects distorting the results. Further, to link the resilient classroom model to existing research, the brief measures of effective classrooms must be correlated with the more complex and comprehensive measures of classroom characteristics that have been used in basic research.

In the past, efforts at classroom reform have suffered from a myopic emphasis on the perspectives of the teachers in the classroom, or of outside observers who were not classroom participants. The perspectives of the students who learn in the classrooms were sadly overlooked. An essential contribution of the resilient classroom assessment must be to assess characteristics from an ecological framework by capturing the perspectives of these overlooked classroom participants.

Finally, measures of classroom resilience, by definition, assess the classroom contexts for learning rather than the needs and competencies of individual students in the classroom. This presents a special challenge because the majority of educational assessment tools are focused on individual students or teachers. Indeed, a good deal of ingenuity is required to adapt existing measurement strategies to the assessment of classroom characteristics while still using strategies that are practical and empirically defensible.

In the remainder of this chapter, we describe several different strategies for assessing classroom resilience. First, we describe the important types of assessment that can evaluate classroom characteristics. Next, we summarize existing measures on the resilience characteristics. Finally, we describe the CMS that we developed and that we use to track the resilience characteristics in elementary and middle school classrooms. A copy of the CMS is provided in Appendix A.

ASSESSMENT STRATEGIES

Classroom characteristics can be assessed through surveys and rating scales, systematic direct observations, or records and permanent products of classroom activities. Each of these assessment strategies carries its own unique advantages and inaccuracies. Surveys and rating scales are indirect measures, capturing the impressions and imprecise memories of the person who completes the scales. However, in some cases, rating scales provide a more powerful index of a classroom's characteristics because they reflect the accumulated experience of people who are highly familiar with the classroom and are less reactive to single isolated events that might occur. Ratings will be most accurate and useful when the person completing the rating knows the classroom well, when questions are carefully worded to be understandable and precise, and when the rating form is sufficiently brief so that raters do not find it tedious to complete. Ratings can be adapted to assess classroom characteristics by carefully planning the questions and by aggregating the results across multiple raters. They can be ecologically broad measures when they are collected from all participants in a classroom.

> **Rating scales reflect the accumulated experience of people who are highly familiar with the classroom and are less reactive to single isolated events.**

Systematic observations are highly valued because they provide objective information about events in a classroom from the perspective of an impartial observer. However, the collection of reliable observation data requires substantial discipline on the part of the observer, who must be strict in following a preplanned observational protocol. Further, completion of a single, systematic observation may not be sufficient to provide reliable data about an event (Hintze & Matthews, 2004). Instead, multiple observations may need to be collected on more than one day to secure a representative sample of classroom activities. More important, observations can only be used to assess classroom characteristics that are visible to someone who is not a participant in the classroom. Some events in classrooms are difficult for objective observers to interpret accurately. As one example, students are better able to tell the difference between jostling and peer aggression than are adult observers. Observations will be most reliable when the observation protocol is simple, when observers have been trained to follow the protocol, and when observer reliability is assessed on an ongoing basis while data is collected.

In some cases, the permanent records of classrooms can be used as classroom assessment data. For example, information about attendance and tardiness rates, work completion, and work performance is frequently available in teachers' class record books. Information about work quality or work completion might be gathered by examining papers that were completed by classrooms' students. The number, frequency, and nature of office discipline reports can sometimes provide an index of the behavioral conduct of a classroom (Irvin et al., 2006). The most glaring weakness of permanent product assessment is that the collection of this information is not always as reliable as one might expect. For example, in one middle school where we worked, school attendance records were highly inaccurate and incomplete. Alternatively, when class records are faithfully kept, they can present very useful assessment data that are very simple to collect.

EXISTING MEASURES OF CLASSROOM CHARACTERISTICS

The focus of most prior research has been on measuring individual student and teacher characteristics that contribute to classroom relationships and supports for student autonomy. Still, it is possible to adapt these individual measures to the task of assessing classroom contexts by aggregating results across all students in a class. As one example, Baker, Kamphaus, Horne, and Winsor (2006) asked 68 teachers in one school district to complete a 148-item behavior checklist for each student in their class, answer questions about how frequently they made accommodations for the student, and rate how much they believed that they could help each student succeed. Results were used to describe the prevalence of and variability in students' behavioral needs, information that could be used to refine the classrooms' behavioral supports. These kinds of district profiles can also be invaluable for planning targeted school mental health services that match the needs of students enrolled in the district.

The strategy of aggregating individual measures might be used with student, parent, or teacher ratings and reports. Still, despite their value, teacher reports are particularly challenging to convert to classwide measures. It is tedious for teachers to complete rating forms on every student; Baker et al. (2006) report that their teachers spent 20 minutes completing the measures for each student. It is not clear that teachers can provide thoughtful and accurate answers to such lengthy ratings scales when completing them for 20 or 30 different students. As one alternative, Asher (1995) has collected teacher ratings for an entire class by writing a single question across the top of a page (e.g., "Who often picks on and teases other students?") and listing the students in the class underneath. Teachers complete the rating by circling the names of students in answer to the question.

The social and emotional competence of individual students has frequently been assessed through systematic observation procedures. Observation protocols that were designed to assess a single student can sometimes be adapted to classwide observation by systematically observing a different student in the class during each interval of the observation. Interpretations of these modified measures must be made with caution. Since such modifications would alter the psychometric properties of the measures, it would be important to reassess the reliability and validity of the observation strategies in their altered format.

The past decade has brought a substantial increase in the number and quality of classwide and schoolwide assessment tools that evaluate the six classroom characteristics (Baker, 2008; Severson, Walker, Hope-Doolittle, Kratochwill, & Gresham, 2007). Most of these tools fit into one of four categories: school and classroom climate surveys that ask students to describe their experience of learning and working in the class; sociometric strategies that ask students to rate characteristics of classmates; tiered rating scales that use a multistep procedure to describe the nature and prevalence of problems within a school or classroom group; and database strategies that carefully analyze archival data describing student success and the conditions of learning.

> **The past decade has brought a substantial increase in the number and quality of classwide and schoolwide assessment tools that evaluate the six classroom characteristics.**

Classroom Climate Surveys

Classroom climate is the perceived social and psychological environment of a classroom as reported by the students and staff who are learning and teaching there. It is most often (but not exclusively) assessed through surveys. Surveys may be completed by all students in a class or by teachers and other adults who work in the classroom. While there is no common agreement about the characteristics that comprise an effective classroom climate (Zullig, Koopman, Patton, & Ubbes, 2010), most climate surveys include components describing the prevalence of positive or negative relationships among peers and positive or negative relationships between students and their teachers. Some, instead, describe relationships among the teachers, administrators, and other adults in the building. Other classroom climate surveys emphasize the amount and threat of student violence and aggression on school grounds, the physical characteristics of classrooms, the degree to which students adhere to school rules, the academic expectations held for students, or respect for diversity among students and school staff. Thus, even though most of the surveys use the word *climate* or *environment* in their title, the content of surveys varies depending on which characteristics are assessed. The strength of a classroom's climate is described by how positive the respondents' perceptions are.

One example is the Yale School Climate Survey (YSCS; Haynes, Emmons, & Comer, 1993). It was developed as part of the Comer (1993) School Development Program, which had the goal of empowering parents and teachers to foster schools that made a difference in children's lives. The YSCS assesses students' perceptions of achievement motivation, fairness, order and discipline, parent involvement, sharing of resources, student interpersonal relationships, and teacher–student relationships. Surveys from all students, teachers, and parents are aggregated into a profile of the schools' learning environments as these have been experienced by its participants.

Importantly, the YSCS does not assess two of the six characteristics of resilient classrooms: students' academic efficacy and their academic self-determination. Thus, we argue that its description of the school environment is incomplete. Indeed, this is the challenge in selecting classroom climate surveys. In addition to establishing that a survey has strong technical properties, it is important to also verify the definition of climate that is implicit to the questions that teachers and students are asked to answer. An extensive discussion of classroom climate surveys can be found in Doll and Dooley (2013) and in Zullig et al. (2010).

Sociometric Assessment

Sociometric measures of a classroom's peer relationships are among the oldest measures of a classroom's ecological system. Sociometric measures of children's competence with peers were developed in the 1930s and used widely in schools throughout the 1950s to describe the social climate of classrooms (Barclay, 1992; Cillessen, 2009; Gresham, 1986). Subsequently, these formed the basis for substantial research on children's peer relationships in the 1980s and 1990s. Their validity, reliability, and stability as measures of peer acceptance and social competence is well established (Cillessen, 2009; DeRosier & Thomas, 2003; Gresham, 1986).

Sociometric assessments can use either peer nomination strategies, in which students list their classmates who match a description (e.g., "friends"), or roster-rating strategies in which students rate each classmate according to a criterion (e.g., "like to play with"; Cillessen, 2009; Gresham, 1986). Peer-nomination strategies sometimes limit the number of classmates that a student can name (e.g., "your three best friends") and sometimes ask for negative instead of positive nominations (e.g., "the children you do not like to play with"). Roster ratings are generally preferred because they reflect a student's overall acceptance by every other student in the class and appear to be more reliable than nominations (DeRosier & Thomas, 2003; Parker & Asher, 1993). When nominations are used, limited-choice nominations that restrict the number of classmates a student is allowed to name are problematic because they underidentify mutual friendships and can artificially lower the measure of peer acceptance. Still, both sociometric ratings and nominations have been shown to be stable over time and across situations (Cillessen, 2009; Coie & Kupersmidt, 1983; DeRosier & Thomas, 2003; Gresham, 1986).

When either roster-rating or peer-nomination procedures are used, the peer acceptance of any single student in a class can be determined by counting the number of nominations that the student receives or computing average peer ratings (Cillessen, 2009; Gresham, 1986). Peer friendships can be identified if two students nominate or give high ratings to each other. Sociometric measures are especially suitable for describing the peer social climate of a classroom, either by computing the average sociometric rating that classmates give to one another or by computing the average number of positive and negative nominations given and received using unlimited list procedures.

The use of sociometric procedures in schools has declined markedly in recent decades (Doll, 1996). This has principally occurred because sociometric ratings offend the sensibilities of schools by asking students to acknowledge that they prefer some students over others or to describe negative judgments that they have of classmates. Researchers have gathered evidence showing that sociometric ratings and nominations do not disrupt classroom peer relationships—they do not prompt students to be more negative about their classmates and do not cause hard feelings among classmates (Bell-Dolan, Foster, & Sikora, 1989; Hayvren & Hymel, 1984). Still, many schools and school districts prohibit the use of sociometric procedures for these reasons, and it is important to check with administrators before using them. (An extensive history of school applications of sociometry can be found in Barclay, 1992.)

Tiered Surveys

Tiered survey strategies use an epidemiological research method to efficiently describe the nature and prevalence of a problem within a community and identify the environmental characteristics that make it more or less likely that the problem will occur (Baker, 2008). Historically, the "problems" assessed with epidemiological methods were diseases that could be described dichotomously—any single community member did or did not have the disease (Short & Strein, 2008). However, modern epidemiological research is used to assess behavioral, educational, or social conditions in addition to diseases, as long as these can be defined dichotomously. For example, some dichotomous conditions with relevance to resilient classrooms include social conditions (students who spend more than half of their recess time playing alone); home–school conditions (parents with whom the classroom teacher has never spoken in person or by phone); or evidence of academic disengagement (students who are absent more than 1 day a month, or students who complete less than 80% of their assignments).

Tiered strategies use a "multiple-gating" design with three or more stages of assessment, each progressively more precise in identifying the members of a school or class who have the condition (Baker, 2008). The first tier is generally a brief assessment that is efficient in sorting out students who clearly do not demonstrate the problem from those who may. The best first-tier assessment strategies are very time- and resource-efficient to use with large numbers of students. The second- or middle-tier assessments generally require more resources or time but are given to fewer, select students. The goal of Tier 2 assessments is identifying those students who very likely do demonstrate the problem. The final tier may be quite time intensive, but has the purpose of verifying that certain students definitely do demonstrate the problem.

As one example, the Systematic Screening for Behavior Disorders (SSBD; Walker & Severson, 1992) has adapted a tiered strategy to identify all students with behavior disorders in an elementary school. In Tier 1, teachers list six students from their class: three who most demonstrate externalizing behaviors and three who most demonstrate internalizing behaviors. In Tier 2, teachers complete critical incident checklists (45 items total) to describe the nature and frequency of critical behaviors that characterize each of the six students. Those students who are rated to exceed normative criteria are systematically observed in both the classroom and the playground in Tier 3. They are referred to the school's child study team for behavior planning when the observations confirm that they engage in excessive amounts of negative behavior, are unusually isolated, or are disengaged in classroom learning activities. The SSBD is a time-efficient screening procedure. For a school with 20 classrooms, administration of the SSBD Stage 1 and 2 ratings would take approximately 60 minutes of each teacher's time, and an additional 100 hours of observation time would be required to complete Stage 3. As an illustration of the pragmatic utility of the SSBD, Walker et al. (2010) describe the use of the SSBD in the Jefferson Parish Public Schools (New Orleans, Louisiana) to screen all elementary students (grades 1–5) for possible behavior disorders. Results were used to align evidence-based behavior interventions provided by the district with student behavioral needs.

Archival Data

Schools and classrooms generate a tremendous amount of data about the work that is done there, and many of the data are never carefully analyzed for status or trends. For example, attendance and tardiness records can provide a beginning index of students' involvement in the classroom, and these records become even more valuable in secondary schools where students have substantial control over being in school and on time. Some classrooms have records of students' behavior—"thinking" worksheets that students complete when they have been asked to sit out because of classroom misbehavior, notes that students wrote home to their parents because of rule violations, or "sign-in" logs that keep track of times when students were sent to the office for disciplinary reasons.

> Schools and classrooms generate a tremendous amount of data about the work that is done there, and many of the data are never carefully analyzed for status or trends.

The value of these archival records is that they are already collected, and so they simply need to be organized and analyzed in order to examine the prevalence of or trends in a problem. A second advantage is that they are often permanent products—parts of a paper trail that can be coded and entered into a database with good reliability. A disadvantage is that these existing data may not be a good match to the problems that teachers are trying to track over time. For example, "academic engagement" means that students are not only attending class and completing their work but also that they are thoughtful and careful in their work, interested in what they are learning, and invested in doing well. Attendance and work completion records only provide an oversimplified index of academic engagement. A second disadvantage of archival records is that they are sometimes quite inaccurate. Teachers might only enter a fourth of required assignments into their record books, and school attendance records might overlook the absences of substantial numbers of students. Thus, an important step is to carefully examine how archival records have been maintained, with an eye toward judging their likely accuracy.

A prominent example of the use of archival data is the School Wide Information System (SWIS; May et al., 2003), which is a data management system to track office discipline referrals. School staff spend an average of 10 to 60 minutes weekly entering disciplinary information into the database, and are then able to generate reports describing rates and trends in office discipline referrals by student, problem behavior, location in the school, time of day, or day per month (Irvin et al., 2006). More important, survey information from SWIS users suggests that they use these reports to make data-based decisions about the nature and extent of discipline problems and changes in these once interventions were put in place. The authors emphasize the importance of clear and simple operational definitions for all referrals that were entered into the database—once procedures became too complex, it was difficult to ensure good reliability in data entry and interpretation procedures.

THE CMS: AN ALTERNATIVE ASSESSMENT STRATEGY

The limited availability of practical and empirically supported measures of classroom resilience has prompted us to develop an alternative assessment, the CMS (Doll, Spies, Champion, et al., 2010; Doll, Spies, LeClair, et al., 2010; Doll et al., 2009). The CMS is a collection of eight brief, anonymous student surveys in which all students rate the six resilience-promoting characteristics of their classroom: academic efficacy, academic self-determination, behavioral self-control, teacher–student relationships, peer relationships, and home–school relationships. The survey is modeled after sociometric rating procedures. Students' sociometric ratings have been shown to provide highly accurate descriptions of their classmates' social strengths, social weaknesses, and interpersonal roles (Cillessen, 2009; Gresham, 1986). This suggested that students might also be able to provide accurate descriptions of their classroom's resilience. Individual student ratings could then be aggregated across all students to provide a classroom measure. A copy of the CMS is included in Appendix A.

Each CMS item describes a characteristic of the classroom or its students. The 55 items are organized into eight subscales. Three of the subscales describe autonomy-promoting characteristics of the classroom. The Believing in Me subscale (eight items) assesses academic efficacy in a class by asking students about their expectations of success. The Taking Charge subscale (eight items) assesses academic self-determination by asking students about their participation in goal setting and decision making related to their learning. The Following the Class Rules subscale (six items) assesses behavioral self-control by asking students about their classmates' behavior.

Five subscales describe relational aspects of the classroom. The My Teacher subscale (seven items) assesses teacher–student relationships by asking students about their experiences interacting with their teacher. The My Classmates subscale (six items) assesses peer friendships by asking if students have friends to play with, talk to, and sit with. The Kids in This Class subscale (five items) assesses peer conflict by asking whether students in the class fight, argue, and tease each other. The I Worry That . . . subscale (eight items) asks students to rate how much they worry about peer aggression. The Talking with My Parents survey (seven items) assesses home–school communication by asking students how much they talk with their parents about school. Items on two of these five subscales describe negative events in the classroom: Kids in This Class and I Worry That. . . . The decision was made to include negatively worded items because the language to describe the positive alternatives to these events was too convoluted and included many double negatives. Items on all other subscales are positive descriptions of the classroom.

Students complete the CMS using a 4-point Likert scale (never, sometimes, often, almost always). For example:

I like school.

    Never   Sometimes   Often   Almost Always

Student responses are coded by assigning 3 points for "Almost Always," 2 points for "Often," 1 point for "Sometimes," and 0 points for "Never." (Negatively worded items on the Kids in This Class and the I Worry That . . . subscales are reverse-coded, assigning 0 points for "Almost Always," 1 point for "Often," 2 points for "Sometimes," and 3 points for "Never.") Then, subscale scores are computed by averaging ratings for all items on each subscale. Subscale scores can range from 0 to 3. Because each subscale is intended to measure different features of a classroom, results are not averaged across all CMS subscales.

We have used the CMS with classrooms from the second through eighth grade. Students have repeatedly said that it is very important to let them know why the surveys are being collected and how their information will be used. Consequently, the following instructions are used when collecting the CMS:

"These questions will ask you about your classroom. When we're done, we'll gather all your answers together and make them into a graph. Here is an example from another class like yours. [Show a data graph that was collected from another class.] This is what a group of fourth graders said about their class. The graph shows that lots of kids were not having fun at recess and too many kids had arguments or no one to play with. Using this information, the class decided to plan some new and different games at recess, and found ways to include everyone in the class in the games. This is what the fourth graders said after they had used their plan for several months. [Show the 'after' graph to the class.]

"Once we have graphs for your class, your teacher and I will show them to you. Then, you and your teacher can plan ways to make your class better, using the information from the surveys."

A simple way to summarize a classroom's CMS results is to compute frequencies (the number of times each response is given) for each survey question. Results can then be graphed using simple stacked bars in which the bottom stack shows "Almost Always" responses, the second stack shows "Often" responses, and the third stack shows "Sometimes" responses. The "Never" responses are often colored bright red to show that they are problem responses. (Of course, these stacks are reversed for the Kids in This Class and the I Worry That . . . results, in which "Never" should be on the bottom because it is the most positive response.) An example of a CMS graph for the Kids in This Class (peer conflict) survey (Figure 5.1) is included in the case study at the end of this chapter. Labeling each bar in the graph with the abbreviated question makes it very easy for teachers and students to understand the results.

Technical Properties of the CMS

The CMS was developed through a systematic cycle of scale evaluation and refinement (Doll, Spies, Champion, et al., 2010; Doll, Spies, LeClair, et al., 2010; Doll et al., 2009). The cycle began with a careful review of empirical research on the characteristics of resilient classrooms from which items were derived and then refined in response to teacher and student feedback. The item format was adjusted so that students could respond quickly and easily. The administration time was monitored closely, and the survey length was adjusted so that most classes could complete a paper version of the CMS in 20 minutes or less. Items were subsequently organized into subscales, and factor structure and internal consistency of the subscales were carefully examined to ensure that the final CMS was both brief and technically sound. Then, the surveys were refined in response

> **The CMS was developed through a systematic cycle of scale evaluation and refinement.**

to these analyses, and the cycle was repeated until each CMS subscale showed adequate internal consistency (coefficient alphas greater than .70) and the factor structure of the CMS matched the predicted eight-subscale structure.

Strong internal consistency is necessary to ensure that each CMS subscale is a dependable measure of the characteristic it purports to assess. Higher alpha coefficients indicate that the items on the scale are all measuring the same characteristic. The CMS goal of creating relatively brief subscales (eight or fewer items) without sacrificing internal consistency (alpha coefficients greater than .70) was a challenging one. In a recent study with elementary students (Doll, Spies, LeClair, et al., 2010), the internal consistency of all subscales was strong (alpha equal to or greater than .75). In a second study with middle school students (Doll, Spies, Champion, et al., 2010), the internal consistency of the CMS subscales was even stronger (alpha equal to or greater than .82).

The CMS was developed as eight related but distinct subscales, with each subscale assessing a slightly different characteristic of resilience in classrooms. Consequently, each subscale should represent a different factor in a factor-analytic study of the CMS results. Evidence that the CMS factored into the intended subscales is available from three elementary school studies: one with 1,615 students (Doll & Siemers, 2004), a second with 420 students (Doll et al., 2007), and a third with 345 students (Doll, Spies, LeClair, et al., 2010).

This was supported by a confirmatory factor analysis examining the factor structure of the CMS with middle school students (Doll, Spies, Champion, et al., 2010).

Some research has compared the CMS subscales to other measures of the six characteristics that have been developed and used by other researchers. Positive correlations with similar measures are important evidence that the CMS subscales are accurately assessing the right characteristics. In one study, parallel scales of the CMS and the YSCS were significantly correlated (.47 to .80; Paul, 2005). In a second study, the correlation between the Friendship Features Scale and the CMS My Classmates subscale was significant and robust ($r = .81$; Doll et al., 2006). A third study demonstrated significant correlations between all subscales of the CMS subscales and the degree to which middle school science students valued their science instruction; between Efficacy for Science and the CMS Believing in Me subscale ($r = .66$); and between Engagement in Science and the CMS Taking Charge subscale ($r = .62$; Doll, Champion, & Kurien, 2008). Finally, preliminary evidence from intervention studies using a small-n design suggest that the CMS scores were responsive to classroom changes (Murphy, 2002; Nickolite & Doll, 2008).

These technical properties are strong enough to justify using any single subscale alone, without administering the full eight-subscale CMS. In most cases, using the full CMS is preferable because it provides teachers with data that review the full spectrum of resilient classrooms characteristics. However, in some cases, teachers know in advance that their intervention will address a single resilient classrooms factor, and so could decide to collect only that CMS subscale from their class. Similarly, the strength of the CMS subscales is sufficient for their use with only one student in a more traditional single-student assessment and intervention. Within the broader classwide assessment, though, student anonymity is essential so that students provide meaningful ratings, and this anonymity precludes examining a single student's data from the classwide set.

Representative national norms are not yet available for the CMS. Consequently, decisions about when a problem exists or when an intervention change is adequate are value-based decisions. Generally, when more than 10% of a class reports that a problem is "almost always" present or more than 30% report that a problem is "often" or "almost always" present, the problem merits attention and intervention. (Of course the reverse is true for positively worded scales—when more than 10% of a class reports that the attribute is "never" present or more than 30% report that the attribute is "never" or only "sometimes" present, the strength may need to be promoted.)

SUMMARY

This chapter has discussed alternative ways to assess classrooms as a first step toward describing a classroom's strengths and weaknesses. The ultimate effect of these evaluations is to make resilience-promoting characteristics visible to the teachers, classroom teams, and students who will be working to strengthen them. Chapter 6 explains how this information is used to guide subsequent interventions, and Chapter 7 explains how to make those results most accessible to students at different grades.

INTRODUCTION TO A CASE STUDY
USING CLASSROOM ASSESSMENT

In the case study immediately following this chapter, Kristin Bieber and Brooke Chapla used the Kids in This Class subscales of the CMS to identify the underlying causes of frequent playground disturbances. It is not uncommon for extraneous factors (in this case, extensive remodeling) to force a school to make the best of limited resources. In this case study, the second-grade teachers were able to use classroom meetings and student surveys to modify recess practices and enhance their students' play. Recess could once again be a welcome rest from rigorous classroom learning.

CASE STUDY

A Temporary Playground

Kristin Bieber and Brooke Chapla
University of Nebraska–Lincoln

The Problem

Recess proved to be a particularly difficult part of the school day for the second-grade students at Great Plains Elementary School. The students and teachers were adjusting to a smaller, temporary school while their building underwent renovations. As first graders at their home school, the students enjoyed an expansive grassy area, a basketball court, and a large play structure. Now in second grade, the students' temporary playground was about the size of a basketball court with a much smaller play structure. In this very confined space their play often overlapped, resulting in a great deal of arguing and fighting. At the beginning of every recess, the students could ask to play soccer on a field across the street, but only if a teacher accompanied them. Once there, the students had to play soccer for the rest of the period.

After recess, teachers struggled to redirect the students' attention to instructional activities because lingering playground arguments distracted classroom learning. To address these concerns, the second-grade teachers partnered with university researchers to reduce arguing and conflict among their students during recess.

The ClassMaps Results

Students completed the CMS in late November. Results on the Kids in This Class subscale showed that 20% of the students believed their classmates "almost always" argued with one another, and nearly 25% reported that their classmates "almost always" hit or pushed one another (see Figure 5.1).

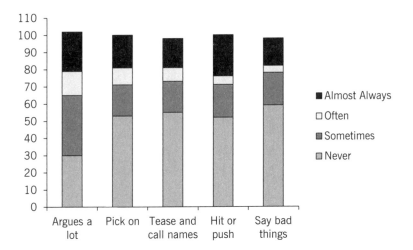

FIGURE 5.1. ClassMaps Survey preintervention graph for the Kids in This Class subscale (second-grade classroom).

Results of the Classroom Meeting

University researchers led classroom meetings to discuss the results with the students. In one class, when asked where the recess problems happened, 14 students voted for the soccer field, 2 students voted for the concrete/basketball court, 1 student voted for the equipment, and none of the students voted for the grassy area. Throwing snowballs, being excluded or ignored, teasing, disagreements about what to play, or arguing about the rules for a game were all situations that students identified as reasons for the problems. Students also listed changes they could make to fix the problem. In general, second graders suggested creating more rules (e.g., no throwing snow or gravel, no line cutting, no kicking) or preventive measures (e.g., "kid patrol," stand up for people who are bullied, take turns). Students also brainstormed possible ways teachers could fix the problem. These included more supervision, teaching kids how to solve their disagreements, and creating schoolwide rules for soccer.

The Teachers' Sense

The teachers were very concerned about the arguing and physical conflict that students reported. They believed the limited number of games and crowding on the smaller playground forced more students to play soccer. As a result, arguments were more frequent because students of different skill levels with varied understandings of the rules for soccer began playing together. They also believed that recess could be improved by increasing communication among supervisors and encouraging them to enforce playground rules consistently.

Plan for Change

A plan was created to teach students a single set of rules for each playground game and encourage communication and consistency among supervisors. The physical education teacher taught students

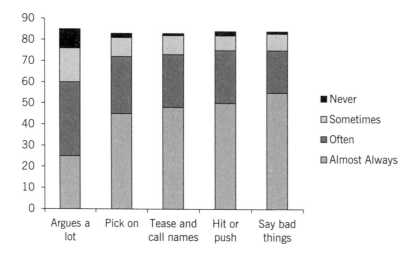

FIGURE 5.2. ClassMaps Survey postintervention graph for the Kids in This Class subscale (second-grade classroom).

school rules for soccer, tetherball, basketball, and four square, and gave the rules to teachers to post in their classrooms. Playground supervisors received additional training in consistently enforcing the rules for playground games. They also brainstormed strategies for promoting positive playground behaviors and developed uniform consequences for problem behaviors.

Results

After several months, students completed the CMS a second time. This time, survey results for the Kids in This Class subscale showed a promising reduction in conflict during recess, seen in Figure 5.2. Just 10% of the students reported that other kids "almost always" argued a lot. Even more encouraging, barely 3% of the students said that kids in their class "almost always" hit or pushed each other.

The Rest of the Story

The second-grade plan reduced conflict and arguing at recess. Some students disliked the increased structure and wanted to play by their preferred soccer rules. Still, the impact of the common rules was quite convincing, and over the summer, the physical education teachers in the district developed districtwide rules for the most popular recess games. The recess supervisors appreciated periodic playground meetings and asked that these be scheduled throughout the coming year. Once repairs were completed, the students would be returning to their home school for their third-grade year, and the teachers will be working to transition their playground rules and routines back to their permanent playground.

CHAPTER 6

Convening the Systems for Change

Transforming a typical classroom into a resilient classroom doesn't quite take a village, but it does require the combined efforts of many different people who participate in and contribute to the classroom learning environment. Consequently, plans for change are most effective when they are made within a classroom team that is led by the teacher and includes other team members such as the school psychologist or counselor, a colleague teacher, a parent, or a student. This classroom team should be carefully selected so that it represents the classroom's members but is small enough to work efficiently and harmoniously. In this chapter, we recommend a collaborative consultation process that classroom teams can use to plan and implement resilient classrooms.

The procedures that underlie collaborative classroom consultation borrow from the extensive research on team consultation (Burns, Wiley, & Biglietta, 2008; Kratochwill, 2008; Rosenfield, 2008; Telzrow, McNamara, & Hollinger, 2000). The principal difference between collaborative classroom consultation and team consultation is that its target is classroom characteristics rather than individual student behaviors. Team consultation uses data-based problem-solving procedures in which problems are identified, analyzed through systematic data collection, and addressed with carefully planned interventions. Then the interventions are evaluated and modified as needed based on the data. The success of systematic team consultation has been directly related to the presence of eight quality indicators (Kratochwill, 2008; Telzrow et al., 2000): precise problem definition, baseline data, clearly identified goals, hypothesized reasons for the problem, a systematic intervention plan, evidence of treatment integrity, data describing the response to treatment, and comparison of student performance with a baseline. Teams whose practices satisfy more of these quality indicators have greater impact on students' academic and behavioral success (Bahr, Whitten, Dieker, Kocarek, & Manson, 1999; Telzrow et al., 2000). Still, teams rarely meet all eight of these indicators, and there is little research to clarify which of the indicators are most essential for changes in student success. In one study, only four of the eight indicators were related to important changes in student performance: precise problem definition, clearly identified goals, evidence of treatment integrity, and availability of treatment data (Kosse & Doll, 2006).

In this chapter, we have organized these quality indicators into a simplified four-step team consultation framework that emphasizes the collection and use of data to describe goals for classroom change, plan interventions, and refine and improve the interventions. The four collaborative classroom consultation steps are:

- *Step 1: Conducting a classwide assessment.* The classroom team gathers information about the classroom and uses that data to describe strengths and weaknesses in the classroom's natural supports for learning. This assessment forms a baseline against which future changes in the class will be measured.
- *Step 2: Making sense of the classroom data.* The team organizes, codes, and graphs the collected information and then shares selected portions of the data with the classroom's students. They listen to students' explanations of the classroom data and ideas for improving the class. Then, the team uses the data combined with student interpretations to set goals for classroom improvements.
- *Step 3: Planning and implementing classroom changes.* Using their own ideas and those contributed by students, the team writes a plan for changing classroom routines and practices. Then, they carry out the plan while keeping careful records to show how well the plan was followed and document any revisions that were made.
- *Step 4: Evaluating and refining the intervention.* The classroom team monitors progress of the intervention by re-collecting classroom data at regular intervals and by refining the plan in response to evidence of progress (or lack of progress) toward classroom goals.

The remainder of this chapter discusses these steps in more detail. In some of the examples, the idea to build resilient classrooms was initiated by a classroom consultant who was not the teacher. Several other examples come from teachers who initiated the change process in their own classrooms, convened a team to help them, and directed the change process with the help of their team. In some cases, a full school of teachers has been engaged in promoting resilient classrooms within the building. While this chapter discusses the process from the perspective of a single classroom, Chapter 10 briefly discusses the process of introducing classroom consultation to a full school. Throughout the chapter, we presume that the CMS will be used as data describing the classroom, but any of the other assessment procedures described in Chapter 5 can be substituted, as long as they provide reliable and valid information about the classroom.

STEP 1: CONDUCTING A CLASSWIDE ASSESSMENT

Teachers generally decide to implement a resilient classrooms intervention because they are dissatisfied with some aspect of the learning environment in their classroom. They may be concerned about the behavioral, social, or academic success of a few individual students or of subgroups within the classroom. Sometimes, they are concerned with the general "climate" of the classroom and its unsatisfactory impact on classwide behavior or learning. During this first step and throughout collaborative classroom consultation, it is important that the team follow the teacher's lead, even if it deviates somewhat from the process recommended in this book. Teachers are ultimately responsible for the management of their classrooms and need to retain final decisions about plans for change.

A necessary first step is to collect data about the classroom's resilience. Chapters 2, 3, and 4 provide a conceptual framework for the classroom characteristics that ought to be described by these data. These include characteristics describing the relationships that exist within the classroom (between and among teachers, students, classmates, and families) and characteristics supporting students' emerging autonomy (including their sense of efficacy, self-determination, and self-control).

> **A necessary first step is to collect data about the classroom's resilience.**

Work begins by assembling a small classroom team to assist with strengthening the classroom's resilience. Team members could include another teacher who is a peer mentor, a related services professional who works with the classroom, a paraeducator or other support person who works in the classroom, or a parent of one of the students in the class. Although their participation can complicate scheduling, parents have a unique understanding of how to coordinate home–school communication and can rally support of other parents for interventions. Students are participants in classrooms, and their unique perspectives may contribute to classroom change strategies. Importantly, students are also the members of classrooms with the most time to contribute to the effort.

To prepare for collaborative classroom consultation, classroom teams should read Chapters 1 through 5 for an overview of the classroom change process and an explanation of how enhancing resilience can improve classroom relationships and achievement. When the team first meets as a group, the team will need to allocate some time to explore their common task and explain the contributions they expect to make to the project. Regardless of the team's membership, teachers' participation in collaborative classroom consultation must be voluntary, and any classroom data that are collected must be kept confidential. In every case example drawn from our own research, we secured the principal's prior agreement that classroom data would belong to the teacher and would not be shown outside the classroom by anyone except the teacher. This ensured that the resilient classrooms intervention would not be transformed into an exercise in teacher evaluation.

The teacher with the team secures any necessary approvals for collecting data about the classroom's resilience. When classroom data are used for instructional purposes only, most school districts do not require a formal approval process. However, in every case, we sent a letter home to parents that told them about the project and how the classroom information would be used. (Of course, if there are plans to publish classroom data as part of a larger research study, the team must follow formal research approval requirements for obtaining school district and school consent, parental consent, student assent, and ensuring confidentiality.)

Next, the team collects data about the classroom characteristics. We developed the CMS for this purpose because we could align the anonymous student questions with the conceptual framework underlying resilient classrooms, because the student surveys were both practical to use and technically sound, and because there are relatively few other measures available to efficiently and effectively assess these characteristics of classrooms. (See Chapter 5 for more information on the CMS.) The CMS requires approximately 20 minutes for a class to complete using paper surveys or 15 minutes of computer lab time when completed online. Because some CMS questions asked about the teacher or teaching practices, we typically had a team member who was not the teacher read questions to the class while the teacher worked in some other part of the classroom. We routinely read each item aloud while another adult circulated around the room to answer any student questions because student reading levels vary widely, even within upper elementary and middle school classrooms.

Students have taught us the importance of explaining why the classroom data are being collected and how the information will be used. For example, one seventh grader asked, "Is this all about fixing our school? Because, if we knew that before we answered the questions, I think we would tell the truth." Since then, the instructions for the CMS have incorporated examples from other classrooms where survey information was used to plan for classroom changes. The verbatim instructions that we used are included in Chapter 5.

STEP 2: MAKING SENSE OF THE CLASSROOM DATA

An important next step is collecting, organizing, and interpreting the data. The resulting "portrait" of the classroom learning environment will be used to describe the goals for change with some precision, consider alternative reasons for classroom weaknesses, and brainstorm alternative interventions for change from multiple perspectives. The Step 2 Worksheet "Making Sense of the Classroom Data," included in Appendix B, will guide this process. Teachers play a central role in making sense of their data because their essential insight into classroom dynamics frames the data interpretations.

> **An important next step is collecting, organizing, and interpreting the data.**

Teams analyze and graph the classroom data and, because classroom graphs will almost always be shown to students, their format needs to be clear, simple, and easy to interpret. For example, CMS graphs are easy for students to understand if each question's responses are described with simple bar graphs that show the number of students giving each response. In secondary classrooms, the graphs might instead show the percentage of students giving each response. (Additional information about data analysis and graphing can be found in Chapters 5 and 7.) Data graphs should always be carefully screened to ensure that there is no distinguishing information, such as the teacher's name or room number, that identify the data should they be misplaced.

Together, the teacher and the classroom team examine the data graphs and identify the classroom strengths and weaknesses these reveal. This is a complicated process, and it can flow more smoothly if the team previews the Step 2 Worksheet "Making Sense of the Classroom Data" (in Appendix B) and pencils in those decisions that have already been made. The worksheet questions refine the team's understanding of the weaknesses and clarify the conditions under which they present a problem for the class. This will lead naturally into a discussion of what else in the class contributes to these weaknesses and to the formation of a hypothesis (an educated guess) about why they have emerged. In effect, these discussions constitute a functional analysis of the conditions under which the classroom weaknesses are evident and the features of the environment that might be supporting them.

In addition to providing a portrait of the conditions supporting classroom weaknesses, the team's discussions of data prompt educated guesses about why the weaknesses occur. Such hypotheses are sometimes dismissed as simply "admiring the problem." However, they are truly much more than glorified descriptions of weaknesses. Instead, the hypotheses bring together the team's shared educator experiences into a rich, albeit tentative, understanding of the mechanisms that might underlie the classroom resilience. These mechanisms are essential for subsequent intervention planning.

Throughout these discussions, it is crucial that the team remains sensitive to the personal responsibility that the teacher holds for the classroom's resilience. Sometimes a teacher's understanding of a classroom's weaknesses is complicated by emotion-laden themes that seem out of proportion to the problem. Professional frustration may cause the teacher to "catastrophize" the problem, and other team members may be tempted to buy into this negative perspective (Caplan, 1970). To restore objectivity, teams can describe more reasonable and likely alternatives than the teacher's worst-case scenario without disputing the teacher's basic description of the problem.

Often, a classroom team will include a school psychologist or other person with substantial experience in interpreting data and frequently that person has some tentative interpretations or interesting contrasts to point out to the team. However, if the team is to remain truly collaborative, this prior knowledge cannot be allowed to dominate the discussion. Good consultation practice recommends that interpretations be offered tentatively (Rosenfield, 2008). Then, all team members can participate equally in decision making, work toward a common goal, and share accountability for outcomes. The Step 2 Worksheet "Making Sense of the Classroom Data" (included in Appendix B) will guide the team's process without the appearance of controlling the meeting.

Care should be taken to focus on strengths of the classroom as well as on weaknesses and to present the classroom as a system with multiple elements that contribute to the learning climate. This system's focus will deter the team from viewing the graphs as a measure of the teacher's competence in leading the class. Other very useful strategies for maintaining the team's focus on strengths and positive goals can be found in manuals describing brief solution-focused therapy (Murphy, 2008). For example, asking when a given weakness is not present or is not a problem can describe conditions that could contribute to a successful solution for the weakness. The classroom's goal can be specified more clearly by asking the team members to describe in detail what they expect to see and not see when the weakness is no longer a concern in the classroom.

Although the team may ask other questions in addition to those on the worksheet, questions on the worksheet systematically lead the team to the ultimate decision—the articulation of a goal for classroom change. Anyone reading the goal should understand what exactly will change; what success will look like and how much change is needed to be meaningful.

In pragmatic terms, the goal should be stated in language that is so clear and precise that everyone will be able to tell when the goal is met. One example of a strong goal would be "First thing every morning, 90% of students will come to class with their homework completed and ready to turn in," whereas a much weaker goal would be "All students will complete their homework."

Stating the goal inevitably identifies other data (frequency counts or student self-monitoring) that could be available in the classroom to mark progress toward the goal. Progress monitoring data could include a weekly administration of a CMS subscale that is closely related to the intervention, existing records such as work completion rates or behavioral referral rates, discipline records, or brief student reports. More examples of classroom assessment strategies are described in Chapter 5. In every case, these data must be brief, easy, relevant to the classroom goal, and graphable so that they can be regularly administered and interpreted without infringing on other responsibilities of team members. It is best to have 7 days or 2 weeks of consistently collected data before the intervention plan is implemented, so baseline collection of these data should begin immediately. Teams should make sure that data collection is as effortless and reliable as possible. Together with the CMS, these data constitute the baseline against which postintervention data will be compared to judge progress of the intervention.

Once they have reviewed the data themselves, the team will seek student perceptions of the classroom's data and their implications for change. Student participation is essential to ecological classroom change because the classroom's multiple participants must share responsibility for intervention in order for changes to be meaningful and large. Consequently, in Step 2, the team convenes a classroom meeting to discuss classroom data with the students. The meeting gives students an opportunity to comment on the accuracy of the classroom data, explain their hypotheses for why weaknesses exist, and suggest strategies for change. To emphasize the students' shared responsibility for classroom change, they are specifically asked to identify things that they could do to make things better in addition to describing what they think the teacher could do. Comprehensive instructions for conducting classroom meetings are described in Chapter 7, and the Step 2 Worksheet "Classroom Meeting Record" is provided in Appendix B. A good strategy is for one team member to lead the meeting while another uses the record sheet to keep the notes. The classroom meeting's questions should not constrict the class discussion. Instead it should proceed normally and comfortably. However, if each of the record's questions are introduced in turn, all key meeting topics will be covered. Copies of the Step 2 Worksheet "Classroom Meeting Record" should be available to all team members.

STEP 3: PLANNING AND IMPLEMENTING CLASSROOM CHANGES

By the end of Step 2, the classroom team will have collected multiple perspectives and ideas about why the classroom weaknesses have occurred and what can be done about them. In Step 3, the team writes a plan for intervention, commits team members to carrying it out, and arranges for the collection of intervention data. The Step 3 Worksheet "Planning and Implementing Classroom Changes" (included in Appendix B) can serve as a guide for this discussion.

Three principles guide the design of an intervention plan. The first, equifinality, means simply that there are many ways to achieve the same outcome (Doll & Lyon, 1998). Teams should be encouraged to explore several alternative intervention strategies before choosing one. This brainstorming may prompt the team to identify resources that would have gone unnoticed otherwise. Some teams may want one member to act as an expert and propose the "correct" intervention to them. However, a wise team member will take a collaborative stance, tentatively adding to the intervention suggestions without displacing other team members' ideas, and encouraging discussion so that an idea is not

> **Teams should explore several alternative intervention strategies before choosing one.**

selected prematurely. A second principle is that a match must exist between a team's skill and the demands that a specific intervention might place on class resources (Kratochwill, 2008). Some interventions can be adapted or changed without impacting their effectiveness, whereas others cannot. Teams should work to anticipate what might go wrong with an intervention, whether it needs to be altered to match classroom resources, and whether it will still be effective if altered. Finally, the acceptability of the intervention to the teacher should be considered (Elliott, 1988). Interventions will be more acceptable if they are described in language that matches the teacher's perspective on the problem (Kratochwill, 2008; Rosenfield, 2008) and the classroom's cultural values (Brown, Pryzwansky, & Schulte, 2001). Teachers will accept interventions if they expect that they will be able to implement them effectively and if they are rewarded for their efforts by outcomes they value (Tollefson, 2000).

It is important that the classroom interventions balance empirical rigor with practicality. Consequently, we have identified two levels of interventions for teams to select from. These levels are articulated for each resilient classrooms factor in Chapter 8. First, microchanges in classroom routines and practices have been identified for each classroom characteristic; these reflect teacher expertise or may have been included as recommendations by researchers investigating each characteristic. For example, a microchange to enhance peer relationships in a classroom is to increase the students' opportunities to engage in enjoyable learning activities within pairs or small groups. The effectiveness of this intervention is suggested by Menesses and Gresham's (2009) research on peer tutoring in general education classrooms and Berndt's (1999) research on the impact of friendships on academic learning. Classroom teams will generally select from these microchanges first because they are easier and faster to implement. However, when classroom data show that these microchanges have not been effective, evidence-based manualized interventions have also been identified to enhance each classroom characteristic. These are interventions with formal intervention manuals that have been demonstrated in well-controlled studies to enhance one or more of the classroom characteristics. Although they require more effort and discipline to implement, they can be effective in situations that require substantial change. Chapter 8 describes both microchanges and manualized interventions for the six classroom characteristics.

Using the Step 3 Worksheet "Planning and Implementing Classroom Changes" (in Appendix B), the team will create a simple plan for intervention together with a plan for collecting data to monitor the intervention's impact. Then, the team will complete the Step 3 Worksheet "Intervention Plan Record" (also included in Appendix B) as a written record of who did what to carry out the intervention, and when they did it. The best records also include a schedule for data collection. Completed weekly, the "Intervention Plan Record" can be used to track plan implementation. The simple "Yes–Partly–No" format allows quick review of each component of the plan and also serves to remind the team of the plan's key steps. Ideally, data collection during intervention should remain consistent with the way data were collected at the baseline so that new data can be compared with baseline data. Data collected from this point forward will be used to determine whether or not the class is successfully reaching its goal or how to modify the plan so that the goal is met.

Next, the intervention activities need to be carried out as planned. The best intervention plans are simple so that the classroom is not overwhelmed with too many changes at one time. Plans that are very complex can be implemented in steps, first making the easiest changes and those that are expected to have the greatest impact. Some teachers will want the team to provide direct help with plan implementation. This help can take the form of modeling some of the activities that another team member will eventually take over or working directly with students in large or small groups. Team members should not make time commitments they cannot reasonably keep. Intervention plans that demand too much of a team will need to be revised, or responsibility for implementation should be shared with others in addition to the core team. Moreover, intervention plans that are too complex will be difficult to incorporate into the regular classroom routines.

A challenge in Step 3 will be to maintain the team's commitment to the plan as written and to make modifications in systematic and thoughtful ways. The integrity of the implementation is especially important since most unsuccessful plans fail because they were never truly carried out. A common error is to expect team members to carry out activities with which they have little or no experience. To guard against unintended deviations, the team should meet at least once a week to review data and monitor the progress of the plan. In some cases, teams have a good reason to deviate from a plan. Careful record keeping can identify aspects of the plan that were difficult to implement, focus efforts to revise the plan as needed, and ultimately lead to greater acceptance and use of the plan over time. In some cases, it will be useful to pull the team back together to consider alternative plans. Effective teams will not revise the plan too quickly. Any plan of action needs a sufficient trial period, usually 2 weeks, before its effectiveness can be determined.

> **Most unsuccessful plans fail because they were never truly carried out.**

STEP 4: EVALUATING AND REFINING THE INTERVENTION

A critical step in collaborative classroom consultation is to monitor the progress of the plan in meeting the classroom's goal. Toward this end, the classroom team should collect continuous classroom data relevant to the goal and analyze and monitor the data to determine whether progress is evident and whether the goal has been met. Typically, the CMS is readministered to verify that the classroom's students, too, see improvements that the team notices. In some cases, the classroom plan will work quickly and efficiently, sometimes in less than a month. At that point, the team can collate the classroom data, reconvene one last time for debriefing, hold a final meeting with the classroom's students, and plan for routinizing the intervention into ongoing classroom practices. Routinization is different from the "general-ization" that completes individual student behavior plans. Generalization is intended to instate students' target behaviors in diverse situations while fading the artificial conse-quences imposed by the intervention. In resilient classrooms interventions, the goal is not to fade the supports for learning that have been introduced into the classroom, but rather to embed them into the classroom's ongoing routines and practices even after the project has ended.

> **Routinizing embeds the changes into the classroom's ongoing routines and practices even after the project has ended.**

In other cases, the classroom's plan will not appear to be working or only some parts of it will be working. In this case, the team should return to Step 3 and consider making revisions to the plan or goal. When interventions are not effective, it may be because the "dosage" of the intervention was insufficient. That is, the intervention activities may be appropriate but may need to happen more often or for longer periods of time. Alternatively, it is possible that the intervention was not implemented with integrity and that the activi-ties strayed so far from the original intervention plan that it was never truly provided to the classroom. In some cases, the classroom may need to institute a more rigorous and ambi-tious intervention, drawing from an evidenced-based intervention whose effectiveness has been documented in the research literature. Finally, it is possible that the original func-tional analysis of the classroom's learning context was inaccurate or overlooked key informa-tion. At any point where an intervention plan is being revised, it is also wise to review and refine classroom data collection procedures to be consistent, objective, and comprehensive.

Some classroom teams will reach the first goal and decide to redirect attention to a second goal. When this happens, it is recommended that comprehensive classroom data be re-collected because progress on one goal can affect the profile of the class in other areas. The same team can remain, or a new team can be convened and the process begun again.

SUMMARY

This chapter has described data-based consultation procedures that will be familiar to any-one who has worked on a school's student assistance teams, but classroom change rather than student change has been made the focus of the process. The ultimate purpose of this collaborative classroom consultation is to design, implement, and assess the impact of class-room interventions to improve the learning supports for students. Chapter 7 follows up on this discussion by providing a further explanation of ways that students can be more fully involved in the intervention process, and Chapter 8 describes alternative intervention strategies that classroom teams might use.

INTRODUCTION TO A CASE STUDY
OF COLLABORATIVE CLASSROOM CONSULTATION

The case study immediately following this chapter describes a team of a classroom teacher, paraprofessional, school psychologist, and colleague who worked together to strengthen the students' relationships with their teacher and with one another. Examples of completed worksheets illustrate how these can guide the resilient classrooms' problem-solving strategies. This teacher's two goals—both peer relationships and her relationship with students—illustrate the close links between the six characteristics of classrooms. Inevitably, classroom changes that affect one characteristic will also affect another. Pay close attention to the collaboration that underlie this team's work to change the classroom—colleagues are some of the best coaches when making classroom refinements.

CASE STUDY

A Collaborative Classroom Consultation Example

Ellie, a third-grade teacher, sought consultation with the school psychologist because she was finding it difficult to interact comfortably with her "very needy group of students." She explained that the students acted "very mean to each other" and frequently argued with her and the classroom aide. She had implemented classroom meetings in an attempt to address these behaviors but was frustrated because the problems didn't seem to be decreasing.

The consultant suggested that a team problem-solving approach could help with her concerns, and together they invited the classroom aide and another third-grade teacher to join them. During the first team meeting, when asked to describe the most important problem to address, Ellie responded, "We need to ask the students . . . they know best." The consultant offered to collect anonymous surveys to reveal the classroom's most pressing concerns and to provide visual feedback to the team.

The consultant graphed the CMS results and brought the graphs along with the Step 2 Worksheet "Making Sense of the Classroom Data" (Figure 6.1) to a team meeting. As the team discussed the graphs, the consultant completed the worksheet. Ellie expressed dismay at the number of students who responded "Sometimes" or "Never" to questions on the teacher–student relationships survey (shown in Figure 6.2). She explained that at the beginning of the school year she had felt so pressured to cover a lot material and bring up sagging test scores that she might have overlooked the importance of establishing rapport and listening carefully to her students. She wondered if her students' perception that they lacked rapport with her could also be affecting their relationships with one another. This led her to a goal for the classroom: to improve her relationship with her students to see if their relationships with one another also improved.

Classroom: *Ellie's third grade*   Date of goal setting: *January 29*

What strengths are shown by your classroom data?

Most kids in the class have someone to eat with at lunch. The students are talking to their parents about school. They're asking for help when they need it.

What weaknesses are shown that you would like to see improve?

Lots of students respond "Sometimes" or "Never" when talking about the teacher relationship. There is a lot of peer conflict reported. Students describe lots of disruptive behavior in the class.

Which is the most important weakness to change?

The relationship between the teacher and students.

In addition to the classroom data, what other evidence do you have that this weakness is a problem for the class?

There are frequent arguments among the students and the teacher and aide. Students are mean to one another.

What are the times and places when this weakness is particularly a problem for the class?

Before and after school. As students come in from lunch recess. During reading groups. When the seatwork is difficult.

What are the times and places when this weakness is **not** present or is **not** a problem for the class?

When having "special lunch" with the students. During times of direct instruction.

What else is happening in the class when the weakness is particularly a problem? Or when is it **not** present? (Examples might include certain individuals who are present, the size of the group, time of day, seating arrangement, expectations for a task, etc.)

There's a lot of emphasis on catching up with academic standards—these kids were behind at the end of last year. These kids are pretty competitive with one another.

What will the classroom be like once the weakness is "fixed"?

- Exactly what will change?

  The number of arguments recorded in class and at recess will decrease.

- How much will it change?

  The number of arguments recorded will decrease to three or fewer per day.

- What will success look and sound like?

  There will be fewer arguments between students, a student and an aide, and a student and the teacher both in the class and at recess.

(continued)

FIGURE 6.1. Completed Step 2 Worksheet "Making Sense of the Classroom Data" for Ellie's third-grade classroom.

Resilient classrooms goal:

Improve relationships with students, and then see if their relationships with one another
also improved.

How will you know if the class meets the goal?

Teacher's daily notes will show fewer student arguments in class.

Students will describe a more positive teacher relationship.

There will be fewer arguments at recess.

What Additional Classroom Data Will Tell You When the Classroom Goal Is Met

What data will be collected?

Daily teacher notes of number of arguments (1) in class and (2) at recess.

Who will collect the data?

Ellie

When and how often?

Each day immediately after recess.

In the Class Meeting

What classroom data would you like to show to the class? (Consider showing one graph reflecting a class strength and a second graph reflecting a class weakness.)

The teacher–student relationships graph.

FIGURE 6.1. *(continued)*

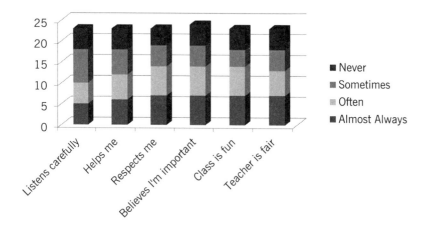

FIGURE 6.2. ClassMaps Survey graph for teacher–student relationships in Ellie's third-grade classroom.

When the consultant showed the teacher–student relationships graph to Ellie's class a few days later, the students agreed that they would like to have a better relationship with their teacher and that the class would also be more enjoyable if they got along with one another better. They came up with the idea of making "friendship bracelets" for each other out of colored string to remind themselves to treat one another like friends rather than people they didn't care about. They also agreed to make sure that everyone was included equally during group activities. The consultant supported their idea and led them in a discussion of how friends treat one another and resolve conflicts. Ellie kept notes on the Step 3 Worksheet "Planning and Implementing Classroom Changes" (Figure 6.3), and as she listened she felt that she was on the right track.

Next, Ellie's team met to plan a classroom intervention to achieve the goal. Using the solution-focused approach (Metcalf, 2008), the consultant asked Ellie to describe the things that were going well in her relations with students. She replied that she often had lunch with the students who were well behaved and finished their work. She commented that she'd never really considered spending "special" time with the students whose behavior was not up to her standards. When the consultant asked if she might consider doing that, Ellie commented, "Looking at these graphs, it's like a light-bulb going off in my head. Of course the struggling students need extra attention—probably more than the kids who are doing well. I should have been paying more attention to that all year."

Continuing the solution-focused approach, the consultant asked if there was anything Ellie could think of doing now to begin turning things around. Ellie commented, "I need to stop looking at giving special time to students as a reward and start thinking of it as a good teaching strategy. After all, I give them extra help when they're having a hard time with math or writing!" This comment led to a discussion among the team members about implementing the "banking time" intervention (Pianta, 1999; Pianta & Hamre, 2001) described more fully in Chapter 8. In banking time, the teacher spends special time with students doing an activity of their choice, thus strengthening the quality of the relationship. The consultant and the team completed the Step 3 Worksheet "Intervention Plan Record" (Figure 6.4), specifying how and when Ellie would spend time with her troubled students individually and with the class as a group and how data to evaluate the intervention would be collected.

The consultation process yielded many benefits for Ellie and the students in her classroom. She gained increased awareness of her students' social–emotional needs and of her own ability to support troubled students. She was able to reframe her construct of "good teaching" to include providing special time and attention to students as they needed it. She no longer perceived the extra attention as "rewarding bad behavior" but as an effective teaching strategy to build positive relationships between herself and at-risk students. Several months into the consultation process, Ellie reported that other teachers in the building were eager to hear about her new strategies and wanted anonymous surveys administered in their classrooms. Ellie's newfound role of an in-house professional development resource provided her with an increased sense of teaching efficacy and optimism for the start of the next school year.

Classroom: _Ellie's third grade_ _____   Date of planning: _February 2_ _____

Your Resilient Classrooms Goal

Improve relationship with students, and then see if their relationships with one another

also improved. _____

What Do Your Classroom Data Show?

What data were collected? _Daily teacher notes of arguments (1) in class and (2) at recess._

Who collected the data? _Ellie_ _____

When and how often? _Immediately after recess every day._ _____

What did the data show? _Lots of students respond "Sometimes" or "Never" when talking about_

the teacher relationship. There is a lot of peer conflict reported. Students describe lots of

disruptive behavior in the class. _____

Planning for Change

What new information was learned from the classroom meeting or data collection?

Kids are mean. We're grumpy most of the time. This is a grouchy classroom.

Sometimes we have a bad day at home. We give our teacher a headache a lot. Kids copy

what they see in other classes. We forget that we like one another. Sometimes other kids won't

let us play. _____

What can be done in this class to reach the goal? Options might include one or more of the following:

☐ Changing classroom routines _____

☐ Changing teacher behaviors _____

☐ Changing student behaviors _____

☐ Increasing teacher skills _____

☐ Changing the physical setting of the classroom (by adding things or rearranging existing things)

    _____

☐ Changing the physical setting of playground or other school facilities (by adding things or rearranging existing things)

    _____

☐ Modifying classroom discipline procedures _____

☐ Anything else? _____

The Plan

What changes will be made in the classroom?

Change 1: _Take turns giving "special time" at lunch to the three kids who are struggling most:_
Matthew, Lisette, Arnie.

Change 2: _Plan a fun learning game for the midmorning break._

_____

(continued)

FIGURE 6.3. Completed Step 3 Worksheet "Planning and Implementing Classroom Changes" for Ellie's third-grade classroom.

Change 3: _Make friendship bracelets to remind us to be kind to classmates._

_____

Change 4: _____

_____

*Next, enter each change into the **Intervention Plan Record,** noting who will make the change, when, and where.

Should Changes Be Made in the Plan for Data Collection?

Collecting different data? _____

Change who collects the data? _____

When and how often? _____

FIGURE 6.3. *(continued)*

Classroom: _Ellie's third grade_ _____   Record for week of: _____

Change/Activity 1

What will be done? _Take turns giving "special time" at lunch to the three kids who are_
struggling most: Matthew, Lisette, Arnie.

Who will do it? _Ellie_

When? _Every Tuesday and Thursday at lunch period._ Where? _In the classroom._

Did this happen?   ☐ YES   ☐ PARTLY   ☐ NO

Change/Activtity 2

What will be done? _Plan a fun learning game for the midmorning break._

Who will do it? _Ellie and the class._

When? _Every day from 10 to 10:20 a.m._ Where? _In the classroom._

Did this happen?   ☐ YES   ☐ PARTLY   ☐ NO

Change/Activity 3

What will be done? _Make friendship bracelets to remind us to be kind to classmates._

Who will do it? _Classroom students._

When? _Week 1._ Where? _In the classroom._

Did this happen?   ☐ YES   ☐ PARTLY   ☐ NO

(continued)

FIGURE 6.4. Completed Step 3 Worksheet "Intervention Plan Record" for Ellie's third-grade classroom.

Change/Activity 4

What will be done? _____

_____

Who will do it? _____

When? _____

Did this happen?   □ YES   □ PARTLY   □ NO

Data Collection

What data were collected? _Daily teacher notes of arguments (1) in class and (2) at recess._

_____

When were the data collected? _____

	Monday	Tuesday	Wednesday	Thursday	Friday
Date	yes	no	yes	yes	no

Attach the actual data records.

FIGURE 6.4. *(continued)*

CHAPTER 7

Including the Classroom's Students in Planning and Decision Making

Thus far, this book has described six essential characteristics of resilient classrooms, the tools and methods that can be used to assess these characteristics, and a data-based problem-solving framework for fostering classroom change. This chapter describes the strategies for engaging the classroom's students in interpreting their classroom's data, setting goals for classroom change, and acting as agents of change within their classroom. Much of this work will be initiated within the context of classroom meetings, with students taking responsibility for following through on the plans that are made during those meetings.

Classroom meetings are the very essence of the resilient classrooms projects, as they are where ideas for intervention are planned collaboratively with students, teachers, paraprofessionals, and other educators who work in the classroom. Classroom meetings are times when teachers and students discuss issues together or make decisions about their classroom routines, activities, and community (Developmental Studies Center, 1996). The collaborative discovery orientation of classroom meetings is very similar to student-centered constructivist teaching. The process is co-crafted with students whose spontaneous ideas may be very different from those that adults had anticipated. It is important that classroom meetings are planned and coordinated events. They include specific steps so that the necessary information is gathered, and they require skilled facilitation so that all class members can participate comfortably and readily. Classroom meetings also require a high degree of focused energy from the facilitators, who are responsible for monitoring both the meetings' content and the process for accuracy and sensitivity. Finally, classroom meetings require flexibility because the methods and strategies must vary to accommodate individual differences in classrooms and their members. Discussion strategies need to be adjusted to the concerns and purposes of each meeting, and these can change over time even within the same classroom.

This chapter describes a collaborative process for conducting classroom meetings that rely upon students and teachers to identify the characteristics of their classroom that need to be enhanced and the methods that will facilitate those changes. Four things generally happen during these meetings: first, data describing the classroom characteristics are presented to students; second, discussions explore student interpretations of the data; third, students make suggestions for ways to change the classroom that may subsequently be incorporated into the classroom's intervention plan; and, fourth, students, teachers, and other team members are assigned responsibilities for implementing the plan. Inevitably, as the plan is carried out, revisions are required and it becomes necessary to evaluate how well the intervention is working. Consequently, follow-up classroom meetings must be convened so that students can participate in these decisions as well. To describe these meetings clearly, a classroom example is provided at the end of this chapter.

Student participation is most active and useful when students know that their ideas are taken seriously and their suggestions probably will be used.

Above all else, student participation is most active and useful when students know that their ideas are taken seriously and their suggestions probably will be used.

The classroom meeting process described in this chapter is derived from numerous approaches to facilitating classroom meetings (Developmental Studies Center, 1996; Glasser, 1969; Murphy, 2002). A few key rules govern their effective facilitation. It is important that leaders ask questions, listen carefully, and confirm what they have heard with students to be certain that they understand how students are perceiving life in the classroom. This requires that the facilitator be an alert and respectful partner in the inquiry process and follow the lead from students and teachers. In turn, this leads to greater student and teacher engagement in the discussions. Initially, it is often easier when the teacher is not the primary facilitator of the classroom's meeting. Teachers play a critical role in determining the classroom characteristics and need to be able to participate freely in discussions about the classroom's data and plans for change. This gives students the implicit message that the teacher is working with them to plan for change. Facilitation responsibilities can be difficult for teachers to juggle simultaneously with student participation. Finally, the social climate created within classroom meetings inevitably spills over into other classroom activities, so it is critical that these meetings strengthen the respect that students have for their teacher and one another.

It is not uncommon for students to be reluctant to engage in classroom meetings. They may believe that their input will not really result in any classroom changes. Students may have experienced previous attempts to modify the classroom learning environment and may have seen little change despite their efforts. Particularly during the first few days of a new school year, teachers often request students' participation in developing classroom rules and routines. Sometimes this becomes a process by which teachers lead students, intentionally or not, to decide upon predetermined teacher or schoolwide rules. Especially when this happens repeatedly, students may not truly believe that their input has been heard and acknowledged. This is particularly true in classrooms in which a few students display unusually challenging behaviors. When students are hesitant to engage in the discussion, it may be necessary to spend additional time discussing the nature of the resilient classrooms process with students. This discussion can convey their teachers' eagerness to engage students in genuine dialogue about how to improve classroom practices. When students view their teachers as partners in facilitating classroom change, and teachers' genuine desire to make classroom changes is voiced to the students, student resistance is softened. In some classrooms, it is helpful to carefully introduce the team member who is working with the teacher during the resilient classrooms process. Students need reassurance that the facilitator is a trusted and reliable partner who will help the class think carefully about the classroom's needs and help the class thoughtfully plan and try out new strategies for change. Providing students with examples from previous resilient classrooms interventions, and the positive outcomes that these held for students and teachers, can promote students' confidence and active participation in data collection and classroom change.

MEETING FORMATS IN RESILIENT CLASSROOMS

Resilient classrooms meetings follow a predictable structure. After presenting the classroom data to students, four questions are posed in turn:

1. "Do you think the data are true?"
2. "What do you think causes this problem in our class?"
3. "What do you think the teacher could do differently to make things better?"
4. "What do you think students could do to make things better?"

One or two people should be responsible for keeping a written record of what the students say during the classroom meeting. In younger classes, at least one record keeper should be an adult. Still, regardless of the students' ages, it is useful to also assign student scribes to share responsibility for the meetings' record. When notes are displayed on a large chart tablet at the front of the room, every student in the class can monitor and reflect on the class's planning. (A blank Step 2 Worksheet "Classroom Meeting Record" is included in Appendix B.) This record will ensure that unexpected and innovative ideas that the class contributes will not be lost during future planning.

PRESENTING CLASSROOM DATA TO STUDENTS

In resilient classrooms meetings, students are shown data about their classroom's characteristics to prompt their planning and guide their decision making. Initially, adults should decide which pieces of the data should be shared with students. Large amounts of data can confuse students and make it difficult for them to draw out meaningful interpretations. Too few data may frustrate attempts to fully understand. Next, a graph of the data can be prepared. Visual displays of data make it easier for students to see the relevance of the data and to estimate the size and importance of differences and trends. These graphs are most effective when they first present the "big picture" to students and then proceed to finer details.

As a rule, students can integrate the key points most easily when fewer, more important facts are provided.

Presentation of these graphs and charts usually is the initiating event in a resilient classrooms meeting. The graphed data are displayed at the front of the group, and the strengths and weaknesses shown in the data are described briefly. Sometimes the discussion of the classroom data may require "stirring the pot" a little. The teacher and other team members may point out apparent contradictions in the data or generate student interest in subtle aspects of the data.

Examples of data charts and graphs that we have used are distributed throughout this book. However, in the early elementary grades, it is sometimes necessary to simplify graphs even further. For example, data diagrams can be restricted to one or two critical pieces of data displayed in a clear, engaging format. Figures 7.1 and 7.2 show two different presentations of data from the CMS Taking Charge subscale. Figure 7.1 is an illustrated chart that describes two important pieces of information for a second-grade urban classroom. Figure 7.2 is a six-bar graph that describes the same kind of information for an eighth-grade class. The simplified chart used with second graders conveys very similar information, but its format allows the younger students to understand the data easily and move comfortably into problem solving.

Figure 7.3 shows a graph from the CMS My Teacher subscale. A third-grade classroom's teacher believed that it would confuse her students, as the class had not yet started their graphing unit. Therefore, in Figure 7.4, the graph was simplified to show only the most important information that required student feedback and discussion. Having fewer bars to focus on and using the "number of students" instead of "percentage of students" on the vertical axis made it possible for students to interpret the data more easily.

In Writing, Math, and Science

Only half the students know when they make mistakes on their work.

Less than half the students know how to get the help they need.

How can we solve these problems?

FIGURE 7.1. An illustrated chart of second-grade classroom's ClassMaps Survey results for the Taking Charge subscale.

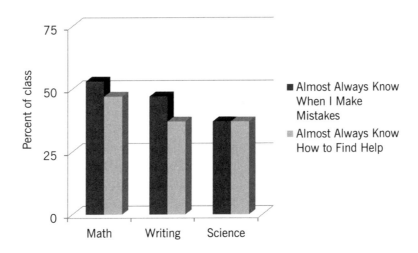

FIGURE 7.2. A six-bar graph of an eighth-grade classroom's ClassMaps Survey results for academic self-determination.

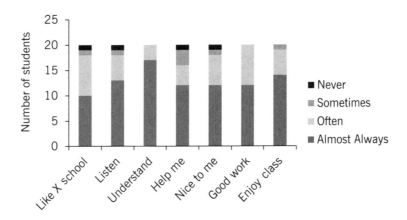

FIGURE 7.3. Original graph of a third-grade classroom's ClassMaps Survey results for teacher–student relationships.

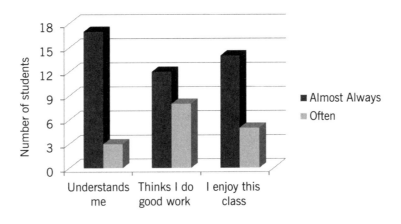

FIGURE 7.4. Simplified graph of a third-grade classroom's ClassMaps Survey results for teacher–student relationships.

	Student 1	Student 2	Student 3	Student 4	Student 5	Student 6
A lot of friends	4	12	1	4	3	1
Like to work with	5	6	0	3	3	0
Like to play with	7	7	1	2	3	1
Bugs kids most	0	0	5	1	1	6
Who finishes their work	6	5	1	2	2	0
Who often breaks the rules	1	0	6	1	2	4

FIGURE 7.5. Complex example of a fifth-grade classroom's sociometric rating survey results.

Chapter 5 included sociometric measures among existing strategies to assess peer relationships in classrooms. Sociometric data can be more complicated than survey data, but they are easily simplified so that students can reflect upon and understand them. Figure 7.5 is part of a sociogram from a fifth-grade urban classroom that was performing well below the norm on state academic standards. This diagram was used to launch a weekly classroom intervention to improve the students' goal-setting skills. (This intervention is described in detail in Chapter 8.) The presentation of sociometric data helped students select their classroom's academic and social goals and plan for ways to reach those goals. While the data described individual students' strengths and weaknesses, they did not identify any students by name. The chart prompted a rich discussion about which student on the chart represented the "ideal" that classmates would like to emulate. Then, the conversation quickly expanded into a discussion about what made some classmates more socially effective than others.

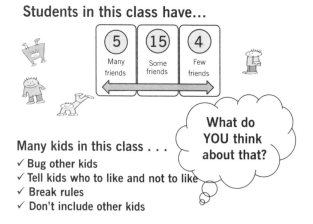

FIGURE 7.6. Simplified example of a third/fourth-grade classroom's sociometric rating survey results.

Figure 7.6 shows a chart that was used to show sociometric data to a third/fourth-grade classroom that was struggling with significant peer conflicts and chronic behavior referrals. This simple visual summary of the data led to a productive conversation without deepening the conflict between any of the students.

ENGAGING STUDENTS IN CLASSROOM MEETINGS

Discussion of the data's meaning typically engages students in a complex problem-solving discussion about the classroom. Students will be asked to describe the nature of the problem in their own words, to make guesses about why it is occurring in their classroom, to generate multiple recommendations for class change, and to suggest the recommendation that they believe will be most effective. They can breathe believability into the data by suggesting why the results occurred, and explaining incidents or anecdotes that illustrate the survey responses. Finally, students can contribute their explanations for what causes the problem in their classroom and what can be done to fix it.

It is important to ask for student recommendations by first asking what they think the teacher could do to help and then asking what the students could do differently to make things better. It is useful to ask about teacher solutions first because these are the first strategies to come to students' minds; once they have those listed, they can think more clearly about student solutions. Without asking for both student and teacher solutions, many students assume that the teacher is the only one who can make changes happen in their classroom. Classroom problem solving is much more useful if students generate lots of recommendations for change. The most effective recommendations are often in the middle of a long list—not at the top where the more obvious recommendations reside, and not at the bottom once the class starts searching for a solution. Consequently, it is important to resist the temptation to prematurely move to planning an intervention before all of the recommendations have been heard. Either the teacher or one of the students should be responsible for completing the Step 2 Worksheet "Classroom Meeting Record" (in Appendix B) during the classroom meeting. This record will ensure that unexpected and innovative ideas that the class contributes will not be lost during future planning.

There are a number of essential ingredients that increase the likelihood that students will participate actively in their classroom's meeting and contribute innovative ideas to the discussion. First, it is important to create a climate of "relaxed alertness" in the classroom (Caine & Caine, 1994). An optimal atmosphere for discussion is one in which students are highly engaged, actively participating, and comfortable with the prospect of sharing their own ideas and opinions. Second, a certain level of disequilibrium must be generated in the students. Students' thinking tends to be more productive and their contributions to be authentic when they are presented with challenging questions, unexpected data, or innovative ideas from one another. Since data usually provide fresh perspectives about the class, the presentation of data in resilient classrooms meetings almost always cues high-quality student participation. Teachers and facilitators can promote higher-order reasoning by arguing for a viewpoint in opposition to the prevailing discussion. Third, discussions generally are most spontaneous when students feel free to say what they think and respond honestly to the views of classmates and their teachers. Further, the social–emotional learning that can occur within these discussions may also contribute to students' understanding of themselves, their relationships, and their places in the classroom. Reluctant students can sometimes be prompted to participate if they are called by name, and inappropriate comments can usually be reframed so that they add to the class discussion.

A classroom's data can guide the progress of each classroom meeting. No two classroom meetings are the same because classroom concerns vary markedly from one classroom to the next and within the same classroom across the year. Because the meetings make no assumptions about the "true" meaning of the data until the students have provided their interpretations, unanticipated interpretations can sometimes shift the focus of the conversation in interesting and very useful ways.

For example, Figure 7.7 shows a graph of recess problems from a fifth-grade inner-city classroom. This very positive assessment of the recess period suggests that there were no concerns about peer interactions in this class. Only a very few children reported problems with arguing or being made fun of, and not one student reported that recess was "bad." Nevertheless, students in this class said that this report described an atypical day and that most of their recesses were fraught with arguments and lost friendships. Ultimately, the class planned an intervention to fix their recess problems because these were more pressing than any of the other issues presented in the meeting.

USING STUDENT SUGGESTIONS FOR CHANGE

The suggestions that students propose to answer complex problems are sometimes ingenious while, at other times, simplistic and shortsighted. Even then, elements in the suggestions can be incorporated into the classroom's co-crafted intervention. For example, a classroom was struggling with excess teasing and one student was convinced that enlarging the classroom's "no teasing" signs would help. While this suggestion was not an essential com-

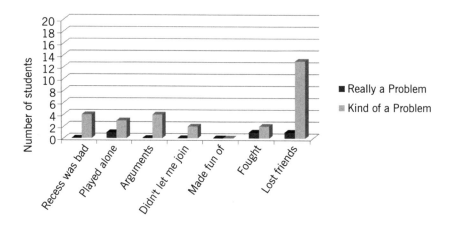

FIGURE 7.7. Graphic depicting recess problems in a fifth-grade classroom.

ponent of the intervention, it was included in the final plan because it would do no harm and would secure student commitment to the intervention. Using pieces of the students' sugges-

tions in the plan for change validates their efforts and makes it more likely that they will buy into the final plan. Classroom interventions must be acceptable to all key participants at multiple levels of the classroom system so that the intervention can be implemented with integrity and enthusiasm.

> **The suggestions that students propose to answer complex problems are sometimes ingenious while, at other times, simplistic and shortsighted.**

Solution-focused counseling techniques (Murphy, 2008) can focus students' contributions to intervention planning so that they build on the classroom's prior successes. The technique provides ground rules that classrooms can fall back on when there are divergent opinions disrupting their discussion. It is helpful to spend time discussing positive, proactive solutions to a problem, rather than complaining about the status quo. For example, it is more helpful for students to think of new and exciting games that they could play at recess rather than complain repeatedly about not being allowed to play football. As another example, it is more helpful for students to examine strategies to organize and simplify their classroom work, rather than focus their attention on how difficult their classwork is. Solution-focused techniques also foster tolerance and acceptance by emphasizing that there are many paths to the same solution and that more than one student can be "right." Using solution-focused strategies, the students can be guided to understand that if something is working well, it makes sense to do more of it and that practices that are not working should be stopped. Minor changes are valued even if they will not solve the whole problem because small changes can lead to bigger ones. The students can be pulled more fully into the intervention activities once they notice and appreciate the improvements that occur from small changes. Solution-focused counseling also discourages the use of absolutes because these are nonproductive and rarely accurate. For example, it's hard to agree to a student's suggestion that a bus driver be fired because he or she is "always" mean. At the same time, engaging the classroom in finding exceptions to absolutes is very productive. Most students can recall the bus driver being "nice" at least sometimes, and those occasions may become the seed that grows into an effective plan for better relationships with the bus driver.

In some classrooms, students may be reluctant to engage in the brainstorming process and have little faith that any real changes can occur. Consider Figure 7.8, which shows the My Teacher graph for a group of eighth-grade students attending a charter school. Students came to this charter school because they were having significant academic and behavior problems in their neighborhood schools. It was very difficult for the teacher in this example to manage the students' behavior and engage their interest in academic tasks. When presented with the My Teacher graph, most of the students agreed the results were accurate, and they described a major concern that their classroom was not fun. This led to a discussion about students' lack of preparation in earlier grades for the work that they were now being assigned. Students also wanted to work more often with a partner and wanted the teachers to pay more one-on-one attention to them. The teacher colleague who led the meeting explained, "I asked the students what they enjoyed doing, what they were good at, and what they considered 'fun' to do." As the students generated a list of activities, it became clear

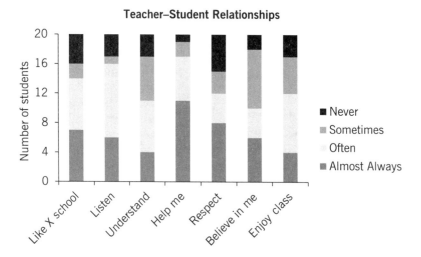

FIGURE 7.8. ClassMaps Survey results for teacher–student relationships in a charter school eighth-grade classroom.

that the students most enjoyed doing things they believed they were good at. Academic work—and the necessary attention, motivation, and goal setting that work requires—was not something they felt good about and enjoyed doing. Simply helping the students understand the source of their resistance to "hard" work (not liking it because they did not feel they were very good at it) was an important first step. The students were encouraged by the teacher's willingness to modify how assignments would be completed (e.g., teaming was OK, if the students could manage their behaviors). They also welcomed the teacher's agreement to make rounds of the class and provide more support shortly after assignments were started. This particular classroom faced some special challenges. Some changes to the classroom routine that would have minimized distractions and off-task behaviors were not endorsed by the administration, leaving the teacher's hands tied when it came to providing more structure and discipline in the classroom. It is not that unusual for teacher practices and administrative guidelines to be at odds with each other—restricting teachers' access to practices that might facilitate more behavioral and academic engagement. Another example of this—and strategies for reconciling such differences—are addressed in Chapter 9.

MAKING STUDENTS PARTNERS IN INTERVENTION

Participation from a classroom's students can also simplify the complex task of implementing classroom interventions. Examples of contributions that students can make are listed in Figure 7.9. Students can contribute to the work of collecting classroom data and graphing or analyzing the data. They can play key roles in implementing classroom interventions and in staffing the new tasks that an intervention might impose. For example, a second-grade class was temporarily housed in a sports arena while the school was undergoing asbestos removal, and the halogen lighting made it impossible to use overhead projectors to show the

- Assign students to take notes during a resilient classrooms class meeting.
- Ask students to organize, count, and graph data from a classroom measure.
- Have students conduct Internet or library research to develop all or part of an intervention. For example, students can find new games that could be added to the recess playground or search for simple rules for soccer.
- Put a student in charge of collecting daily classroom data. For example, students could count the number of homework folders that were returned each morning or gather classmates' daily responses to a one-item survey ("How much teasing happened at recess today?").
- Allow students to conduct a resilient classrooms research project as part of their science fair activities: identify the research question; pick out a measure; collect, collate, and graph the data; make some interpretations and recommendations for the future.
- Assign students to write, format, and copy newsletters to parents, telling them about the classroom's resilient classrooms project.
- Give students the job of creating materials or supplies for a resilient classrooms intervention.
- Allow students to advertise the resilient classrooms project in "public service announcements" targeted to families, other school employees, or community leaders.
- Have students keep track of whether or not each step in the intervention occurred using the intervention worksheet.

FIGURE 7.9. Strategies for involving students in resilient classrooms.

class data. Two students drew up a large copy of the classroom's data graph so that the class could discuss it together. A fifth-grade classroom was collecting daily surveys about recess problems as part of their classroom project to reduce playground conflicts. A student was assigned the task of collecting the surveys as the students came in from recess while the teacher prepared for the afternoon lesson. A fourth-grade class modified their lunchtime soccer game so that the rules were clear and were consistently enforced by the referee. Because playground paraprofessionals were not available to referee the game, the class assigned students to that role and arranged for a "referee-training curriculum" to make sure that the students would be successful. Another fourth-grade class established problem-solving notes for students to complete when they were caught up in a conflict; the notes minimized the need for adult intervention. In each case, the students' participation carried a dual benefit. It not only eased the work of the classroom's intervention but also enhanced the students' autonomy and self-determination.

> **Students can contribute to the work of collecting classroom data.**

SUMMARY

Until now, this book has emphasized the essential role that students play as members of the classroom ecological system. This chapter has emphasized the contributions that students can make toward understanding the classrooms' needs, identifying key strategies for change, and implementing classroom interventions. It is not clear where the upper limits of student contributions lie, and it is important that their potential not be underestimated. Students are a great untapped resource of classrooms, and their contributions to classroom change can make many more things possible.

INTRODUCTION TO A CASE STUDY OF STUDENT PARTICIPATION IN RESILIENT CLASSROOMS

David Fourmy and Kate Churley's case study, immediately following this chapter, demonstrates the power of student participation in classroom change efforts. Class 8C had a reputation as one of the most difficult in the school, and it would have been easy for the teacher to focus on tightening up the rules and imposing severe consequences for disruptions. Instead, by including the students in collaborative planning for solutions, the teacher was able to direct classroom changes that furthered the students' autonomy and respected their competence. Classroom changes supported by such shared decision making is more likely to endure into the future.

CASE STUDY

"Oh No, Not 8C . . . ": A Secondary School Class Changes Its Reputation

David Fourmy and Kate Churley
London Borough of Camden

The Problem

The head teacher's observation of a lesson in 8C confirmed teachers' views that it was a highly problematic class. The class was aware of the school's perception. A request for support from the Educational Psychology and Behavior Support Services resulted in an offer of the ClassMaps strategy as a way of promoting whole-class resiliency.

The ClassMaps Results

An analysis of the survey results indicated that students rated themselves highly in regard to academic efficacy and self-determination, but two main areas of concern emerged: peer relationships and behavioral self-control (see Figure 7.10).

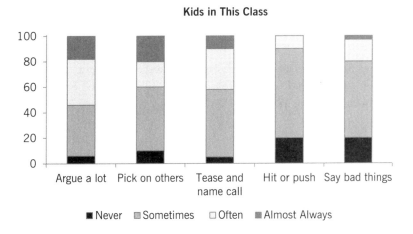

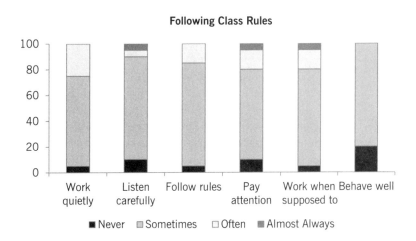

FIGURE 7.10. ClassMaps Survey preintervention results for peer relationships (top) and behavioral self-control (bottom) in 8C.

The Teachers' Sense

Incident reports from teachers across the curriculum had identified verbal aggression, a lack of respect for teacher authority, and poor engagement with learning as problems. The ClassMaps results made clearer the strengths within the class and the areas that students and staff needed to address collaboratively. All subject teachers completed a 10-point Likert scale to gain a clearer picture of their experiences of this class, their concerns, and the goals they would like to achieve. This process raised their awareness of the benefit of considering whole-class interpersonal relationships, rather than just focusing on individual characteristics of children. They also became more aware of their role in influencing classroom climate and promoting positive relationships, and its impact on achievement.

Results of the Classroom Meeting

A summary of the findings was presented to the whole class, and they all agreed that they would like things to change. Students completed the 10-point Likert scale to gain a more concrete sense of where they felt they were currently and where they would like to be (see Figure 7.11). Small-group solution-focused discussions then took place about how they would like to proceed.

Plan for Change

The students decided to take on the role of researchers themselves and were keen to take responsibility for changing their behavior. They also suggested ways that teachers could help improve the classroom environment. The class requested regular meetings during tutor time to review progress and get teacher feedback. Teachers agreed to allocate time in lessons to help students resolve any ongoing issues, allowing them to let problems go and give their attention back to learning. Additional support was provided by the mentoring team, and a restorative approach to solving conflict was used with the class.

Results

By giving the students the opportunity to use the ClassMaps framework to think together and take collective responsibility, a significant shift occurred quite quickly. This suggests that the ClassMaps process itself became a tool for facilitating change; as one student put it: "I wish we had more time to do this kind of thing." In the final evaluation meeting with the class, students rated themselves again using the ClassMaps Survey. There was whole-class consensus that they had made significant improvements in both areas, particularly in the area of interpersonal relationships (see Figure

Students' Likert ratings during the classroom meeting										
Kids in This Class	1	2	3	4	5	6	7	8	9	10
Where we are now		2			13	5				
Where we want to be							9	9	2	
And at the end of the year										
Where we are now									21	1

Students' Likert ratings during the classroom meeting										
Following Rules	1	2	3	4	5	6	7	8	9	10
Where we are now				11	8	1				
Where we want to be							4	14	1	1
And at the end of the year										
Where we are now							16	4	1	1

FIGURE 7.11. Results of Likert scale ratings for peer relationships and behavioral self-control.

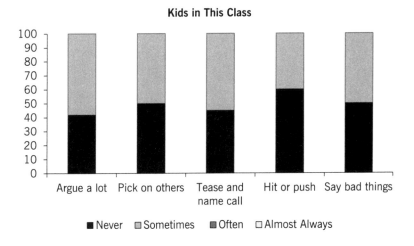

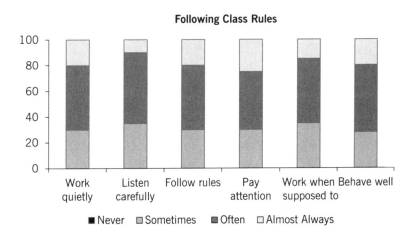

FIGURE 7.12. ClassMaps Survey postintervention results for peer relationships (top) and behavioral self-control (bottom) in 8C.

7.11). School data confirmed the students' views (see Figure 7.12): there was a marked reduction in incident reports and teachers found 8C more enjoyable to teach, saying that students were more cooperative and engaged in their lessons. When the head teacher observed a lesson at the end of this program, she praised the class and asked them what had made the difference: "We've been doing all this work as part of our research." Certificates were given to class members to acknowledge their role as researchers. At an end-of-year outing, their head of year reported that out of the whole-year group, only one class stayed together to decide what they wanted to do: 8C.

CHAPTER 8

Developing and Implementing
Effective Strategies

The student and teacher comments, interpretations, and suggestions that emerged during Chapter 7's classroom meetings are the raw materials from which a plan for change will be crafted. These provide the teacher and classroom team with an elaborated understanding of the classroom's strengths and weaknesses, the most important goals for classroom change, and the dynamics that might be contributing to classroom weaknesses. In some cases, these comments and suggestions will point inevitably to simple changes in classroom routines and practices that will strengthen the classroom's relationships or students' growing autonomy. We call these "microchanges" because they represent small but highly beneficial shifts in classroom practices that students and their teachers can immediately implement with existing classroom resources. Ideas for these microchanges might come from teachers' own experiences, the experiences of their colleagues, professional journals, or professional development workshops. While many of these changes have not been endorsed as "evidence based" by any professional group, they are made within a resilient classrooms project and classroom data will be available to evaluate their impact. If the microchanges are successful, there may be no need to implement an ambitious, resource-hungry, evidence-based intervention. On other occasions, microchanges might not be effective and the classroom's need for change could be pressing. In these cases, a classroom team might select an evidence-based intervention program identified in professional clearinghouses or research publications. In this chapter, we provide intervention strategy sheets listing microchanges and evidence-based interventions for each of the six characteristics of resilient classrooms, together with a conceptual framework for understanding how each characteristic is likely to change, and strategies for identifying additional evidence-based interventions as these emerge within the professional literature.

Microchanges and evidence-based interventions each have particular advantages and disadvantages. Microchanges tend to be resource efficient and, because they are usually quite simple, they can often be routinized seamlessly into the daily practices of a classroom. Thus, their impact can persist indefinitely because, once routinized, they never truly go away. They frequently emerge out of the students' and teachers' understanding of each unique classroom, and so readily accommodate the individual nature of the classroom. They build on the mechanisms that appear to underlie a particular classroom's problems. In contrast, evidence-based interventions tend to be resource costly, both with respect to time and money. They may require a realignment of classroom routines and so require a deeper and more persistent commitment by the teachers and students.

> **Evidence-based interventions often produce larger effects if implemented with good fidelity.**

Still, evidence-based interventions often produce larger effects if implemented with good fidelity, and they are sometimes effective in classrooms that are resistant to less ambitious interventions.

While everyone on the classroom team will participate in selecting the intervention, it is particularly important that the teacher make the primary decisions about classroom change. Interventions will be implemented more completely and will be maintained longer when those affected have a voice in their selection. For each resilient classrooms characteristic, this chapter includes a strategy sheet that lists examples of microchanges and evidence-based interventions that are relevant to that characteristic. Copy-ready versions of each strategy sheet are included in Figures 8.2–8.7. The strategy sheets play an important role in engaging teachers in intervention planning. Microchanges listed on each sheet act as catalysts for the teachers' brainstorming: they broaden teachers' thinking about possible interventions, remind them of familiar practices they might have used previously, and provide "seed" ideas that can be grown into very suitable changes for the teachers' own classrooms. The evidence-based interventions listed on each sheet alert the team to manualized programs for change. The one-page strategy sheet format allows all members of the classroom team to scan through these ideas quickly during the course of a discussion so that their planning is informed by others' work while also shaped by their own professional expertise. In some cases, in which a team's planning might cut across two or more strategy sheets, we have copied each sheet on a different color of paper so that the team members can communicate quickly with each other about the fourth idea on the yellow sheet or the second idea on the pink sheet. Over time, teams in a school might revise and refine strategy sheets in any particular domain, so that these capture the new and innovative practices that have emerged within a school's classrooms.

The plan for intervention also needs to be tailored to the unique concerns of an individual classroom. Again, all key classroom participants should be included in planning for these modifications. In particular, the more involved students are in crafting, selecting, and modifying an intervention, the more likely they are to adhere to the classroom's plan. Chapter 7 describes ways to fully include students in resilient classrooms planning. Consider an example from a seventh-grade classroom. Figure 8.1 shows the data about peer relationships that were presented to students in a classroom meeting. Table 8.1 is an abbreviated transcript of the students' discussion of the data. Toward the end of the classroom discussion, students began generating some strategies that would help them feel more empowered

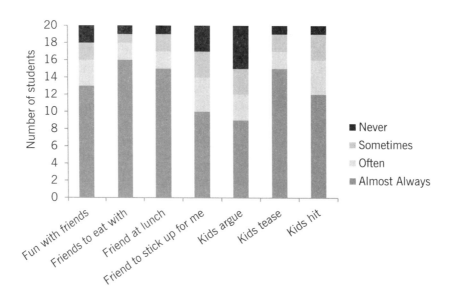

FIGURE 8.1. ClassMaps Survey graph for peer relationships in a seventh-grade classroom.

in the class and, at the same time, more accepting of one another. Ultimately, their participation strengthened their active involvement in the classroom changes.

Evidence-based interventions should be selected with an eye toward their empirical support. An intervention is more likely to have an important impact on the classroom when there are objective research data showing that it has worked in similar classrooms. Interventions should also be selected because they suit the specific attributes of a classroom. Key attributes that can alter the impact of an intervention include the demographics of the community, the resource personnel available to the classroom, or the philosophical orientation and skill of the teacher. Because of attributes such as these, an anti-bullying program that proved highly successful in Des Moines might not be appropriate for a classroom in Los Angeles. Even comprehensive, evidence-based programs might not be suitable for a particular classroom without being adapted to that classroom's unique needs. Nevertheless, when modifying interventions, practitioners must consider the degree to which the program can still yield positive results despite the alterations. In some cases, it may be more appropriate to select a different intervention strategy than to lose the integrity of an evidence-based program.

Over the past two decades, educators and other researchers have clearly articulated the standards for establishing that an intervention has evidence that it is effective. Interventions are evidence based when they have been examined in at least two well-designed group studies or a series of well-conducted small-n studies, in which participants were randomly assigned to treatment and control groups, and the results demonstrated that improvements occurred and were caused by the intervention. Interventions are most convincing when their effects are at least as strong as the effects of competing interventions, and when the studies have been conducted by researchers who were not the intervention's author. Using this or similar definitions as criteria, there are several national websites that review inter-

TABLE 8.1. Seventh-Grade Students' Discussion of ClassMaps Survey Peer Relationships Results

Q. What do you notice about this graph? Is it accurate?

A. Yes. It's accurate. Lots of kids in this class have friends to spend time with but lots of kids are saying there is hitting in the class—maybe they're the ones who are being pushed around by other kids.

Q. What do you think about that?

A. It's not OK because that makes this class not a good place. . . . It's not OK because usually if you are getting hit, even if the kid is playing around, you'll end up hitting back. There's definitely a lot of arguing that goes on all day and in other classes too.

Q. Why do you think there's so much arguing?

A. Because we are all different. People tease other kids because they're different. Sometimes it can just be fun. Yeah, but sometimes when kids finished their work they bother kids who are still working. Some kids don't even do their work. They bother lots of kids!

Q. How come that happens?

A. It's easy to lose attention if work is not at your level. Then you start bugging kids. The people who are ahead on their work should walk around and help keep an eye on things and help other kids.

Q. Raise your hands if you'd like there to be less arguing in this class.

A. (*Most of the students raised their hands.*)

Q. How could that happen?

A. We should learn how to accept other people more. It has to be individual, you have to want to not hit other kids and stop arguing. We just need to learn to respect rules before we'll ever really follow them.

Q. What would make kids respect rules more?

A. They're not our rules—we didn't make them.

Q. What if you did?

A. It would be easier to follow them. We never get to make the rules, we're just kids.

Q. Are you saying that if we let kids help make the class rules, and if we were sure to give work that was at kids' level, and if we can help kids figure out ways to accept other kids who are different, then there'd be less arguing, teasing, and hitting?

A. (*Most kids agreed.*)

Q. What should we work on first?

A. We can make some different rules in the class.

Q. What kind of different rules?

A. The kids who finish their work should help other kids. . . . I mean really help, not make fun of them. Then the teacher could give good reports for kids to take home. We should also have a rule about accepting other kids. If the class was more fun and interesting, we wouldn't bother each other so much. Everyone should eat breakfast! And shut off the air conditioner. . . . It's too noisy!

vention research and list interventions meeting these criteria. The most prominent of these are:

- U.S. Department of Education's What Works Clearinghouse
  http://ies.ed.gov/ncee/wwc
- Center for the Study and Prevention of Violence
  www.colorado.edu/cspv
- Model Program Guide of the U.S. Office of Juvenile Justice and Delinquency Prevention
  www.ojjdp.gov/mpg

What follows is a sampling of microchanges and evidence-based interventions that can be used to enhance the resilience of classrooms. Even though each of these is listed under one of the six characteristics, many have the potential to affect several characteristics simultaneously. This is because, as explained in Chapters 3 and 4, characteristics of resilient classrooms are strongly interconnected and effectiveness in one area is often related to or caused by effectiveness in another.

In all cases, evaluation of the success of these interventions should be embedded into the intervention plan. Even evidence-based interventions that have strong empirical support may not show the same results in the unique setting of a specific classroom. Evaluation will be even more important for microchanges that may have little empirical data supporting their use. The purpose of these embedded evaluations is to verify whether the resilient classrooms characteristics have been adequately enhanced or whether alternative interventions are necessary. Chapters 5 and 9 provide further guidance on planning and conducting these evaluations.

TEACHER–STUDENT RELATIONSHIPS

Interventions to strengthen teachers' relationships with their students inevitably rest upon the two simple principles of mutual respect and enjoyable time together. This is somewhat counterintuitive; it makes more sense that strong relationships ought to emerge out of carefully crafted prosocial interchanges between the teacher and the students. Early teaching manuals sometimes scripted particular ways of speaking to children so that only positive words were used and children were uniformly praised and prompted to feel good. However, human relationships are more fundamentally authentic than these scripts might suggest. Even awkward and inexperienced exchanges can be touching when both parties sense that the interaction is trustworthy, real, and caring. Respect is conveyed when these interactions reflect ambitious expectations of the students, and joy emerges out

> **Interventions to strengthen teachers' relationships with their students inevitably rest upon the principles of mutual respect and enjoyable time together.**

of interactions in which students and teachers have fun together. A comprehensive description of the mechanisms by which teacher–student relationships support student success can be found in Chapter 3.

Microchanges for Teacher–Student Relationships

The microchanges listed in Figure 8.2 emphasize the creation of such moments with students. Of course, the immediate objection of most teachers is that schools are busy places and class schedules are rarely flexible enough for these moments to occur. An experienced

---

EXAMPLES OF MICROCHANGES IN ROUTINES AND PRACTICES

- Create brief moments when teachers and other adults check in with students—to share a student's successes and struggles and to show interest and respect.
- Warmly greet students at the beginning of class, quickly review the day ahead, and remind them of one thing that they can do to make the day successful.
- Actively listen to students during brief conversations—reflect back what they have said to show that you have truly listened.
- Hold regular classroom meetings to make decisions, prepare for classroom changes, and gather student perceptions of challenges.
- Play games with students—learning games, playground games, waiting games—and inject more fun into the classroom.
- Celebrate students' strengths and interests. Draw attention to their successes, explain why they are likely to succeed again, and remind them of how much they have accomplished in the last week or month.
- Match struggling students with an adult at school who meets regularly with them and pays particular attention to them.
- Add more humor to the classroom—tell jokes, post cartoons, or read funny stories. Have a "bad joke" moment each day.
- Give students a chance to cool off when things get tense, and then return to work once they have collected their sense of control.
- Hold high expectations for students and make sure that they know you do.

EVIDENCE-BASED INTERVENTIONS

- **Students, Teachers, and Relationship Support (STARS) Program** (Pianta & Hamre, 2001). This is one of the few teacher–student relationship programs. It describes a systematic procedure in which teachers enhance their relationships with students by scheduling positive interactions each day (banked time) and then mastering effective conduct management strategies. Evidence shows that the program strengthens teachers' relationships with the students, reduces discipline problems, and enhances students' attachment to school.

FIGURE 8.2. Strategies for promoting teacher–student relationships.

teacher explained, instead, "I don't have time for all of the disruptions and distractions that occur unless I check in regularly with my students." Joy and caring does not always need to interrupt the ongoing work of a classroom. On an oppressively hot day, one teacher sprayed cooling mint water into the air over students while they worked. Another led small word games with students while they waited in the cafeteria line. A third went outside with the class at recess a few times each month and taught them new games to play. While the scripts of teacher–student conversations are of secondary importance, it still can be useful to think carefully about the language that teachers use with students. Faber and Mazlish (1995) describe an active-listening approach to conversations between teachers and their students. Classroom teams might draw upon this reference to plan new ways of interacting that would foster more comfortable teacher–student conversations.

Evidence-Based Interventions for Teacher–Student Relationships

There are very few evidence-based strategies for strengthening teacher–student relationships. One exception is Pianta and Hamre's (2001) Students, Teachers and Relationship Support (STARS) program, which describes a systematic, data-tested procedure for consulting with teachers in order to enhance their relationships with their students. A striking component of the STARS is its "banking time" intervention in which the teacher spends between 5 and 15 minutes daily with a target student doing some activity of the student's choice. This positive time creates a reserve of emotional goodwill that allows the teacher–student relationship to withstand later conflict without deteriorating. While banking time is designed to be a dyadic intervention, it might be modified for classwide implementation. One teacher created a personal moment board on which each student selected a weekly time to be "heard" and receive some private attention. This is a variant of banking time that is available to all students in the classroom.

PEER RELATIONSHIPS

Interventions to foster a caring and engaging community of students require careful attention to classroom friendships, peer conflict, and peer aggression. The foundation of interventions is friendships. Students will be more invested in the peer community when they have friends to talk with, eat with, and hang out with. Inevitably, these friendships will have some conflict, but as long as disputes are resolved and do not unduly interrupt the friendships, they will not detract from the classroom's peer community. Still, a special case of unresolved conflict is particularly troublesome: peer aggression in which one student deliberately acts to harm another student. Microchanges described in Figure 8.3 may address any or all of these three aspects. A comprehensive description of these aspects of peer relationships and of the

> The foundation of interventions to foster a caring and engaging community of students is friendships.

EXAMPLES OF MICROCHANGES IN ROUTINES AND PRACTICES

Peer Friendships

- Find multiple tasks for students to complete with a classmate and, occasionally, assign them to unexpected partners. These can be classroom chores, instructional tasks, or classroom privileges.
- Teach students to play noncompetitive games that are appealing but have no clear winners and losers.
- Add many more attractive and developmentally appealing games to the playground with special attention to games that can be played by students with limited athletic ability, games for small and large groups, and games that are very physical or very sedate.
- Hold "game clinics" in which a new game is taught at recess—start with a small group that includes a few isolated students. Once the game starts, anyone can join.

Peer Conflict

- Solve frequent and predictable arguments in advance with classroom meetings.
- Have students who argue complete a "conflict worksheet" together to talk through what happened and how to fix it.
- Relocate playground games so that they don't bump into each other.
- Write simple school rules for the common playground games (soccer, basketball, four square) that students often argue about.
- Make a routine for choosing teams once a week (balancing the skills on teams) and use those same teams until the next week.
- Add more supervisors to the playground or change where they are located.
- Change what supervisors do: have them actively circulate on the playground and prompt students to play and resolve conflicts.
- Shorten the length of the recess.
- Conduct a "recess workshop" in which all students tour the playground together while reviewing the routines, rules, proper use of equipment, entry/exit procedures, strategies for having fun together, and supervisors' actions when there are problems. Add a booster workshop midway through the year.
- Hold "recess school" for students who accrue more than three "sit outs" in a month. In the school, students should overpractice the right ways to play games or use recess equipment and relearn the routines and rules.
- Invite a prominent local athlete to the school to talk about good sportsmanship.

Aggressive Conflict and Bullying

- Have students mark playground maps with the places where bullying occurs and plan extra supervision of these places.
- Encourage students who are the targets of bullying to play near supervisors.
- Conduct classroom meetings to increase empathy in the students who observe bullying and prepare them to stop it.
- Meet with all playground supervisors to discuss aggressive conflict and ways to interrupt it.
- Sensitize students to bullying by using a video or read-aloud book (e.g., *Bridge over Terabithia*) to prompt a class discussion of what it feels like to be bullied.

(continued)

FIGURE 8.3. Strategies for promoting peer relationships.

EVIDENCE-BASED INTERVENTIONS

- There are several anti-bullying programs that have been shown to reduce rates of bullying in schools. Examples include:
  - **Bullying Prevention Program** (Olweus, Limber, & Mihalic, 1999). This program alerts teachers, students, and parents to the varying and subtle forms of bullying and prepares them to respond promptly and decisively to discourage such behavior.
  - **Bully Busters.** A teacher's manual (Newman, Horne, & Bartolomucci, 2000) provides teachers with strategies to intervene to reduce bullying and prevent future incidents with classroom meetings and activities.
  - **Second Step** (Frey, Hirschstein, & Guzzo, 2000). This program teaches students social and emotional skills for violence prevention.
- **Promoting Alternative Thinking Strategies (PATHS) Program** (Greenberg, Kusche, & Mihalic, 1998). Evidence has demonstrated that this classwide program strengthens the social competence of preschool and elementary children. The program includes 20-minute lessons taught three times each week on emotional literacy, self-control, social competence, and interpersonal problem-solving skills.
- **Strong Kids** (Merrell, Gueldner, & Tran, 2008). This curriculum provides classroom teachers with 10 to 12 half-hour lessons on diverse topics related to social–emotional learning. One component of the program addresses students' competent peer interactions. Versions of the Strong Kids curricula are available for preschool, early elementary, late elementary, and middle school grades. Evidence shows small but robust improvements in students' social–emotional competence.
- **I Can Problem Solve** (Shure, 1997). This was one of the earliest social learning programs and it continues to demonstrate significant increases in children's prosocial behaviors and decreases their social impulsivity. It is a yearlong curricula that teaches students to think about the social problems that they encounter, consider alternative solutions, carefully consider the feelings of other students and themselves, and translate these into competent social behaviors.

FIGURE 8.3. *(continued)*

mechanisms by which peer relationships support student success can be found in Chapter 3.

Microchanges for Peer Relationships

Peer Friendships

Teachers have struggled mightily to find classroom strategies that foster friendships for students without friends. Inevitably, adults will try to nudge self-isolating students into asking a classmate to play at recess, or they will prompt an empathic student to adopt an isolated classmate into their play. Still, the dominant principle underlying peer friendships is quite simple. Like teacher–student relationships, students' friendships with classmates are strengthened when they have fun doing things together. The friendship-promoting microchanges described in Figure 8.3 create frequent and diverse opportunities for students to work together with different students on various enjoyable tasks around the classroom. Small classroom chores are particularly effective because these are brief and nonthreatening, and students may learn that they enjoy having a moment to share a few words with a less familiar classmate.

Peer Conflict

Much of teachers' time and attention has been devoted to stopping conflicts when these occur and (by enforcing rules with consequences) to preventing conflicts altogether. Still, a practical reality is that interpersonal conflicts are ubiquitous—and people of all ages inevitably have conflicts when sharing resources, asserting needs, and defending themselves. As evidence, consider adult work environments—it is a rare setting that does not have its share of work "politics." Thus, while the frequency of peer conflicts can be reduced, they will never go away altogether. The peer relationships microchanges described in Figure 8.3 emphasize repairing conflicts when they occur so that the free flow of relationships is uninterrupted and so that all students who are involved are comfortable with the resolution.

Peer Aggression

When one student is deliberately acting to harm another student, adults will need to intervene to protect the vulnerable students, stop subsequent aggression, and ensure that the students know better strategies for dealing with future conflicts. Certain microchanges in Figure 8.3 work to reduce the frequency of peer aggression by limiting the number, place, type, and benefit of peer aggression in the classroom. Then, additional microchanges or evidence-based interventions may be needed to teach the social–emotional competencies that students need to cope effectively with peer aggression in the future.

Classroom meetings have great potential for altering all three aspects of the peer climate in classrooms while fostering prosocial peer relationships among students (Developmental Studies Center, 1996; Murphy, 2002). Classroom meetings also provide a fertile environment for bibliotherapy strategies that can help students talk through classroom concerns. Doll and Doll (1997) provide a practical overview of children's mental health needs and the bibliotherapy tools that teachers and classroom teams can integrate into classrooms' reading instruction, recreational reading, or instruction in other content areas. In particular, children's books have been used to assist classrooms when students are talking through friendship issues and bullying.

Evidence-Based Interventions for Peer Relationships

There are numerous evidence-based interventions that foster positive peer relationships in classrooms, proof that considerable importance is attached to managing the peer climate of a class. Still, most of these interventions have a goal of preventing bullying and related forms of aggression. One of the oldest of these is the Bullying Prevention Program (Olweus, Limber, & Mihalic, 1999), which alerts teachers, students, and parents to the varying and subtle forms of bullying and prepares them to respond promptly and decisively to discourage such behavior. It has been identified as Blueprint Model Programs by the Center for the Study and Prevention of Violence. Other bullying prevention programs include Bully Busters (Newman, Horne, & Bartolomucci, 2000) and Bully-Proofing Your School (Garrity, Jens, Porter, Sager, & Short-Camilli, 1997).

Some evidence-based programs target students' overall social competence. In their book *Promoting Social and Emotional Learning*, Elias et al. (1997) describe a wide range of school-based interventions designed to promote student's social and academic competence and the quality of peer and adult interpersonal relationships. When integrated into the school curriculum, social and emotional learning (SEL) strategies have demonstrated success in promoting students' attachment to school, school completion, receptivity to learning, and academic success (Blum, McNeely, & Rinehart, 2002; Osterman, 2000; Wilson, Gottfredson, & Najaka, 2001). One example of an evidence-based SEL programs is the Committee for Children's Second Step program. This program works to strengthen students' empathy, emotional regulation, and social problem solving. It has been identified as a model program by the U.S. Department of Education, the Substance Abuse and Mental Health Services Administration, and the Office of Juvenile Justice and Delinquency Prevention. Similarly prominent, Greenberg, Kusche, and Mihalic's (1998) Promoting Alternative Thinking Strategies (PATHS) Program teaches children emotional literacy, self-control, social competence, and interpersonal problem-solving skills. It has been designated a Blueprint Model Program by the Center for the Study and Prevention of Violence.

Social skills training programs are used frequently by school mental health professionals to improve the quality of peer relationships. While there is some evidence to suggest that children with peer problems can benefit from such training (Bullis, Walker, & Sprague, 2001), meta-analytic studies suggest that social skills training programs typically fail to show large treatment gains (Luellen, 2003). Gresham, Sugai, and Horner's (2001) review of the social skills research revealed generally weak effect sizes. Disappointing results were also reported in meta-analyses by Quinn, Kavale, Mathur, Rutherford, and Forness (1999) and Mathur, Kavale, Quinn, Forness, and Rutherford (1998). Subsequently, researchers have suggested that it is the generalization of social skills to actual class environments that presents the difficulty, and contemporary studies are examining the impact of social skills instruction when it is conducted in natural rather than pull-aside locations (Corkum, Corbin, & Pike, 2010; DuPaul & Weyandt, 2006).

HOME–SCHOOL RELATIONSHIPS

Schools are placing increasing emphasis on home–school relationships in the face of growing evidence that they are potent predictors of students' ultimate academic success (NRC/IOM, 2004). In the past 10 years, advances in both research and practice have articulated a clearer understanding of the characteristics of effective relationships (Christenson, 2004; Hoover-Dempsey et al., 2005). Above all, effective home–school relationships are partnerships in which families and schools value each other's perspectives and recognize the important contributions both make for student success. Building these partnerships is most difficult when there are large disconnects in social class, physical distance, or spoken language between schools and their families. Working around these constraints requires high-quality communication in which parents are kept informed about the school curriculum and their students' learning and behavior, and schools are kept informed about family strengths and the goals that families hold for their students. A comprehensive description of the mechanisms by which home–school relationships support student success can be found in Chapter 3.

Microchanges for Home–School Relationships

Most microchanges that promote home–school partnerships routinely invite families to participate in the classroom; create student-centered events that attract families' interest and celebrate their children; and work around family constraints related to work schedules, low income, transportation limitations, or language differences (see Figure 8.4). The most promising microchanges for connecting classrooms and families are often crafted from scratch. For example, in Chapter 3 we described a teacher who created videotapes of the teacher and their child working together on typical homework problems. Then, the tapes were sent home for parents to view, and the taped interactions made it easy for parents to understand what "helping with homework" looked like. Similarly, students in an urban middle school created an art exhibit portraying their views of the community. Both of these projects fostered a great deal of home–school conversation and, because students carried out most of the work, these did not intrude unnecessarily into teachers' workdays. Similarly, students can write and mail letters home, create class newsletters, or post announcements on a class website. We have worked with teachers who assign students the task of interviewing their parents about the changes they have seen in schooling since they were children. Others have assigned students to ask their parents for contributions to the "suggestions-from-home" box each week. Students can invite their grandparents or parents into the class to teach a wide range of talents such as cooking, astronomy, carpentry, law, or the history of their community. In every case, these microchanges invite families to become involved in a student-centered activity in the school and because their own children "star" in the activities, they are inherently more engaging to families.

Evidence-Based Interventions for Home–School Relationships

An evidence-based strategy for promoting effective home–school collaboration can be found in Sheridan and Kratochwill's (2008) model of conjoint behavioral consultation (CBC). CBC provides specific guidelines for engaging the mutual efforts of parents, teachers, and school psychologists in developing and implementing behavioral or learning plans for students (Sheridan, Eagle, Cowan, & Mickelson, 2001). While the focus of CBC is typically on the problems experienced by a single student, the process can be adapted to explore solutions to classroom-level concerns. The problem-solving, collaborative nature of CBC can provide a medium for constructive, goal-directed, solution-oriented home–school partnerships. A second innovative evidence-based program, Linking the Interests of Families and Teachers (LIFT; Eddy, Reid, & Fetrow, 2000), provides parents with instruction in effective discipline through six meetings at their child's school at the same time as teachers are taught more effective classroom management strategies. LIFT has been identified as a Blueprint Promising Program by the Center for the Study and Prevention of Violence.

EXAMPLES OF MICROCHANGES IN ROUTINES AND PRACTICES

- Send regular communications home to families—let students write and illustrate the notes, newsletters, or entries on a classroom webpage.

- Have students write letters or make phone calls to their family to celebrate their successes. Or take a photo of the classroom celebration and send it to the family.

- Every once in a while, assign activities in which one part can be completed at school but the second part is completed at home with a family member.

- Hold regular 1-hour "open class" times when families can come in to discuss different topics of concern to them and their child.

- Videotape a classroom presentation or activity and let students take the video home to show their family.

- Construct book bags holding a book, an object or picture related to the book, and a journal notebook. Students will read the book with their families, talk about the object, and the family will write a note in the journal to send back to class with the book bag.

- Keep a classroom website where families can go to find out what the students are learning and what homework has been assigned. To ease the upkeep of a website, have students help compose it and keep it up to date.

EVIDENCE-BASED INTERVENTIONS

- **Conjoint Behavioral Consultation** (CBC; Sheridan, 1997). This is a unique form of systematic consultation in which teachers and parents meet together with a behavioral consultant to devise solutions to student learning or behavior problems. The intervention uses systematic data-based problem-solving procedures and requires adequate meeting time. However, the time is well spent; results show significant improvements in students' success and improved communication between home and school.

- **Linking the Interests of Families and Teachers Program** (LIFT; Eddy, Reid, & Fetrow, 2000). This preventive intervention has been shown to be effective in reducing rates of conduct problems and substance use among children living in communities with high rates of delinquency. Students participate in classroom lessons promoting positive behaviors while parents are instructed in the use of similar discipline strategies in the home, and teachers are taught more effective classroom management strategies.

- **Seattle Social Development Project** (Hawkins et al., 1992). This intervention also provides parent management training for parents while teachers learn strategies in proactive classroom management and cooperative learning. Variations on the training are provided at each of grades one through six. When implemented across all school years, evidence shows that the program reduces delinquency and strengthens children's prosocial attachments to families and school.

FIGURE 8.4. Strategies for promoting home–school relationships.

ACADEMIC EFFICACY

In very simple terms, two things interfere with students' expectations that they will succeed in school: they are overwhelmed by the enormity of the academic task that they face, or they believe that success on that task is wholly outside of their own control. Unfortunately, the current circumstances in schools often lead students (and sometimes their teachers) to believe that their failure is inevitable: the state and national standards require performance on standards assessments that may appear entirely too ambitious; and success, when it occurs, seems accidental. Brophy (2004) calls these "pie-in-the-sky" beliefs and explains that these beliefs lead inevitably to student expectations for failure.

Fortunately, convincing students of their potential for excellence simply requires reversing these two perceptions: show students that overwhelming expectations can be reached in a series of smaller and very achievable steps, and prove to students that they can successfully reach these steps one at a time. While most of the microchanges and interventions described in Figure 8.5 capitalize on these sorts of success experiences, some also take advantage of two additional principles for fostering self-efficacy that were described by Bandura (1993, 1997). Efficacy beliefs can be shaped vicariously by observing other students succeed on similar tasks, and they can be prompted through persuasion in which teachers or other students express their own confidence that a student will succeed. Managing verbal persuasion might require reshaping the discourse in the classroom so that students notice and draw attention to one another's successful achievements. A comprehensive description of the mechanisms by which academic efficacy supports student success can be found in Chapter 4.

Microchanges for Academic Efficacy

The microchanges listed in Figure 8.5 embed these simple strategies into the daily routines of classrooms. Large steps are broken into a series of smaller steps, and attention is carefully drawn to the myriad small successes that students experience when working toward these smaller steps. Small celebrations of students' successes need not rely on teachers alone; classmates, too, contribute to the shared efficacy of all students in a class. Teachers can use numerous daily practices to foster students' academic efficacy, even within the constraints of typical classroom grading policies and standards-based assessment (Brophy, 2004). These include teaching for and carefully monitoring student understanding, even if this means slowing the pace of instruction. Covering less material

> **Efficacy beliefs can be shaped vicariously by observing other students succeed on similar tasks.**

with the goal of uncovering deeper understanding is a solid instructional strategy that also enhances efficacy. Efficacy is enhanced when classroom procedures provide quick, accurate, and detailed feedback to students so as to strengthen their control over their own learning. Instruction is efficacy enhancing when it emphasizes student effort and personal understanding and avoids comparisons with other students.

EXAMPLES OF MICROCHANGES IN ROUTINES AND PRACTICES

- Deliver "strong praise" to students several times a day: one sentence describing what the student did; a second sentence saying why it mattered; and a third sentence stating how much you appreciated it.

- Coach students to use "strong praise" with one another. Begin by giving students small tokens or chips for a job well done; then, let students take over responsibility for awarding tokens to classmates when they catch them being great. Make sure the tokens reward effort, diligence, careful work, and helpfulness—not just success. Script some words that classmates will say to each other as they award the tokens.

- Provide prompt, accurate, and specific feedback to students about their successes on classroom work.

- Teach a "strategy of the week" that students can use to succeed on schoolwork. Give each strategy a name, model it, have the students practice it three or four times on simple tasks, and then prompt them to use the strategy several times a day. At the end of the week, add the strategy to the classroom's "book of learning tricks" and periodically review previous strategies.

- Use a "task ladder" to teach unfamiliar tasks by first discussing a model of a completed task; then assign a task for two or three students to complete together and then check against a key; next assign a task for students to complete independently and check against a key; and finally assign a task for students to complete independently and turn in.

- Guide students through step-by-step planning for large assignments: break the assignment down into six or eight steps, complete one step at a time, review and check the whole assignment, and track their progress over time while they work through the assignment. And always, always have students "pat themselves on the back" as each step is done.

- Identify times and places that students can use to get extra help if they need it: a 20-minute lunchtime open house, a bit of "catch-up" time carved out of class, or a half-hour "think about it" time after school. Students who are caught up can use that time to earn extra credits by helping a classmate.

- Immediately and forcefully confront any shaming, embarrassing, or cajoling comments about students by classmates or others.

EVIDENCE-BASED INTERVENTIONS

Evidence-based interventions that address academic efficacy generally incorporate efficacy units into larger multiunit programs to strengthen their overall autonomy and social competence:

- **Positive Action Program** (PA; Flay, Allred, & Ordway, 2001). This is a wellness-oriented program that teaches students in kindergarten through twelfth grade to self-assess, set, and work toward self-improvement goals. Some of the units foster students' sense of efficacy. At each grade level, there are scripted classroom units and a manualized intervention for school mental health professionals to use with students at greater risk. Evidence suggests that this program strengthens students' social–emotional skills.

- **Unique Minds School Program** (Linares et al., 2005; Stern, 1999). This manualized curriculum provides lessons for kindergarten through fifth-grade students to enhance their self-efficacy, problem solving, and social–emotional functioning.

- **Strong Kids** (Merrell, Gueldner, & Tran, 2008). This curriculum provides classroom teachers with 10 to 12 half-hour lessons on diverse topics related to social–emotional learning. As part of its broader target of strengthening social–emotional competence, the program includes several units addressing students' recognition of their personal strengths and success. Versions of the Strong Kids curricula are available for preschool, early elementary, late elementary, and middle school grades. Improvements in social–emotional competence are modest but significant, and the program is easier to implement than many therapy-based interventions.

FIGURE 8.5. Strategies for promoting academic efficacy.

Evidence-Based Interventions for Academic Efficacy

Despite the very rich research on the nature of academic efficacy and its strong relation to students' school success, there are relatively few evidence-based efficacy interventions. Those that are available typically embed efficacy-promoting strategies into a broader SEL curriculum. Thus, the foundational units of the Positive Action (PA) Program (Flay, Allred, & Ordway, 2001) are units on Self-Concept and Positive Actions for Your Body and Mind. PA is predicated on the principle that students who feel good about themselves will also act and interact in positive ways. An advantage of PA is that it is written to be provided for teachers, school mental health providers, families, and community members; evaluations of its impact have shown increased academic achievement and school completion, and fewer discipline referrals (Flay & Allred, 2003; Li et al., 2011). The program is listed on the U.S. Department of Education's What Works Clearinghouse. As another example, the Strong Kids programs (Merrell, Carrizales, Feuerborn, Gueldner, & Tran, 2007a, 2007b) include units on "Clear Thinking" emphasizing refuting negative thought patterns and "The Power of Positive Thinking." An advantage of the Strong Kids programs is that they are teacher ready and can be implemented by classroom teachers with minimal training. Preliminary evidence suggests that the curricula foster small but robust improvements in students' social and emotional competence (Tran & Merrell, 2010).

ACADEMIC SELF-DETERMINATION

The simple purpose of academic self-determination interventions is to help students assume ever-increasing responsibility for their own learning. Ultimately, self-determined students will be adept at all facets of goal setting and decision making: setting goals for their learning and development; monitoring their own progress toward these goals, knowing multiple and varied strategies that they can use to overcome challenges, selecting the best strategy to use, and revising their plan as needed so that they are indeed more successful. Students' self-determination is closely related to their academic efficacy because students who believe that they can make a difference in their learning are more likely to try; students who actively manage their learning are more aware that their strategic efforts are related to their subsequent success. Thus, many intervention strategies simultaneously address academic self-determination and academic efficacy. A comprehensive description of the mechanisms by which academic self-determination supports student success can be found in Chapter 4.

Microchanges in Academic Self-Determination

Figure 8.6 draws upon the wealth of microchanges promoting academic self-determination that are described in cognitive research on instructional practices. Most of these microchanges integrate scaffolded support for student-directed problem solving and decision making into the daily practices of classrooms. In an early and classic example, Elias and Tobias (1996) used a combination of inservice training programs for teachers and practical SEL strategies to infuse the same eight problem-solving steps into instruction (math-

EXAMPLES OF MICROCHANGES IN ROUTINES AND PRACTICES

- Give students frequent practice, feedback, and direct instruction in setting goals, making decisions, solving problems, and self-evaluating their skills and behavior.

- Practice goal setting by having students set a goal for mastering a task and make a plan to do at least one thing to improve their progress. Then include a daily or weekly "check-in" during class when students chart their progress, post their progress onto a graph, decide how to change their plan, and celebrate their successes. One wall of the classroom could be used to post a classwide graph showing how close students are to achieving their goals.

- Teach students to use "stair steps" to take on challenging goals. Draw five to nine steps on a piece of paper. Write the student's goal on the top step. On the bottom step, write what he or she is doing now. Then fill in the steps in between. Students should keep a calendar of the step that they are on each day, set a goal for moving to the next step, and do one thing each day to help them move up a step.

- Let students make frequent and varied choices: about where to sit, between two optional assignments, or which book to read.

- Model mastery self-talk in the classroom: "I need to finish this report, but making graphs is not my strong suit. I think I'll sketch it out first and decide if it makes sense. Then, I'll start entering the data into the spreadsheet. I'll tell Mrs. Luther that I'm working on this, and see if I can ask her for help if I get stuck. If I do this one step at a time, I can do a good job."

- Give students a checklist for good goals and let them self-rate their goals using the checklist: good goals are clear (other people understand them). It is easy to tell whether or not you have met them. They can be met within 2 weeks. (Change the time to match students' age and development.) They are important. And they are something that you want to be able to meet.

EVIDENCE-BASED INTERVENTIONS

- **Promoting Alternative Thinking Strategies (PATHS) Program** (Greenberg, Kusche, & Mihalic, 1998). Evidence has demonstrated that this classwide program strengthens the self-determination of preschool and elementary children. The program includes 20-minute lessons taught three times each week on self-control and interpersonal problem-solving skills.

- **Strong Kids** (Merrell, Gueldner, & Tran, 2008). The Strong Kids curricula script half-hour lessons on diverse topics related to social–emotional learning. Some of these lessons teach goal setting, decision making, and becoming a self-determined student. Versions of the Strong Kids curricula are available for preschool, early elementary, late elementary, and middle school grades. Evidence shows small but robust improvements in students' social–emotional competence.

- **Positive Action Program** (PA; Flay, Allred, & Ordway, 2001). This is a wellness-oriented program that teaches students in kindergarten through twelfth grade to self-assess, set, and work toward goals to strengthen their learning and behavior. Some of the units foster students' self-determination. At each grade level, there are scripted classroom units and a manualized intervention for school mental health professionals to use with students at greater risk. Evidence suggests that this program strengthens students' self-regulation.

FIGURE 8.6. Strategies for academic self-determination.

ematics, language arts, social studies) and school discipline procedures (academic organization, conflict management). Their impressive schoolwide alignment made it possible for students' attention to focus on the content of their decisions because the problem-solving steps became second nature.

Schoolwide alignment is not always possible but classwide alignment is usually a viable alternative. Instruction in self-determination can be embedded into any subject curriculum by first modeling learning strategies for students and then helping them master the strategies through coaching and scaffolding (Randi & Corno, 2000). For example, teachers in a secondary humanities course provided students with explicit instruction in self-regulation strategies, and then they gave students the assignment of finding these strategies in stories that the class read (Deno, 2002; Deno, Fuchs, Marston, & Shin, 2001). Students' essays compared the self-management strategies of story characters to their own goal-oriented efforts. In another study, students compared their task success to self-monitoring notes that they kept about their use of study time and their efficacy (Zimmerman, Bonner, & Kovach, 1996). Then, students evaluated the impact that their strategies and efficacy had on subsequent test performance. The systematic record keeping made students more aware of how they could impact their own task success by what they believed and what they did.

> **Instruction in self-determination can be embedded into any subject curriculum.**

High school and college students composed a written goal for their achievement ("I will solve as many math problems as I can") and also specified when, where, and how they would act on the goal (Bayer & Gollwitzer, 2007). Some students also added a statement designed to strengthen self-efficacy ("And if I start a new problem, then I'll tell myself: 'I can solve it' "). The goal and efficacy statements gave students a very portable script for thinking about their purpose in a broad range of learning situations. The addition of the self-efficacy statement was especially useful in strengthening students' success. Although a bit contrived initially, these scripts eventually contributed to students' habitual attention to what they were learning, how they should learn it, why it was important, and their likely success.

Evidence-Based Interventions in Academic Self-Determination

Although multiple empirical studies have examined classroom practices, few of them have been organized into manualized intervention programs to promote self-determination. However, units and components that address self-determination are integral to several SEL curricula. For example, the Strong Kids programs (Merrell et al., 2007a, 2007b) that were mentioned as evidence-based interventions for academic efficacy also include units on "Solving People Problems" and "Setting Goals and Staying Active." Because these curricula can be delivered by classroom teachers, they are easier to implement with current school resources; the trade-off, of course, is that their effect sizes appear to be somewhat smaller than more intensive and specialized curricula (Tran & Merrell, 2010). Alternatively, the Positive Action (PA) program (Flay et al., 2001) includes a unit on "Improving Yourself Continually" that emphasizes setting and achieving goals. Also mentioned earlier as a program emphasizing students' academic efficacy, there are multiple formats for delivering PA through home, school, and community programs, and there is evidence of its impact on students' school success (Flay & Allred, 2003; Li et al., 2011). Several other evidence-based programs teach students to use problem-solving and decision-making frameworks to manage their learning and behavior. These include Linking the Interests of Families and Teachers (LIFT; Eddy et al., 2000), which uses a problem-solving framework to teach students strategies for managing their behaviors, and Promoting Alternative Thinking Strategies (PATHS; Greenberg et al., 1998), which uses problem-solving frameworks to strengthen students' peer relationships and social understanding.

BEHAVIORAL SELF-CONTROL

Many interventions have been created for school classrooms with the primary purpose of managing student behavior but, in most cases, they promote teachers' control over student behavior (Bear et al., 2005). The defining essence of behavioral self-control is that students manage their moment-to-moment behavior so that it satisfies school rules and community mores and also advances their progress toward personal goals for learning and development. Experienced and sensitive teachers are adept at imposing control over students' behaviors by clearly stating the rules and expectations, delivering positive consequences for appropriate behavior, and responding immediately and definitively to inappropriate behavior. Ultimately, resilient students need to be able to self-impose this behavioral monitoring. Most interventions that successfully transfer adult control to the students use one of four methods: (1) providing students with direct instruction in, practice with, and feedback on simple classroom routines to shape positive behaviors; (2) embedding "ways of acting" into a larger problem-solving strategy and reinforcing students' commitment to acting consistent with their decisions; (3) teaching students to stop and think before acting, as a strategy for overcoming some students' predisposition to act impulsively; and (4) teaching students strategies to recognize, understand, and manage their emotional responses so that they do not short-circuit self-enhancing behaviors. Both microchanges and evidence-based interventions listed in Figure 8.7 draw from these methods for shaping student self-control. A comprehensive description of the mechanisms by which behavioral self-control supports student success can be found in Chapter 4.

Microchanges in Behavioral Self-Control

One of the microchanges listed in Figure 8.7, direct instruction in classroom routines, is unique in its preventive emphasis on the classroom context for instruction. Several examples are included in Witt et al.'s (1999) practical handbook on teaching routines: if the noise and placement of the classroom pencil sharpener interrupts students' concentration, teach the class a routine to presharpen pencils for the full day. If students are rowdy when leaving the classroom for recess, have them repeatedly practice the routine for entering and leaving the classroom. If the class inevitably descends into pandemonium when a substitute teacher

EXAMPLES OF MICROCHANGES IN ROUTINES AND PRACTICES

- Identify when the behavior trouble spots occur in the classroom, and create a classroom routine for students to use instead. Give the routine a name. Describe the routine, model it, have students practice it several times in a row on the first day, and then once or twice for the rest of the week. Then use the routine as part of the regular classroom routines and reteach occasionally as needed.

- Reframe the classroom rules so that there are fewer rules, described in words that the students can understand and phrased positively so that they are a list of "Things to Do" and not a list of "Things Not to Do."

- Put 25 tokens in your pocket at the beginning of the day and hand one to students when you catch them following the "Things to Do" rules. As one variation, have a "tootling time" when students can nominate a classmate for a token because of something good that the classmate did.

- Teach students to use calming strategies when angry or upset: "touch your heart" (how are you feeling); "take a deep breath, count to five slowly"; "put your hand on your heart and think or say 'Slow down'"; "breathe in—breathe out."

- Create some steps that students can follow if they are angry: first, move to a "safe place" where students can go but not be in trouble. Students can still do their work in that place. If this doesn't help, quietly draw the situation that is a problem. Decide what to do, and write that down. Then, return to the class.

- Teach students to stop and think about problems before reacting using "Stop and think" or "Before you react get the facts!" steps.

- Teach students self-control by showing them how to keep a simple record of their own behavior and to enter their data onto a simple graph. Students can connect each data "dot" with a line and decide whether their graph is going up (behavior improving), staying the same, or going down. Then, they can write a contract describing what they will do to make their line go up.

EVIDENCE-BASED INTERVENTIONS

- **Promoting Alternative Thinking Strategies (PATHS).** This is a universal competence-building intervention that has been shown to improve students' self-regulation and problem-solving skills (Kam, Greenberg, & Kusché, 2004; Kusché & Greenberg, 1994). The program's 20-minute lessons are taught three times a week in the general education or special education classroom.

- **I Can Problem Solve** (Shure, 1997). This is a yearlong curricula that teaches students to think about the social problems that they encounter, consider alternative solutions, carefully consider the feelings of other students and themselves, and translate these into competent social behaviors. Evidence shows that the program strengthens children's prosocial behaviors and decreases their social impulsivity.

- **Coping Power** (Lochman, Powell, Boxmeyer, & Baden, 2010). While the principal component of this program is a therapeutic intervention for highly aggressive children, there is also a classwide Coping Power curriculum that teaches students to use goal-setting, problem-solving, and anger-management skills. The classwide curriculum has shown small improvements in all students' behavior and social competence, but it has shown larger effects in improving the behavioral competence of highly aggressive children whose classroom has been trained in Coping Power skills.

FIGURE 8.7. Strategies for promoting behavioral self-control.

is in charge, guide students in overlearning routines for behaving with substitute teachers. Repeated practice forms these new routines into behavioral habits that students perform with little to no teacher oversight, contributing to students' competence in self-managing their own behavior.

Other microchanges listed in Figure 8.7 teach students to use familiar problem-solving steps to decide, in advance, how they intend to behave in particular situations. Reasoning in advance is useful when students are facing uncommonly difficult circumstances (e.g., being picked on by a group of older kids) or when they are predisposed by temperament or disability to act in self-defeating ways (e.g., inattention by students who are easily distracted, self-isolation by students with limited social competence). Thinking through a problem helps students assume the perspectives of other people who they are dealing with and provides them with a framework for making important decisions about their own preferences in behavior. Initially, once they have a plan, students need gentle reminders to follow through with their decision. For example, teachers might whisper a prompt ("remember your words") or use a subtle signal (touching an ear) to remind students to listen. Sometimes, students learn to prompt each other with similar reminders. Ultimately, students can self-remind and will have less need for teacher prompts.

Stop and think strategies borrow from one of the earliest intervention manuals for children. Kendall and Braswell's (1985) "Stop and Think" strategy taught impulsive students to pause and evaluate their behavior before acting. The practice of interrupting children's behavior with cognitive self-instructions draws from an overarching principle of cognitive-behavioral psychology—that cognitions, like overt behaviors, can be targeted, taught, reinforced or punished, and shaped. Like the problem-solving steps, once students have practiced stop and think strategies, they will generally need prompts and cues as reminders to use the strategies in actual settings.

Microchanges that teach students about their own emotions build students' feelings vocabularies, and a strong feelings vocabulary incidentally alerts them to the occurrence of emotions and makes it possible for them to talk articulately about their emotional experiences. Conversations about emotions build students' construct "maps" for emotions, including two key understandings: that emotions sometimes distort their understanding of their experiences, and emotions sometimes drive them to behave in ways that create bigger problems. Simple strategies to counteract the maladaptive impact of emotions are easily integrated into classroom routines—allowing quick-to-anger students to go to a special spot in the classroom to cool down, or creating classroom "scripts" for students to say when they are overwhelmed by anxiety or anger.

Evidence-Based Interventions for Behavioral Self-Control

Evidence-based behaviors to strengthen behavioral self-control are among the most numerous programs available to schools. In Figure 8.7, programs are listed only if they can be implemented in a classwide format and if they have a purpose of building students' autonomous control (rather than teacher-directed control) over their behavior. As one example, Eddy and colleague's LIFT Program (Eddy et al., 2000), also mentioned as an evidence-based intervention supporting home–school relationships, has been shown to strengthen students' problem-solving and conflict-resolution skills and lower students' aggression and conduct problems. A classroom-based preventive adaptation of the Incredible Years child program (Webster-Stratton, Reid, & Hammond, 2001) teaches students a collection of behavioral literacy skills including problem solving, following school rules, and how to be successful at school. The Incredible Years programs also include teacher-training and parent-training components and are identified as a model Blueprint for Violence Prevention by the Center for the Study and Prevention of Violence. The Coping Power Program (Lochman, Wells, & Lenhart, 2008) was originally designed as an individual child and family intervention program for highly aggressive students. Among the program objectives are activities to strengthen students' goal setting, anger management, study skills, social problem solving, and perspective taking. The program has been identified as an exemplary program by the Office of Juvenile Justice and Delinquency Prevention. Recently, a universal classroom component has been developed for the Coping Power Program that prepares all students in a class in the behavioral literacy skills (Lochman, Powell, Boxmeyer, & Baden, 2010). Early results suggest that the impact of the individual intervention program is magnified when aggressive students are in classrooms receiving the universal classroom component.

Local, state, and national educational agencies have also strongly endorsed positive behavioral supports: schoolwide and districtwide policies and practices that predispose students to act in ways that are safe, respectful, and positive. A prominent positive behavioral system is positive behavioral interventions and supports (PBIS; Sugai & Horner, 2001). PBIS provides schools with technical assistance for identifying, adapting, and sustaining effective schoolwide disciplinary practices. More than 500 schools in the United States across 13 states, elementary to high school, have implemented PBIS, and the program has demonstrated benefits in decreasing behavior referrals, increasing academic instruction time, and improving academic achievement.

IMPROVING THE RESILIENT CHARACTERISTICS OF CLASSROOMS: AN ILLUSTRATION

A novel intervention that targeted several characteristics of resilient classrooms began with the administration of a sociogram. Students nominated three peers each for items describing a wide range of social and academic behaviors (e.g., "The kids who have a lot of friends are _____"; "The kids who finish their work are _____"). Figure 8.8 shows a portion of the sociogram results, tallied to represent the number of nominations a particular student received for each of the sociogram questions. Each number along the top represents a student in the classroom. The numbers were assigned randomly to ensure student anonymity.

During classroom meetings, the sociogram was placed on an overhead projector at the front of the classroom and one line at a time was uncovered as students speculated about the meaning of the numbers. Inferences were strongly encouraged as students attempted

Student Numbers	#1	#2	#3	#4	#5	#6	#7	#8	#9	#10
Sociogram Questions										
Who has lots of friends?	3	7	0	2	2	3	11	2	5	1
Who do you want to work with on class projects?	9	1	1	1	3	3	9	1	2	0
Who do you like to play with?	5	4	0	2	4	1	4	3	4	2
Who is liked by everyone?	3	5	0	2	2	2	8	2	4	0
Who gets good grades?	10	2	0	3	1	5	10	1	1	1
Who does not pay attention?	1	6	2	0	4	1	0	8	3	5

FIGURE 8.8. Results of a sociogram used in an intervention.

to discern why a particular student may have seven votes for "Who has a lot of friends?" yet only one vote for "Who do you want to work with on class projects?" Student inferences such as "Maybe they never pay attention" or "Maybe they're not very good at finishing their work" helped them see the relationship between classroom behaviors and their social or academic standing with their peers. The intervention helped students define specific academic and social goals they want to achieve and determined the teacher, classroom, and/ or parental supports they needed to achieve those goals. In response to these discussions, students began to develop classroom-based strategies to acquire the prosocial attributes and good academic habits of a "student number" on the sociogram that they wanted to emulate. They also received considerable feedback and support from other students and the teacher.

Some students chose to tape their two most important goals to their desks. The students decided to reinforce one another's progress through the use of yellow sticky notes that would quietly reinforce the efforts of their classmates. To help keep one classmate from continually talking to his neighbors, nearby students adopted a "zipping the lips" pantomime, coupled with a good-natured smile, to help their classmate stay focused. Teacher participation was crucial to reinforce the language and strategies of effective goal setting and prosocial behaviors on a daily level in the classroom. Through ongoing classroom meetings the adult facilitators fostered a social context for learning that supported academic goal setting, supportive relations among students and teachers, and the development of effective behavior regulation skills.

SUMMARY

This chapter described the various resources and principles that guide classroom teams in selecting effective classroom interventions. We recommend that teams initially rely on innovative microchanges because simple changes are often sufficient to alter important characteristics of classrooms and are easier to maintain over time. Even when using evidence-based interventions, teams will need to make clinical judgments about the suitability of a particular intervention for a specific class. Classrooms vary widely in their human and material resources, the nature and extent of their needs, and the unique combination of intervention activities that will shift their ecological systems. Interventions' effectiveness will vary in interaction with these unique classroom conditions. Consequently, appropriate selection of classroom interventions will always need to be preceded by a careful analysis of classroom strengths and weaknesses (Chapter 6) to identify the classroom conditions that might constrain or potentiate an intervention. These will always need to be monitored through the ongoing collection of classroom data (Chapter 5) to verify that the intervention is effective in each specific classroom.

INTRODUCTION TO A CASE STUDY OF RECESS INTERVENTIONS

Bullying is a common concern in many schools, and the case study immediately following this chapter describes use of the CMS to plan and carry out a bullying prevention program. Kadie Dooley, Kristin Bieber, and Courtney Wimmer describe a three-pronged intervention to address the third graders' bullying. Teachers in Central Elementary were especially concerned because repairing the damage done on the playground was eating into their instructional time—and this, too, is a common complaint. Notice that the use of microchanges by the teachers were effective and yet fit naturally into the school day. If these had not been effective, the teachers could have moved to an evidence-based intervention, but in this case, that proved unnecessary.

CASE STUDY

Recess Worries

Kadie Dooley, Kristin Bieber, and Courtney Wimmer
University of Nebraska–Lincoln

The Problem

Administrators and teachers had concerns about bullying during the third-grade recess at Central Elementary School. Teachers often had to take time away from instruction to settle students' disagreements and smooth over their hurt and angry feelings. They partnered with university researchers to develop recess strategies that would stop much of the playground bullying and aggression from occurring.

The ClassMaps Results

To understand the problems from the students' perspective, all third-grade students completed the CMS. Teachers were particularly interested in students' responses to the I Worry That . . . subscale (see Figure 8.9). Results showed that 37% of students worried a lot (almost always or often) about other kids doing mean things to them. Also, 43% of the third graders were often worried that other students would tell lies about them. Just as important, 30% of students reported frequent worries that others would hurt them on purpose. After discussing these results, the teachers wanted to ensure that all students felt safe and included at recess.

Results of the Classroom Meeting

Classroom meetings were then held to show the results to the students and ask what they thought was causing the problems. During the meeting, the students were asked, "Why do you worry about these things?" "What can adults do to help?" and "What can you do to help?" One class described the specific areas on the playground that they believed were most problematic (e.g., behind the equipment, in the slide, and places where the teachers couldn't see the students well). Students suggested that teachers could help by spreading themselves out and not standing in a big group when supervising the playground, checking the places where students could hide, and taking action when

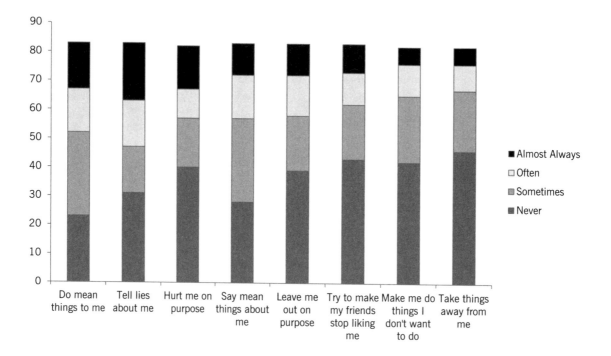

FIGURE 8.9. ClassMaps Survey preintervention graph for the I Worry That . . . subscale (third-grade students).

students report bullying. They suggested that students could help by telling a teacher, standing up for one another, telling the bullies that they would have more friends if they were nice, and ignoring the bullies.

Plan for Change

Based on the students' ideas, the teachers decided to implement three strategies to improve recess. First, they held anti-bullying meetings with the classes to discuss how bullying affects the students and describe ways that students could respond to bullying; the best ideas were posted on each classroom's wall. Second, the teachers assigned a peer mentor to students who often bullied classmates. The peer mentors walked and played with their partners during recess or other unstructured times, prompted them to stop if they started to bully, and modeled prosocial peer interactions. Third, the teachers concluded that certain recess games caused problems because students played by several different sets of rules. They enlisted the help of the PE teacher to teach game rules during gym class. For example, four square was a popular but particularly challenging game because students often argued about when a ball was out. The physical education teacher taught the students a consistent set of rules so that all students made these decisions the same way.

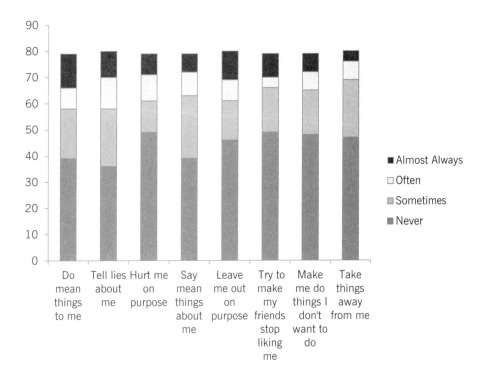

FIGURE 8.10. ClassMaps Survey postintervention graph for the I Worry That . . . subscale (third-grade students).

Results

After the teachers implemented these strategies, the CMS was given to the third-grade students a second time. The results are presented in Figure 8.10. Students now reported fewer worries about bullying. Students' worries (almost always or often) about other kids doing mean things to them decreased by 10%. Also, 43% of the third graders indicated on the first survey that they were often worried that other students would tell lies about them, but on the second survey only 28% of students worried (almost always or often). Last, 30% of students had reported frequent worries that others would hurt them on purpose. After the intervention, this number decreased to 23%.

CHAPTER 9

Evaluating the Impact of Resilient Classrooms for External Audiences

National policymakers suggest that the route to improving schools and classrooms is very simple (No Child Left Behind Act, 2002). Schools simply need to find out "what works" and do it. There is good truth in this logic. Educators should provide solid empirical evidence that the services they provide are effective in improving the academic and personal success of their students. Still, the "what works" argument underestimates the difficulty for researchers in identifying effective programs and for schools in restricting their practices to only those programs. National leaders are still debating the criteria that must be met for an intervention to be declared effective (Bumbarger, Perkins, & Greenberg, 2010; Odom et al., 2010; Weisz & Gray, 2008), and the task of identifying effective classwide interventions is even more daunting (Doll & Cummings, 2008; Doll, Pfohl, et al., 2010). In the meantime, while the national debates proceed, educators will often need to document the impact of their services on a case-by-case basis. This chapter explains how to conduct evaluations that can demonstrate to the satisfaction of administrators, school boards, and community members that resilient classrooms interventions have "worked" and are worth the time and resources that teachers spend on them.

Until this point, this book has described data collection as an integral part of classroom intervention so that teachers can tell whether a classroom's goal for change has been met. It is tempting to equate the evaluation of resilient classrooms programs with this simple measurement task. If a classroom's peer relationships were contentious initially, and if classmates are then interacting frequently and comfortably after a classwide intervention, it seems reasonable to claim that the intervention worked. These simple before–after resilient classrooms projects may not be convincing to external audiences. In this example, the classroom could have changed for reasons that are completely independent of the resilient classrooms intervention. For example, the frequency of recess conflicts dropped dramatically once an assistant principal replaced the missing tetherballs, moved the four-square court to a better location, and had goals and sidelines painted onto the soccer fields; or when a school librarian began to allow some students to spend recess in the computer lab instead of going outside; or when a school's physical education teachers revised their curriculum to teach children a number of games that they could play at recess. School changes like these could have been the cause of a classroom's improved peer relationships instead of the resilient classrooms intervention.

Not every resilient classrooms intervention needs a comprehensive and rigorous evaluation. When a teacher and a classroom team are working together to enhance a classroom's characteristics, they simply need to know that the conditions for learning have improved. If student conflicts drop or teacher–student relationships improve, it is relatively unimportant to know who should receive credit for the improvement. In some situations, however, a school's allocation of resources or a classroom's access to funding may be influenced by evidence that a classroom intervention program worked. More rigorous evaluations can sway the opinions of school board members, community leaders, or administrators who control classroom resources.

Convincing program evaluations not only demonstrate that conditions in classrooms improve once an intervention is implemented but also examine whether the improvements were due to the intervention and assess the size of the impact on student success. Some elements of these evaluations are already included in a resilient classrooms project. A well-conducted evaluation begins with a clear decision about the purpose of the intervention program: what will be changed and how much must it change in order for the program to be considered a success? Chapters 2, 3, and 4 of this book discuss the intervention goals that are likely to make classrooms more resilient communities for children. Next, a measurement strategy that allows for the collection of data that is objective and quantifiable must be identified. Chapter 5 describes several alternative assessment tools to assess classroom characteristics. Chapters 5 and 6 explain how the CMS could be used for this purpose. One key difference is that a program evaluation must include data that are gathered continuously (and preferably daily) before, during, and after the intervention. Only some of Chapter 5's assessment tools lend themselves to continuous administration. While the CMS would be too long to administer daily, it is possible to administer a single subscale several times each week when the subscale addresses the purpose of the program.

> **Convincing program evaluations examine whether classroom changes were due to the intervention and assess the impact on student success.**

For a program evaluation, baseline data must be gathered to determine the preintervention characteristics of classrooms. As is true for a resilient classrooms project, the intervention must be described as a very specific step-by-step plan, and careful records must be kept to document whether it is implemented exactly according to the plan in all classrooms participating in the intervention. A distinctive feature of program evaluations is that they require the use of a meticulous evaluation design that specifies a schedule for collecting data and implementing the intervention so that it is possible to know whether classroom improvements are due to the intervention. Finally, the evaluation data must be reviewed and used to decide whether and how to refine the intervention to improve its effectiveness.

CLARIFYING THE PURPOSE

Resilient classrooms interventions will have one of six immediate goals: to improve a classroom's teacher–student relationships, peer relationships, home–school relationships, academic efficacy, self-determination, or behavioral self-control. In some cases, one or more components of these goals will be selected instead. For example, a goal for classroom change might be to reduce the number of fights and conflicts that occur on the playground or to increase the frequency with which children talk with their parents about their schoolwork. When the CMS was used to assess classroom characteristics, teachers frequently built their goals for change around one or more items on the survey. Each of these goals is designed to alter the classroom's ecology so that it becomes a more successful place for children to learn and interact. Because they are immediate goals of the intervention, these are the goals that are most likely to be met. Immediate goals should always be defined for an evaluation.

Still, these immediate goals may not be highly valued by administrators, community members, government officials, or policymakers, especially if they are not convinced that resilient classrooms contexts will improve students' academic success. The external audiences to the classroom are typically interested in goals that target student outcomes rather than classwide improvements: higher test scores, lower grade retention rates, lower dropout rates, lower suspension or expulsion rates, and higher student grades. These are indirect goals of the intervention and, because they are somewhat removed from the immediate activities of the classroom interventions, they are less likely to be met over a short period of intervention. Still, the importance of these goals cannot be underestimated because they may determine whether or not resources will be available to continue an intervention, promote a teacher, or allocate staff time to a classroom or building. Student outcome goals should be established whenever important decisions might be made about resources, access, or school policy based on results of the evaluation.

Intermediate goals lie in between immediate intervention goals and student outcome goals. An assumption of resilient classrooms is that effective classroom environments will increase children's availability for learning by increasing their academic engagement and enhancing their behavioral discipline. Examples of intermediate goals include work completion rates, attendance and lateness, or discipline referrals. Consequently, goals set for improvements in academic engagement and class discipline will represent middle steps between goals for effective classroom environments and goals set for improved student outcomes. While external audiences might not value attainment of these intermediate goals as highly as they value student outcomes, the relationship between increased time on task and academic success is more apparent and easier to defend than is that between classroom characteristics and academic success. Moreover, changes in these intermediate goals will occur over shorter time intervals than those for the student outcome goals. For these reasons, it can be very useful to track progress toward these intermediate goals.

> **An assumption of resilient classrooms is that effective classroom environments will increase children's availability for learning by increasing their academic engagement and enhancing their behavioral discipline.**

Goals may also differ depending on whether they are set by the teacher alone, with the participation of the classroom's student or families, or by an administrator or policymaker. The purpose of the evaluation can shift decidedly depending on whether the audience is the classroom only or a building-level administrator and whether urgent decisions are being made based on the evaluation.

Time is a critical component of any intervention goal. The purpose of an intervention is never to alter a classroom "eventually" or given sufficient time. Instead, the intervention is successful if it accomplishes its goal within a reasonable time frame. It is reasonable to expect a classroom social skills curriculum to alter the social behaviors of a classroom's students within some 8–12 weeks. It is less reasonable to expect such a curriculum to alter the children's social behaviors within a few days. Consequently, well-stated goals include a statement about the time interval over which change is expected to occur. When a classroom's students are participants in the goal setting, it is important to recognize the developmental differences that exist in children's ability to track goals over time. As a rule of thumb, most middle school students can track progress toward a goal that they are expected to achieve within a month's time but find it very difficult to stay focused on goals that will be achieved a semester or a year into the future. For example, a sixth-grade teacher had a very difficult time motivating students to work toward a trip to the Mesa Verde prehistoric cliff dwellings in southwestern Colorado scheduled for 2 years later. Elementary school students can easily track progress toward goals that they expect to achieve within a week or even two, but they generally lose interest in working toward goals that are several weeks in the future. Many high school students can work toward goals that are a semester away but may not plan well toward goals that are displaced a year or more into the future.

Most evaluation designs require the replication of an intervention across more than one classroom. Consequently, evaluations of classroom interventions are usually directed toward high-frequency goals that are shared by multiple classrooms: increasing homework or seatwork completion, enhancing teacher relationships, improving communication with families, or reducing peer conflict.

MEASUREMENT STRATEGIES

The selection of measures for classroom characteristics has been described in some detail in Chapter 5. These assessment strategies are satisfactory for gathering data about the immediate goals of resilient classrooms interventions. Particular attention has been paid to the CMS, which was developed for the purpose of evaluating immediate classroom goals. When one or more subscales of the CMS matches the purpose of the program, those subscales could be administered several times a week to monitor shifts in student perceptions over time. Alternatively, teachers have sometimes selected out two to three key items on the CMS that matched their program goals. In this instance, however, the measure would not have the same reliability and stability as might be seen in one of the six- to eight-item subscales.

Information about student outcome goals—suspension and expulsion rates, test scores, graduation rates, report card grades—are collected as a matter of course in most schools.

The only challenge in assessing these goals is accessing information for one or more specific classrooms.

Assessments of intermediate goals related to academic engagement and behavioral discipline are more challenging. In most cases, indicators related to these goals are integral to the record keeping of a classroom. For example, student attendance, work completion rates, and homework completion rates ought to be recorded in classroom record books. However, in actual practice, these records may be very haphazard and lack the dependability necessary for data collection. In these cases, keeping stricter records of classroom performance may become part of the intervention plan.

A strategy for tracking the academic engagement of students with disabilities is integral to the Check and Connect Program for dropout prevention (Christenson & Reschly, 2010). The program maintained daily records of student tardies, truancies, and behavioral referrals. In addition, teachers completed weekly rating forms describing student work completion and classroom time on task. The Check and Connect Program intervened with students when these records showed a pattern of disengagement from school. Like many of the measures that have been described in Chapter 5, the Check and Connect record keeping is intended to focus on individual students at risk and would need modification before being used to track classroom engagement.

It is also possible to use direct observation to record academic time on task within a classroom. Squires and Joyner (1996) describe a simple procedure for observing academic engaged time in a classroom. A trained observer spends ten 10-minute intervals in a classroom. During each interval, the observer looks at each individual student for 2–3 seconds, decides whether that student is on task, and enters a tally mark on an observation form if the student is not engaged. The observer continues until all students in the class have been observed, then repeats the process for each of the 10-minute intervals. At the end of the observation, a simple calculation yields the engagement rate for the classroom.

Regardless of the data collection procedures that are used, an effective program evaluation requires that the data be gathered strictly, precisely, and completely. Missing or incomplete data seriously impair the ability to draw firm conclusions from the evaluation. A corollary rule is that the data must be extremely simple to collect. Complicated data collection procedures are easily violated, whereas sensible and easy-to-follow procedures are more likely to yield complete information. Only people who have no

> **An effective program evaluation requires that the data be gathered strictly, precisely, and completely.**

vested interest in the evaluation results should collect evaluation data. For example, when students in a classroom participate in evaluating CMS information and plan a classroom intervention with the teacher, it is important that the students not be the only source of evaluation data. Because of their participation, they will want to believe that things are getting better in their class and may not provide entirely objective information about class changes.

There are a number of strategies that classroom teams can use to simplify data collection. Especially when multiple measures are being collected, more than one person should be participating in data collection. For example, we have had good success in assigning a responsible classroom student with the task of collecting an after-recess survey. It is sometimes possible to use data that are already being collected for another purpose. If existing data are not available, often it is feasible to use data that can be constructed from permanent products of the system and can be coded retrospectively. Finally, the team should construct simple forms, charts, and tables as memory and organizational aids to capture the data.

BASELINE DATA

The purpose of baseline data is to show the status of classrooms prior to any intervention. To accomplish this task, sufficient baseline data must be collected to provide a convincing description of the preintervention classrooms. Preferably, this requires at least seven data points. If these data points provide a consistent and stable picture of the classroom's characteristics, intervention activities can then begin. However, if these data points are highly inconsistent or show that the classroom's status is gradually improving or gradually worsening, a longer period of baseline data collection might be required. Ideally, the baseline data should provide a clear, uncontested prediction about the projected future status of the classroom if no intervention were to occur.

The collection of baseline data can be difficult to defend in schools. When assessment has provided clear evidence of a problem in a classroom, there can be tremendous pressure to proceed immediately into the intervention without pausing for more baseline assessment. For these reasons, the lack of baseline data is the most frequent violation of school-based program evaluations. Without baseline data, it is virtually impossible to determine whether a classroom is improving.

In some cases, existing data may provide a good baseline for an intervention. For example, when a second-grade classroom decided to plan a homework completion project, the teacher's record book had 3 months of baseline data on the rates of homework completion. Existing records may also document preintervention attendance rates, grades, test performance, or home–school communications. In some classrooms, there is an archive of completed work in student folders that might provide preintervention baseline data on work accuracy rates. Office discipline records may note when and how often students were sent to the school office because of behavioral violations. In some cases, the baseline rates might be known to be zero. For example, a teacher may know that he or she has never had a phone call from a parent or that students have never volunteered to create a lesson for the class.

INTERVENTION PLAN

When a team is working to alter the characteristics of a single classroom, decisions about how to intervene should be made in collaboration with the teacher and students who teach and learn there. Not only are these the participants with the most immediate understanding of what is needed in the classroom but they are also the ones who will be responsible for implementing any intervention. However, when practitioners are working to demonstrate the impact of an intervention program in multiple classrooms, decisions about how to intervene must be based on what is likely to work in most classrooms. At the same time, intervention programs need to be selected with an eye toward what has been shown to be effective. While few classroom interventions have been verified as "evidence based," there are a number of promising practices in each of the six resilience characteristics, which have been described in Chapters 3, 4, and 8.

Once an intervention plan is made, it is critically important that a written plan describe what to do, when to do it, and to whom to assign the task. Like individual classroom interventions, if this plan is written in a checklist format, it can be used to keep a weekly record of the steps that were carried out and those that were inadvertently omitted. These written records will verify that the intervention was actually used as planned in all classrooms participating in the evaluation.

Good intervention plans will specify the time over which the intervention will be used. In some cases, interventions will incorporate permanent changes to classroom routines and practices. However, in other cases, an intervention will die a natural death once it is no longer necessary. There needs to be a decision about the reasonable interval for an intervention plan to be implemented, and this time frame should become uniform across the classrooms participating in the intervention.

EVALUATION DESIGN

Standards governing the evaluation of interventions have been discussed at length in the research literature. To be proven effective, an intervention should have been evaluated through random-assignment control group designs in which two groups of participants are randomly assigned to intervention and no-intervention groups, and the same baseline and intervention data are collected throughout the study (Doll & Yoon, 2010; Weisz & Gray, 2008). At the end of the study, the difference between the intervention group and the control group can be used to estimate the effect of the intervention. In the best case, these differences will be both significant (statistical verification that there is a true difference in means) and meaningful (with a difference that is large enough to be important for children's success). In a resilient classrooms evaluation, however, the participant in the intervention is a classroom and not a student. Outside of a funded research study, it is rarely practical to recruit sufficient classrooms to participate in a traditional control group study. Moreover, given the diversity of conditions that exist in classrooms, it is unlikely

> **Evaluations of classrooms are best conducted using small-*n* research designs.**

that the same intervention would be appropriate to large numbers of classrooms. Consequently, evaluations of classrooms are best conducted using small-*n* research designs in which the classroom acts as its own control group.

Case Studies

A case study provides the weakest evidence of all of the single-case designs. In a systematic case study, baseline data are collected (Condition A), then the intervention is implemented

(Condition B) and intervention data are collected. This is also called an A–B design. The problem with the A–B design is that there is no good evidence that changes in the classroom are different from those that would have occurred without the intervention. While the baseline data provide a prediction of the future status of the classroom, that prediction is not confirmed. Kennedy (2005) suggests that case study designs are a simple way to establish the initial promise of an intervention but should always be followed up by designs with better controls. Still, if sufficient numbers of well-controlled case studies have been conducted, they can be aggregated to provide an estimate of the impact of the intervention across multiple conditions. For example, Sheridan et al. (2001) demonstrated the impact of conjoint behavioral consultation by aggregating effect sizes across 57 consultation case studies. Aggregated case studies are most convincing if the different case examples had similar goals or used similar interventions.

One variation of an A–B design provides more convincing evidence of intervention effectiveness. In an A–B design with follow-up, the progress of the classroom continues to be monitored through data collection even after an intervention has been completed and discontinued. Then, if the classroom's characteristics begin to decline, the intervention is implemented once again. If conditions improve after the intervention is reinstated, there is good support for suggesting that the intervention was effective in creating the change.

Withdrawal Designs

In a withdrawal design, baseline data are collected (Condition A), the intervention is implemented (Condition B), and once intervention data are stable the intervention is withdrawn and the classroom returns to its baseline condition (Condition A). Withdrawal designs are sometimes called A–B–A designs and include many variations: A–B–A–B designs are withdrawal designs that end on an intervention phase rather than a baseline phase; A–B–A–C designs are withdrawal designs that examine two interventions (Conditions B and C) rather than a single one. These can be powerful designs to use when a classroom needs to know which of two interventions is more effective.

Withdrawal designs are powerful because each classroom serves as its own baseline. However, these designs can be used only when the intervention is something that can be taken away. For example, if an intervention involved teaching a group of students a new strategy for resolving peer conflicts, it could not be assumed that they unlearned that strategy during the withdrawal period. Consequently, a withdrawal design would not be appropriate for this kind of intervention. However, if an intervention involved holding regular classroom meetings to resolve conflicts from recess, it would be simple to stop holding the meetings during the withdrawal period. A withdrawal design would be appropriate in this instance.

There are times when it would be unethical to withdraw an intervention that appears to be working. For example, when a sixth-grade teacher found that his students' suspension and expulsion rates dropped once games were provided for the recess playground, he was unwilling to withhold those games for fear that physical fights and the accompanying suspensions would resume. In most instances, these ethical issues can be solved because the withdrawal period will be of short duration and will be followed by reinstatement of the intervention.

Multiple-Baseline Designs

When the same intervention will be used to change more than one characteristic of a classroom or when the same intervention will be used for the same goal in multiple classrooms, a multiple-baseline design can be used. To use a multiple-baseline design across goals, baseline data should be collected for both intervention goals. Then, once the baseline data are stable, the intervention should be used to change one characteristic of the classroom only.

Intervention data are then collected for that goal while baseline data continue to be collected for the other goal. Once the intervention data are stable, the intervention can be used to also change the second characteristic of the classroom. There is evidence that the intervention was responsible for the classroom change if the data show that the first characteristic improved when the first intervention began and that the second characteristic did not improve until the second intervention began. For example, a classroom might use classroom meetings as an intervention to discuss and problem-solve peer conflicts that occur during the lunchtime recess and those that occur in class during small-group time. Baseline data would be collected to count both recess conflicts and group-time conflicts. Then, the class meetings would begin to discuss recess problems while data were still collected about both recess and group-time conflicts. Once recess conflicts declined, the class meetings could begin to discuss group-time conflicts. If these conflicts also declined, there would be good evidence to claim that classroom meetings were effective in reducing peer conflicts.

Multiple baselines can be used in the same way to evaluate an intervention that occurs in more than one classroom. If three third-grade classrooms had difficulties with students' homework completion, a multiple-baseline design would collect data on homework completion in all three classrooms until the baseline data were stable. Then, a parent involvement program could be initiated in Classroom 1 while data collection continued in all three classrooms. Once the intervention data were stable in Classroom 1, the parent involvement program could be added in Classroom 2. Similarly, once intervention data were stable in Classrooms 1 and 2, the program could be added to Classroom 3. If the data showed that homework completion rates improved only once the parent involvement program was added to each class, there would be good evidence that the improvements were due to the intervention program.

REVIEW AND FEEDBACK

A critical step in any program evaluation is the periodic review of the evaluation results, followed by planning revisions in response to those results. Where intervention programs have not been effective, revised plans might include strengthening the dosage of the intervention, implementing it more accurately, persisting with it for an additional period of time, or changing to a new intervention. Again, careful evaluation designs will require that these modifications be made uniformly across classrooms and that data be collected systematically before, during, and after modifications.

Where interventions have been effective, it is important to decide whether the classroom goals have been met to the satisfaction of participants in the classroom. Meaningful change in classrooms should not only be empirically detectable but should also be sufficient to satisfy the classrooms' teachers, students, and parents.

To document the classroom satisfaction with the intervention, program evaluators could adapt the Behavioral Intervention Rating Scale (BIRS; Elliott & Von Brock Treuting, 1991; Von Brock & Elliott, 1987) for use by teachers and parents. The BIRS has been used with good reliability in similar school-based studies of treatment effectiveness (Sheridan & Steck, 1995). Alternatively, Goal Attainment Scales can be used to assess students' and teachers' beliefs about whether classroom goals were met (Kiresuk, Smith, & Cardillo, 1994). A Goal Attainment Scale is a simple 5-point line stretching from –2 to +2 that is drawn on a paper (see Figure 9.1). Students or teachers would circle –2 if the classroom's situation had got significantly worse, they would circle +2 if the classroom goals had been completely met, or they could mark any point in between. The midpoint of the line (0) would represent the case where nothing had changed. The validity and reliability of Goal Attainment Scales has been shown to be high when they are used in similar evaluations (Kirusek et al., 1994).

> **Meaningful change in classrooms should not only be empirically detectable but should also be sufficient to satisfy the classroom's teachers, students, and parents.**

PRESENTATION OF EVALUATION RESULTS

Once an evaluation has provided convincing evidence of an intervention's effectiveness, results should be disseminated in ways that influence key decision makers. Presentations are more striking if they are brief and highly focused on the most essential information about the intervention program: What was done in the intervention? What resources were required to implement it? How much impact did it have on student success? And what policies, resources, and/or decisions are necessary to continue to use the intervention in future classrooms? Bulleted lists, highlighting, and liberal use of headings and titles will draw the audience's eye to important information. The use of data graphs and diagrams will be more influential than numbers in tables. Evaluations that occur without careful plans for dissemination will have minimal impact.

FIGURE 9.1. Goal Attainment Scale.

An Evaluation of a Classroom Intervention

P. S. Murphy (2002) evaluated the impact of classroom meetings on the recess problems of fourth- and fifth-grade students. He identified three classrooms that had too many recess problems with student conflicts (identified in Figure 9.2 [p. 134] as "conflict") and with students being left out (identified in Figure 9.2 as "inclusion"). In all three classrooms, he immediately began collecting two recess reports each week by having students complete a seven-item survey describing problems they had immediately as they came in from recess. Baseline data collection continued in all three classrooms from Weeks 1 through 3. During Weeks 4 and 5, once his baseline data was stable, he began to hold one classroom meeting each week in Classroom 1 only. The meetings used a problem-solving format in which he asked students to describe the recess problems, suggest alternative solutions, anticipate the consequences of each solution, choose one strategy, and try it out. The classroom teacher sat at the back of the class and took notes to make sure he followed the agreed-upon meeting format. Figure 9.2 shows that the number of recess problems dropped once the meetings began. In Week 6, the classroom meetings were stopped in Classroom 1 and started in Classroom 2; at that point, recess problems rose in Classroom 1 but did not show any apparent change in Classroom 2. In fact, over the entire period of Classroom 2's classroom meetings, recess problems seemed to increase. In Week 7, classroom meetings were resumed in Classroom 1 and were initiated for the first time in Classroom 3, and recess problems dropped in both classrooms. Murphy's assessment is an example of a simple evaluation of a classroom intervention. His results suggest that the classroom meetings were responsible for slight declines in recess problems in Classrooms 1 and 3 but were not effective in Classroom 2.

SUMMARY

Rigorous evaluation of resilient classrooms interventions will not always be necessary. In many classrooms where the immediate task is to refine the classroom context for learning, simple case study collection of baseline and intervention data can demonstrate that this goal has been accomplished. When rigorous evaluation is necessary, the purpose of evaluation will almost always be to justify school or classroom resources. In this event, three key questions will need to be answered: Were the resilient classrooms interventions effective in improving classroom environments? Did students experience more success as a result? And how big was the effect?

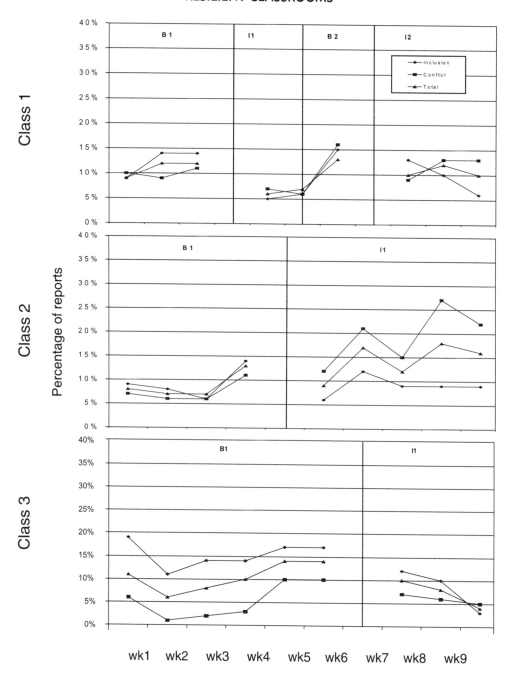

FIGURE 9.2. Trend line of student's weekly report of overall recess problems. From P. S. Murphy (2002). Reprinted by permission of the author.

CHAPTER 10

Integrating the Resilient Classroom with Existing School Mental Health Services

Like classrooms, schools are ecological systems. Introducing change into schools requires the same careful attention as is required by changing classrooms. Large and sudden changes are difficult to sustain because they impose too many unfamiliar demands on the system. Small and subtle changes are easily co-opted; what appears at first to be a change comes to look very much like the same old practice given time. The true challenge is to integrate change into the existing practices of school while still protecting the innovative and important modifications that it represents. This chapter describes how to integrate the resilient classrooms thinking into existing practices of schools. First, we describe how resilient classrooms are similar to current practices of schools, because this familiarity should ease acceptance of the change and should point to the competencies that schools already have that can support classroom interventions. Then, we review the features of resilient classrooms that are distinctive from current school practices and explain once again why these ought to be protected.

THE FAMILIAR

Much of what has been described in this book should be familiar to schools. For example, the data-based decision making that characterizes resilient classrooms practices is also integral to diagnostic teaching, in which teachers systematically identify their students' strengths and weaknesses, deliver instruction that addresses the weaknesses, and reassess the results to determine whether the instruction has been successful. Data collection and analysis are also characteristic of action research, in which teachers and other practitioners systematically investigate problems of practice that they encounter in their daily work and identify optimal teaching strategies or preventive practices to address these problems. In special education programs, the progress of students is tracked through continuous collection of data so that the programs can demonstrate that the students' individual educational programs are appropriately accommodating for the disabilities. As a result of schools' growing emphasis on data-based decision making, much of the expertise that is required by resilient classrooms practices already exists in schools. Most schools already have staff members who understand how to collect and record data; have a foundation of knowledge about alternative ways to assess academic, social, behavioral, and emotional variables; and have a tacit understanding of ways in which data can support effective decision making.

Much of what has been described in this book should be familiar to schools.

The systematic consultation that underlies resilient classrooms strategies is also familiar to schools. For the past 30 years, school mental health professionals like school psychologists, school counselors, and school social workers have been engaging in professional consultation to support teachers with unusually difficult student problems. It has been repeatedly demonstrated that consultation is more effective when it is deliberate, structured, and data driven. More recently, schools have established team consultation programs in which a group of colleagues works together to address persistent learning or behavior problems of students. Data-based decision-making teams have been highly effective in promoting the academic and behavioral success of students (Burns & Symington, 2002; Erchul & Martens, 2002; Gutkin & Curtis, 2009; Martens & DiGennaro, 2008). Also called "student assistance teams" or "instructional consultation teams," they are typically composed of regular and special education teachers and special service providers. Consultation is a familiar practice in schools, and teachers and other educators have become accustomed to working in teams with colleagues to make decisions on behalf of students.

Functional behavior assessment is an ongoing practice in most schools. It examines functional relationships between environmental variables and the occurrence or nonoccurrence of a student's behavior. Hypotheses are developed about the variables that might be causing the problem behavior, and these variables are manipulated in order to test the hypotheses. Experience with functional behavior assessment prepares schools to understand and identify the functional relationships that resilient classrooms teams identify between classroom characteristics and students' success and achievement.

School have responded to public demands for excellence with buildingwide and districtwide school reforms that raise academic standards and prepare students for future employment (Dwyer, 2002). To guide reforms, many schools have a building leadership team with representatives who span the school's professions, grades, and subject matter. Like resilient classrooms strategies, these reform initiatives are intended to strengthen schooling practices that will contribute to student success and high achievement. Because such school teams have assumed responsibility for the goals and activities that underlie schoolwide reform, they tend to support the principles that underlie the classroom reforms of resilient classrooms.

Finally, teachers and other educators have a pragmatic understanding of the impact of context on students' behavior and their learning. Incidental to their daily work in schools, they observe large numbers of students moving from classrooms to lunchrooms to playgrounds and note the very different ways that students act under such different conditions. Across their years of teaching, they have observed students move from one year's classroom to the next and understand that the same student can behave very differently in a different teacher's classroom. Because of their routine observations of context, the ecological framework underlying resilient classrooms has strong face validity with teachers.

THE UNFAMILIAR

Other features of resilient classrooms may well be less familiar to teachers. For example, schools habitually attribute students' learning, behavior, and emotional problems to their own disabilities and disturbances. Past practices have emphasized providing students' with remedial services to correct the disabilities and accommodations to allow them to succeed despite the disabilities. Resilient classrooms practitioners break with this tradition by proposing that some of the problems may reside within the classroom context and not within the students.

In schools, responsibility for the mental health of students is traditionally vested within educational specialists—psychologists, counselors, and social workers—and not within teachers. Students with exceptional emotional or behavioral difficulties are provided with supports through individual and small-group counseling activities that often occur outside of the classroom. The provision of these mental health supports is understood to fall outside of the core responsibilities of schools, and schools have relatively few mental health practitioners to address these needs (Adelman & Taylor, 2008). In contrast, resilient classrooms strategies emphasize natural supports like teachers, friends, and families as the principle source of socioemotional support for students. Like Adelman (1996; Adelman & Taylor, 2008), we believe that schools cannot achieve the vision implied by educational reform if they fail to address the psychosocial needs of children.

Prominent definitions of school success emphasize students' mastery of local, state, and national standards in math, reading, writing, science, and social sciences. In contrast, resilient classrooms strategies emphasize academic engagement as a proximal indicator of students' success in school. One indicator of academic engagement is on-task behavior such as completing assignments, complying with teacher requests, seeking help when appropriate, volunteering to answer questions, and engaging in assigned tasks (Greenwood, 1991; Liaupsin, Umbreit, Ferro, Urso, & Upreti, 2006). Still, students must be actively thinking about the material and reflecting on its meaning to show sustained learning (Fredericks, Blumenfeld, & Paris, 2004; Reschly & Christenson, 2006). Students who also strive for knowledge, set personal goals for success, and regulate their concentration and effort will show even higher levels of school success (Pintrich, 2003). Ultimately, the most successful students will be those who are personally entranced with learning, are part of a strong social network within their school, or lead efforts to strengthen schoolwide conditions for learning. (Fredricks et al., 2004; NRC/IOM, 2004).

Above all else, the goal of schooling has always been to change the student—increasing student achievement, skill mastery, and success. The measure of school success is an increase in the number of students who pass a mastery exam, who obtain an average score on a curricular exam, or who graduate with a high school diploma. Resilient classrooms strategies suggest that in some cases the route to greater student success is by changing the classrooms.

EMERGING INNOVATIONS

Resilient classrooms interventions reflect three interlocking innovations that are emerging in contemporary schools: response to intervention (RTI), PBIS, and multi-tiered systems of support (MTSS). RTI, a special case of data-based decision making, was recognized in the most recent Individuals with Disabilities Education Improvement Act (IDEIA, 2004) as an appropriate procedure for identifying students with learning disabilities. School districts around the nation collect continuous data describing students' performance in reading, mathematics, language arts, or science and use these data to examine the impact of trial instructional interventions on student learning (Brown-Chidsey & Steege, 2005). Resilient classrooms interventions are a logical extension of RTI procedures even though the subject of inquiry is a classroom learning environment, rather than a single student. The key question in a resilient classrooms project is whether the classroom environment improved once an intervention was put in place.

IDEIA 2004 also acknowledged the importance of PBIS in schools. PBIS is a decision-making system through which schools establish routines and practices prompting students to engage in adaptive, prosocial behaviors using clear descriptions of the adaptive behaviors that teachers expect from students and ensuring that there are positive consequences for students to behave in these ways (Sugai, Horner, & McIntosh, 2008). Resilient classrooms share the PBIS emphasis on data and data-based decision making and mimic the PBIS focus on the systems of schools that influence students' success. One important contribution that resilient classrooms make to PBIS is an operational description of the positive classroom characteristics that contribute to student success.

Prominent frameworks for RTI and for PBIS use a tiered prevention model, also called "MTSS," to describe the continuum of services that are provided to students. The lowest tier of services (Tier 1) describes universal programs and strategies that are integral to every student's experience in the school. Effective Tier 1 services maximize the success of most students in the building. Resilient classrooms is an example of a Tier 1 service that fosters highly effective learning environments for students in a school. Tier 2 supports are provided to students who are not fully successful despite the universal supports available to them at Tier 1. In many schools, RTI programs are Tier 2 services used to identify effective behavioral or instructional interventions with individual students. Services at the higher tiers represent successively more intensive strategies and supports for students who are still not fully successful.

In an optimal system, schools and classrooms would use sound data-based decision-making strategies to establish a strong foundation of highly effective instruction and very favorable classroom learning environments for every student in the school. Goals for classrooms and for students would be defined in precise, operational, and positive language. When classwide or schoolwide data suggested that either the instruction or the learning environments were less than ideal, interventions guided by data-based decision-making strategies would be used to refine and strengthen these. Regardless, students who continued to struggle with learning, behavior, or academic engagement would be provided with more intensive supports at an upper tier, always guided by data to verify that the students' response to these supports was successful. RTI, PBIS, MTSS, and resilient classrooms all contribute in shared and distinct ways to this vision.

INTEGRATING RESILIENT CLASSROOMS INTO SCHOOLS

How can the resilient classrooms approach be integrated into the fabric of schools so that it becomes one of many threads that are woven together to support student success? Systems change principles suggest that it is first necessary to identify gatekeepers as the people who have decision-making power, the ability to distribute resources, and the authority within the system (Curtis & Stollar, 2002). In schools, they typically include the principal but may also include highly influential teachers, school board members, or community leaders. Then, it will be essential to identify stakeholders who will be affected by the change, such as the school's parents and teachers, and devise ways to involve them in planning and decision making from the beginning. An important next step will be to formulate realistic, concrete goals for the broader change process that includes resilient classrooms. Is its purpose to increase student success? To reduce the number of students served through special programs? To increase teacher participation in school reform efforts? Finally, it will be useful to anticipate other effects that implementation will have on the school beyond those that are inherent in the resilient classrooms approach. For example, will parents want to participate in other aspects of school functioning, and will there be resistance to change from any individual or group?

A very simple way to introduce resilient classrooms into a school is to identify a single teacher who would accept the idea readily and work closely with that teacher. The ideal "groundbreaking" teacher would be one who is influential in the building, excited about trying new things, and has effective and innovative teaching strategies that might enrich the classroom change strategies that are planned. The resilient classrooms approach appeals to many of the needs that teachers experience but that may go unmet in some schools, such as a sense of community, an avenue for professional growth, and enhanced teaching and management efficacy (Adelman & Taylor, 2008). When presenting the model to a teacher, we briefly summarize the model for classroom resilience and then provide one or two examples of successful classroom change projects. Nothing breeds success like success, and word will spread about resilient classrooms when this early effort is successful.

> **Identify a single teacher who would accept resilient classrooms readily and work closely with that teacher.**

In many schools, teacher interest in trying new practices is related to perceived support by the principal (Vadasy, Jenkins, Antil, Phillips, & Pool, 1997). Resilient classrooms can be presented to principals by appealing to their concerns for discipline and high achievement scores and the central importance of academic engagement for strengthening these areas. Principals appreciate a written proposal that outlines the basic ideas of resilient classrooms how it directly addresses their goals and concerns and a plan for how the consultant will support the program. It is important to explain how the resilient classrooms activities fit naturally within the team's existing duties and how they will affect other tasks the team members regularly perform.

Once principals understand how the resilient classrooms approach can enhance classroom functioning, they may seize upon it as an opportunity to obtain help for struggling teachers. Consultants should curb this kind of enthusiasm by emphasizing that the strategy will work best when everyone participates voluntarily. Although some struggling teachers may be among the first to request assistance in their classrooms, others will wait to see if the strategy works before committing themselves to participation in the program. Once resilient classrooms projects are under way in one or more classrooms, it will be important to update the principal periodically on the number of classrooms that are implementing resilient classrooms interventions and the general issues being addressed. Care should be taken, however, to keep these reports general so that teacher identity and confidentiality concerning progress are maintained.

A third avenue is to integrate resilient classrooms projects into school programs that are already serving children successfully. For example, schools with strong prereferral student assistance teams can be helped to use classroom-changing rather than student-changing strategies in some instances. Alternatively, the school's accountability or school improvement team could incorporate the resilient classrooms approach as a strategy for moving reform efforts down to the classroom level. Resilient classrooms practices provide strategies that student assistance teams or school improvement teams can use to tailor their efforts to fit each classroom's unique environment and to involve the people who must interact in that system.

Inevitably, resilient classrooms projects will need to become team efforts. Teams can reasonably assume leadership for classroom intervention programs because the knowledge base that underlies the interventions is cross-disciplinary, the prerequisite skills are not unique to any single profession, and the team member role is compatible with diverse educational roles. Even with partners sharing the responsibility for classroom changes, it is important that the team not overcommit.

AN EXAMPLE OF SCHOOL CHANGE

A veteran school psychologist was assigned to a bilingual inner-city school that was performing poorly on state standards. The district also assigned a new principal to the building and allowed the school 3 years to improve the lagging test scores or it would become a charter school. The school psychologist, in collaboration with the principal, invited the teachers to participate in weekly classroom meetings that could enhance students' academic and social goal-setting skills and foster satisfying relationships among students in the class. (The intervention is described in greater detail in Chapter 8.) Through the class meetings, the school psychologist was able to address the state standards, directly support student achievement in the classroom, and model new strategies that teachers could imitate to address students' motivation and interpersonal needs. Just as important, the school psychologist served a broad selection of students throughout the school, and the principal was able to participate by reinforcing prosocial behaviors and attainment of students. Teachers responded quite favorably to these suggestions for change and, before long, classroom meetings were occurring on a weekly basis in all third- through fifth-grade classrooms. The impact of the intervention on students and teachers was notable. Many teachers held classroom meetings more frequently than once per week because their communications with students improved so dramatically. Students were excited about reaching their own academic and social goals and looked forward to receiving their certificate of accomplishment from the principal. Figure 10.1 is an example of such a certificate. Some students took these certificates home to share with their parents, while others posted them in their classrooms or in the hallways.

FIGURE 10.1. Example of an achievement certificate.

SUMMARY

This book has proposed a framework for resilient classrooms in which classrooms are assessed, weaknesses in their supports for learning are identified, interventions are systematically planned and implemented, and data are used to assess the impact of the plan. This framework is proposed not as a substitute for current change-the-child strategies for educational intervention but as a supplement to them. Dwyer (2002) has suggested that students' behavior and socialization problems frequently reflect normal responses to irritating factors in the environment rather than emotional conflicts within the child. The resilient classrooms framework provides an alternative form of service delivery that can reduce these irritations. A middle school administrator explained it this way: "It's like a fish bowl. All the other people come into our school and try to fix the fish. You're trying to clean up the water." Cleaning up the water does not always fix the fish, but it's almost impossible to keep the fish healthy until the water is clean.

> It is impossible to keep the fish healthy until the water is clean.

ClassMaps Survey

ClassMaps

DIRECTIONS: These questions ask what is true about your class. For each question, circle the choice that is true for you. Do not put your name on the paper. No one will know what your answers are.

I am a: ☐ boy/male ☐ girl/female I am in the _____ grade.

Believing in Me

1. I can do my work correctly in this class.

    Never   Sometimes   Often   Almost Always

2. I can do as well as most kids in this class.

    Never   Sometimes   Often   Almost Always

3. I can help other kids understand the work in this class.

    Never   Sometimes   Often   Almost Always

4. I can be a very good student in this class.

    Never   Sometimes   Often   Almost Always

5. I can do the hard work in this class.

    Never   Sometimes   Often   Almost Always

6. I can get good grades when I try hard in this class.

    Never   Sometimes   Often   Almost Always

7. I know that I will learn what is taught in this class.

    Never   Sometimes   Often   Almost Always

8. I expect to do very well when I work hard in this class.

My Teacher

9. My teacher listens carefully to me when I talk.

    Never   Sometimes   Often   Almost Always

10. My teacher helps me when I need help.

    Never   Sometimes   Often   Almost Always

11. My teacher respects me.

    Never   Sometimes   Often   Almost Always

12. My teacher likes having me in this class.

    Never   Sometimes   Often   Almost Always

13. My teacher makes it fun to be in this class.

    Never   Sometimes   Often   Almost Always

(continued)

14. My teacher thinks I do a good job in this class.

  Never   Sometimes   Often   Almost Always

15. My teacher is fair to me.

  Never   Sometimes   Often   Almost Always

Taking Charge

16. I want to know more about the things we learn in this class.

  Never   Sometimes   Often   Almost Always

17. In this class, I can guess what my grade will be when I turn in my work.

  Never   Sometimes   Often   Almost Always

18. I work as hard as I can in this class.

  Never   Sometimes   Often   Almost Always

19. I find and fix my mistakes before turning in my work.

  Never   Sometimes   Often   Almost Always

20. I learn because I want to and not just because the teacher tells me to.

  Never   Sometimes   Often   Almost Always

21. When the work is hard in this class, I keep trying until I figure it out.

  Never   Sometimes   Often   Almost Always

22. I know the things I learn in this class will help me outside of school.

  Never   Sometimes   Often   Almost Always

23. I can tell when I make a mistake on my work in this class.

  Never   Sometimes   Often   Almost Always

My Classmates

24. I have a lot of fun with my friends in this class.

  Never   Sometimes   Often   Almost Always

25. My friends care about me a lot.

  Never   Sometimes   Often   Almost Always

26. I have friends to eat lunch with and play with at recess.

  Never   Sometimes   Often   Almost Always

27. I have friends who like me the way I am.

  Never   Sometimes   Often   Almost Always

(continued)

28. My friends like me as much as they like other kids.

| Never | Sometimes | Often | Almost Always |

29. I have friends who will stick up for me if someone picks on me.

| Never | Sometimes | Often | Almost Always |

Following the Class Rules

30. Most kids work quietly and calmly in this class.

| Never | Sometimes | Often | Almost Always |

31. Most kids in this class listen carefully when the teacher gives directions.

| Never | Sometimes | Often | Almost Always |

32. Most kids follow the rules in this class.

| Never | Sometimes | Often | Almost Always |

33. Most kids in this class pay attention when they are supposed to.

| Never | Sometimes | Often | Almost Always |

34. Most kids do their work when they are supposed to in this class.

| Never | Sometimes | Often | Almost Always |

35. Most kids in this class behave well even when the teacher isn't watching.

| Never | Sometimes | Often | Almost Always |

Talking with My Parents

36. My parents and I talk about my grades in this class.

| Never | Sometimes | Often | Almost Always |

37. My parents and I talk about what I am learning in this class.

| Never | Sometimes | Often | Almost Always |

38. My parents and I talk about my homework in this class.

| Never | Sometimes | Often | Almost Always |

39. My parents help me with my homework when I need it.

| Never | Sometimes | Often | Almost Always |

40. My parents and I talk about ways that I can do well in school.

| Never | Sometimes | Often | Almost Always |

41. My parents and I talk about good things I have done in this class.

| Never | Sometimes | Often | Almost Always |

42. My parents and I talk about problems I have in this class.

| Never | Sometimes | Often | Almost Always |

(continued)

I Worry That . . .

43. I worry that other kids will do mean things to me.

Never   Sometimes   Often   Almost Always

44. I worry that other kids will tell lies about me.

Never   Sometimes   Often   Almost Always

45. I worry that other kids will hurt me on purpose.

Never   Sometimes   Often   Almost Always

46. I worry that other kids will say mean things about me.

Never   Sometimes   Often   Almost Always

47. I worry that other kids will leave me out on purpose.

Never   Sometimes   Often   Almost Always

48. I worry that other kids will try to make my friends stop liking me.

Never   Sometimes   Often   Almost Always

49. I worry that other kids will make me do things I don't want to do.

Never   Sometimes   Often   Almost Always

50. I worry that other kids will take things away from me.

Never   Sometimes   Often   Almost Always

Kids in This Class

51. Kids in this class argue a lot with each other.

Never   Sometimes   Often   Almost Always

52. Kids in this class pick on or make fun of each other.

Never   Sometimes   Often   Almost Always

53. Kids in this class tease each other or call each other names.

Never   Sometimes   Often   Almost Always

54. Kids in this class hit or push each other.

Never   Sometimes   Often   Almost Always

55. Kids in this class say bad things about each other.

Never   Sometimes   Often   Almost Always

APPENDIX B

Worksheets

Classroom Meeting Record

Classroom: _____ Date of class meeting: _____

Question 1: Do you think the classroom data are accurate?

Response: _____

Question 2: What do you think caused the problem?

Response: _____

_____

_____

_____

Question 3: What do you think the teacher could do differently to make things better?

Response: _____

_____

_____

_____

Question 4: What do you think students could do to make things better?

Response: _____

_____

_____

_____

Did the class think that the classroom data are accurate? Check one.

- ☐ Completely inaccurate
- ☐ Kind of inaccurate
- ☐ Neutral
- ☐ Accurate with a few inaccuracies
- ☐ Very accurate

(continued)

What words did the class use to describe the problem?

_____

_____

_____

_____

What did the students think caused the problem?

_____

_____

_____

_____

What did the students think they could do to make things better?

_____

_____

_____

_____

What did the students think the teacher could do to make things better?

_____

_____

_____

_____

Making Sense of the Classroom Data

Classroom: _____ Date of goal setting: _____

What strengths are shown by your classroom data?

_____

_____

_____

_____

What weaknesses are shown that you would like to see improve?

_____

_____

_____

_____

Which is the most important weakness to change?

_____

_____

_____

_____

In addition to the classroom data, what other evidence do you have that this weakness is a problem for the class?

_____

_____

_____

_____

What are the times and places when this weakness is particularly a problem for the class?

_____

_____

_____

_____

(continued)

What are the times and places when this weakness is **not** present or is **not** a problem for the class?

_____
_____
_____
_____

What else is happening in the class when the weakness is particularly a problem? Or when it is **not** present? (Examples might include certain individuals who are present, the size of the group, time of day, seating arrangement, expectations for a task, etc.)

_____
_____
_____
_____

What will the classroom be like once the weakness is "fixed"?

- Exactly what will change?

    _____
    _____
    _____

- How much will it change?

    _____
    _____
    _____

- What will success look and sound like?

    _____
    _____
    _____

Resilient classrooms' goal:

_____
_____
_____

How will you know if the class meets the goal?

_____
_____
_____

(continued)

What Additional Classroom Data Will Tell You When the Classroom Goal Is Met

What data will be collected?

_____

Who will collect the data?

_____

When and how often?

_____

In the Class Meeting

What classroom data would you like to show to the class? (Consider showing one graph reflecting a class strength and a second graph reflecting a class weakness.)

_____

Planning and Implementing Classroom Changes

Classroom: _____ Date of planning: _____

Your Resilient Classrooms' Goal

_____

_____

_____

What Do Your Classroom Data Show?

What data were collected? _____

Who collected the data? _____

When and how often? _____

What did the data show? _____

_____

Planning for Change

What new information was learned from the classroom meeting or data collection?

_____

_____

_____

What can be done in this class to reach the goal? Options might include one or more of the following:

☐ Changing classroom routines _____

☐ Changing teacher behaviors _____

☐ Changing student behaviors _____

☐ Increasing teacher skills _____

☐ Changing the physical setting of the classroom (by adding things or rearranging existing things)

_____

☐ Changing the physical setting of playground or other school facilities (by adding things or rearranging existing things)

_____

☐ Modifying classroom discipline procedures _____

☐ Anything else? _____

(continued)

The Plan

What changes will be made in the classroom?

Change 1: _____

_____

_____

_____

Change 2: _____

_____

_____

_____

Change 3: _____

_____

_____

_____

Change 4: _____

_____

_____

_____

*Next, enter each change into the **Intervention Plan Record,** noting who will make the change, when, and where.

Should Changes Be Made in the Plan for Data Collection?

Collecting different data? _____

Change who collects the dtata? _____

When and how often? _____

Intervention Plan Record

Classroom: _____ Record for week of: _____

Change/Activity 1

What will be done? _____

_____

Who will do it? _____

When? _____ Where? _____

Did this happen?   ☐ YES   ☐ PARTLY   ☐ NO

Change/Activity 2

What will be done? _____

_____

Who will do it? _____

When? _____ Where? _____

Did this happen?   ☐ YES   ☐ PARTLY   ☐ NO

Change/Activity 3

What will be done? _____

_____

Who will do it? _____

When? _____ Where? _____

Did this happen?   ☐ YES   ☐ PARTLY   ☐ NO

Change/Activity 4

What will be done? _____

_____

Who will do it? _____

When? _____ Where? _____

Did this happen?   ☐ YES   ☐ PARTLY   ☐ NO

(continued)

Data Collection

What data were collected? _____

_____

When were the data collected? _____

	Monday	Tuesday	Wednesday	Thursday	Friday
Date					

Attach the actual data records.

References

Adams, K. S., & Christenson, S. L. (2000). Trust and the family–school relationship: An examination of parent–teacher differences in elementary and secondary grades. *Journal of School Psychology, 38,* 447–497.

Adelman, H. S. (1996). Restructuring educational support services and integrating community resources: Beyond the full service school model. *School Psychology Review, 25,* 431–445.

Adelman, H. S., & Taylor, L. (2008). School-wide approaches to addressing barriers to learning and teaching. In B. Doll & J. Cummings (Eds.), *Transforming school mental health services* (pp. 277–306). Thousand Oaks, CA: Corwin Press/National Association of School Psychologists.

American Psychiatric Association. (2000). *Diagnostic and statistical manual of mental disorders* (4th ed., text rev.). Washington, DC: Author.

Anderson, K. J., & Minke, K. M. (2007). Parent involvement in education: Toward an understanding of parents' decision making. *Journal of Educational Research, 100,* 311–323.

Andriessen, I., Phalet, K., & Lens, W. (2006). Future goal setting, task motivation and learning of minority and non-minority students in Dutch schools. *British Journal of Educational Psychology, 76*(4), 827–850.

Ang, R. P. (2005). Development and validation of the teacher–student relationship inventory using exploratory and confirmatory factor analysis. *Journal of Experimental Education, 74*(1), 55–73.

Annie E. Casey Foundation. (2010). KidsCount. Retrieved June 12, 2012, from *http://datacenter.kidscount.org/data/acrossstates/rankings.aspx?ind=43.*

Asher, S. R. (1995, June). *Children and adolescents with peer relationship problems.* Workshop presented at the Annual Summer Institute in School Psychology: Internalizing Disorders in Children and Adolescents, Denver, CO.

Assor, A., Kaplan, H., & Roth, G. (2002). Choice is good, but relevance is excellent: Autonomy-enhancing and suppressing teacher behaviours predicting students' engagement in schoolwork. *British Journal of Educational Psychology, 72,* 261–278.

Bahr, M. W., Whitten, E., Dieker, L., Kocarek, C., & Manson, D. (1999). A comparison of school-based intervention teams: Implications for education and legal reform. *Exceptional Children, 66,* 67–83.

Baker, J. A. (2006). Contributions of teacher–child relationships to positive school adjustment during elementary school. *Journal of School Psychology, 44,* 211–229.

Baker, J. A. (2008). Assessing school risk and protective factors. In B. Doll & J. A. Cummings (Eds.), *Transforming school mental health services* (pp. 43–65). Thousand Oaks, CA: Corwin Press/National Association of School Psychologists.

Baker, J. A., Kamphaus, R. W., Horne, A. M., & Winsor, A. (2006). Evidence for population-based perspectives on children's behavioral adjustment and needs for service delivery in schools. *School Psychology Review, 35,* 31–46.

Bandura, A. (1977a). Self-efficacy: Toward a unifying theory of behavioral change. *Psychological Review, 84,* 191–215.

Bandura, A. (1977b). *Social learning theory.* Englewood Cliffs, NJ: Prentice Hall.

Bandura, A. (1989). Human agency in cognitive theory. *American Psychologist, 44,* 1175–1184.

Bandura, A. (1993). Perceived self-efficacy in cognitive development and functioning. *Educational Psychologist, 28*(2), 117–148.

Bandura, A. (1997). *Self-efficacy: The exercise of control.* Englewood Cliffs, NJ: Prentice Hall.

Bandura, A., Caprara, G., Barbaranelli, C., Gerbino, M., & Pastorelli, C. (2003). Role of affective self-regulatory efficacy in diverse spheres of psychosocial functioning. *Child Development, 74*(3), 769–782.

Barclay, J. R. (1966). Sociometric choices and teacher ratings as predictors of school dropout. *Journal of Social Psychology, 4,* 40–45.

Barclay, J. R. (1992). Sociometry, temperament and school psychology. In T. R. Kratochwill, S. Elliott, & M. Gettinger (Eds.), *Advances in school psychology* (Vol. 8, pp. 79–114). Hillsdale, NJ: Erlbaum.

Barth, J. M., Dunlap, S. T., Dane, H., Lochman, J. E., & Wells, K. C. (2004). Classroom environment influences on aggression, peer relations, and academic focus. *Journal of School Psychology, 42*(2), 115–133.

Bassi, M., Steca, P., Delle Fave, A., & Caprara, G. V. (2007). Academic self-efficacy beliefs and quality of experience in learning. *Journal of Youth and Adolescence, 36*(3), 301–312.

Bayer, U. C., & Gollwitzer, P. M. (2007). Boosting scholastic test scores by willpower: The role of implementation intentions. *Self and Identity, 6*(1), 1–19.

Bear, G. G. (2010). *School discipline and self-discipline: A practical guide to promoting prosocial student behavior.* New York: Guilford Press.

Bear, G. G., Cavalier, A. R., & Manning, M. A. (2005). *Developing self-discipline and preventing and correcting misbehavior.* Boston: Allyn & Bacon.

Bell-Dolan, D. J., Foster, S. L., & Sikora, D. M. (1989). Effects of sociometric testing on children's behavior and loneliness in school. *Developmental Psychology, 25,* 306–311.

Bempechat, J., Graham, S. E., & Jimenez, N. V. (1999). The socialization of achievement in poor and minority students: A comparative study. *Journal of Cross-Cultural Psychology, 30,* 139–158.

Bergin, C. C., & Bergin, D. A. (2009). Attachment in the classroom. *Educational Psychology Review, 21,* 141–170.

Berndt, T. J. (1999). Friends' influence on students' adjustment to school. *Educational Psychologist, 34,* 15–29.

Black, A. E., & Deci, E. L. (2000). The effects of instructors' autonomy support and students' autonomous motivation on learning organic chemistry: A self-determination theory perspective. *Science Education, 84,* 740–756.

Blum, R. W., McNeely, C. A., & Rinehart, P. M. (2002). *Improving the odds: The untapped power of schools to improve the health of teens.* Minneapolis: University of Minnesota, Center for Adolescent Health and Development.

Bouffard-Bouchard, T. (1989). Influence of self-efficacy on performance in a cognitive task. *Journal of Social Psychology, 130,* 353–363.

Bridgeland, J. M., DiIulio, J. J., & Morison, K. B. (2006). *The silent epidemic: Perspectives of high school dropouts.* Washington, DC: Civic Enterprises and Peter D. Hart Research Associates for the Bill and Melinda Gates Foundation.

Bronfenbrenner, U. (1979). *The ecology of human development: Experiments by nature and design.* Cambridge, MA: Harvard University Press.

Brooks, R., & Goldstein, S. (2007). Developing the mindset of effective students. In S. Goldstein, R. B. Brooks, S. Goldstein, & R. B. Brooks (Eds.), *Understanding and managing children's classroom behavior: Creating sustainable, resilient classrooms* (2nd ed., pp. 208–225). Hoboken, NJ: Wiley.

Brophy, J. (2004). *Motivating students to learn* (2nd ed.). Mahwah, NJ: Erlbaum.

Brown, D., Pryzwansky, W. B., & Schulte, A. C. (2001). *Psychological consultation: Introduction to theory and practice* (5th ed.). Boston: Allyn & Bacon.

Brown-Chidsey, R., & Steege, M. W. (2005). *Response to intervention: Principles and strategies for effective practice.* New York: Guilford Press.

Buerkle, K., Whitehouse, E. M., & Christenson, S. L. (2009). Partnering with families for educational success. In T. Gutkin & C. Reynolds (Eds.), *The handbook of school psychology* (pp. 655–680). Hoboken, NJ: Wiley.

Buhs, E. S., & Ladd, G. W. (2001). Peer rejection as antecedent of young children's school adjustment: An examination of mediating processes. *Developmental Psychology, 37,* 550–560.

Bullis, M., Walker, H. M., & Sprague, J. R. (2001). A promise unfulfilled: Social skills training with at-risk and antisocial children and youth. *Exceptionality, 9,* 67–90.

Bumbarger, B. K., Perkins, D. F., & Greenberg, M. T. (2010). Taking effective prevention to scale. In B. Doll, W. Pfohl, & J. Yoon (Eds.), *Handbook of youth prevention science* (pp. 433–444). New York: Routledge.

Burns, M. K., Codding, R. S., Boice, C. H., & Lukito, G. (2010). Meta-analysis of acquisition and fluency math interventions with instructional and frustration level skills: Evidence for a skill-by-treatment interaction. *School Psychology Review, 39*(1), 69–83.

Burns, M. K., & Gibbons, K. A. (2008). *Implement-*

ing response-to-intervention in elementary and secondary schools: Procedures to assure scientific-based practices. New York: Routledge.

Burns, M. K., & Symington, T. (2002). A meta-analysis of prereferral intervention teams: Student and systemic outcomes. *Journal of School Psychology, 40*(5), 437–447.

Burns, M. K., Wiley, H. I., & Biglietta, E. (2008). Best practices in implementing effective problem-solving teams. In A. Thomas & J. Grimes (Eds.), *Best practices in school psychology* (5th ed., pp. 1633–1644). Bethesda, MD: National Association of School Psychologists.

Caine, R., & Caine, G. (1994). *Making connections: Teaching and the human brain.* Menlo Park, CA: Addison-Wesley/Innovative Learning.

Cairns, R. B., & Cairns, B. D. (2000). The natural history and developmental functions of aggression. In A. J. Sameroff, M. Lewis, & S. M. Miller (Eds.), *Handbook of developmental psychopathology* (2nd ed., pp. 403–430). New York: Kluwer Academic/Plenum.

Caplan, G. (1970). *The theory and practice of mental health consultation.* New York: Basic Books.

Chan, J. C. Y., & Lam, S. (2008). Effects of competition on students' self-efficacy in vicarious learning. *British Journal of Educational Psychology, 78,* 95–108.

ChildrensDefense.org. (2010). Children's Defense Fund. Retrieved June 12, 2012, from *www.childrensdefense.org.*

Christenson, S. L. (2004). The family–school partnership: An opportunity to promote the learning competence of all students. *School Psychology Review, 33,* 83–104.

Christenson, S. L., & Godber, Y. (2001). Enhancing constructive family–school connections. In J. A. Hughes, A. M. LaGreca, & J. C. Conoley (Eds.), *Handbook of psychological services for children and adolescents* (pp. 455–476). Oxford, UK: Oxford University Press.

Christenson, S. L., & Reschly, A. L. (2010). Check and connect: Enhancing school completion through student engagement. In B. Doll, W. Pfohl, & J. Yoon (Eds.), *Handbook of youth prevention science* (pp. 327–348). New York: Routledge.

Christenson, S. L., & Sheridan, S. M. (2001). *Schools and families: Creating essential connections for children's learning.* New York: Guilford Press.

Christenson, S. L., Whitehouse, E. M., & VanGetson, G. R. (2008). Partnering with families to enhance students' mental health. In B. Doll & J. A. Cummings (Eds.), *Transforming school mental health services* (pp. 69–101). Thousand Oaks, CA: Corwin Press/National Association of School Psychologists.

Ciani, K., Ferguson, Y., Bergin, D., & Hilpert, J. (2010). Motivational influences on school-prompted interest. *Educational Psychology, 30*(4), 377–393.

Cihak, D. F., Kirk, E., & Boon, R. T. (2009). Effects of classwide positive peer "tootling" to reduce the disruptive classroom behaviors of elementary students with and without disabilities. *Journal of Behavioral Education, 18,* 267–278.

Cillessen, A. H. N. (2009). Sociometric methods. In K. H. Rubin, W. M. Bukowski, & B. Laursen (Eds.), *Handbook of peer interactions, relationships, and groups* (pp. 82–99). New York: Guilford Press.

Coie, J. D., & Kupersmidt, J. (1983). A behavior analysis of emerging social status in boys' groups. *Child Development, 54,* 1400–1416.

Collaborative for Academic, Social, and Emotional Learning. (2003). *Safe and sound: An educational leader's guide to evidence-based social and emotional learning programs.* Chicago: Author. Retrieved September 22, 2012, from *http:// casel.org/publications/safe-and-sound-an-educational-leaders-guide-to-evidence-based-sel-programs.*

Comer, J. P. (1993). *School power: Implications of an intervention project.* New York: Free Press.

Comer, J. P., Haynes, N. M., Joyner, E. T., & Ben-Avie, M. (1996). *Rallying the whole village: The Comer process for reforming education.* New York: Teachers College Press.

Corkum, P., Corbin, N., & Pike, M. (2010). Evaluation of a school-based social skills program for children with attention-deficit/hyperactivity disorder. *Child and Family Behavior Therapy, 32,* 139–151.

Cowen, E. L. (1994). The enhancement of psychological wellness: Challenges and opportunities. *American Journal of Community Psychology, 22,* 148–180.

Cowen, E. L., Hightower, A. D., Pedro-Carroll, J. L., Work, W. C., Wyman, P. A., & Haffey, W. G. (1996). *School-based prevention for children at risk: The primary mental health project.* Washington, DC: American Psychological Association.

Curby, T. W., Rimm-Kaufman, S. E., & Ponitz, C. C. (2009). Teacher–child interactions and children's achievement trajectories across kindergarten and first grade. *Journal of Educational Psychology, 101,* 912–925.

Curtis, M. J., & Stollar, S. A. (2002). Best practices in system-level change. In A. Thomas & J. Grimes (Eds.), *Best practices in school psychology IV* (pp. 223–234). Bethesda, MD: National Association of School Psychologists.

Deci, E. L., & Ryan, R. M. (2008a). Facilitating optimal motivation and psychological well-being across life's domains. *Canadian Psychology, 49,* 14–23.

Deci, E. L., & Ryan, R. M. (2008b). Self-determination theory: A macrotheory of human motivation, development, and health. *Canadian Psychology, 49,* 182–185.

Deno, S. L. (2002). Problem solving as best practice. In A. Thomas & J. Grimes (Eds.), *Best practices in school psychology IV* (pp. 37–55). Bethesda, MD: National Association of School Psychologists.

Deno, S. L., Fuchs, L. S., Marston, D., & Shin, J. (2001). Using curriculum-based measurement to establish growth standards for students with learning disabilities. *School Psychology Review, 30,* 507–524.

DeRosier, M. E., & Thomas, J. M. (2003). Strengthening sociometric prediction: Scientific advances in the assessment of children's peer relations. *Child Development, 74*(5), 1379–1392.

Developmental Studies Center. (1996). *Ways we want our class to be: Class meetings that build commitment to kindness and learning.* Oakland, CA: Author.

DiBenedetto, M. K., & Zimmerman, B. J. (2010). Differences in self-regulatory processes among students studying science: A micro-analytic investigation. *International Journal of Educational and Psychological Assessment, 5,* 2–24.

Doll, B. (1996). Children without friends: Implications for practice and policy. *School Psychology Review, 25,* 165–183.

Doll, B. (2005, July). *The successful student study: Examining precursors to academic, social and behavioral success.* Workshop presented at the Second Annual Summer Conference Critical Skills and Issues in School Psychology, Philadelphia, PA.

Doll, B. (2006, July). *Resilient classrooms: Places where all kids succeed.* An invited workshop at the Third Annual NASP Summer Conference: Critical Skills and Issues in School Psychology, Chicago, IL.

Doll, B., Boyer, J., Lestino, J. C., Marino, R., Kurien, S., LeClair, C. M., et al. (2007, March). *Promoting school mental health . . . so all kids succeed.* Symposium presented at the annual convention of the National Association of School Psychologists, New York.

Doll, B., & Brehm, K. (2010). *Resilient playgrounds.* New York: Routledge.

Doll, B., Champion, A., & Kurien, S. (2008, February). *Social and psychological context for high quality classrooms.* Poster presented at the 2008 annual convention of the National Association of School Psychologists, New Orleans, LA.

Doll, B., & Cummings, J. A. (Eds.). (2008). *Transforming school mental health services: Population-based approaches to promoting the competency and wellness of children.* Thousand Oaks, CA: Corwin Press/National Association of School Psychologists.

Doll, B., & Doll, C. (1997). *Bibliotherapy with young people: Librarians and mental health professionals working together.* Englewood, CO: Libraries Unlimited.

Doll, B., & Dooley, K. (2013). Classroom climate. *Encyclopedia of quality of life research.* New York: Springer.

Doll, B., Kurien, S., LeClair, C., Spies, R., Champion, A., & Osborn, A. (2009). The ClassMaps Survey: A framework for promoting positive classroom environments. *Handbook of Positive Psychology in Schools* (pp. 213–227). New York: Routledge/Taylor & Francis Group.

Doll, B., & Lyon, M. (1998.) Risk and resilience: Implications for the practice of school psychology. *School Psychology Review, 27,* 348–363.

Doll, B., Murphy, P., & Song, S. Y. (2003). The relationship between children's self-reported recess problems, and peer acceptance, and friendships. *Journal of School Psychology, 41,* 113–130.

Doll, B., Pfohl, W., & Yoon, J. (Eds.). (2010). *Handbook of youth prevention science.* New York: Routledge.

Doll, B., & Siemers, E. (2004, April). *Assessing instructional climates: The reliability and validity of ClassMaps.* Poster presented at the annual convention of the National Association of School Psychologists, Dallas, TX.

Doll, B., Spies, R., Champion, A., Guerrero, C., Dooley, K., & Turner, A. (2010). The ClassMaps Survey: A measure of middle school science students' perceptions of classroom characteristics. *Journal of Psychoeducational Assessment, 28*(4), 338–348.

Doll, B., Spies, R., LeClair, C., Kurien, S., & Foley, B. (2010). Student perceptions of classroom learning environments: Development of the ClassMaps Survey. *School Psychology Review, 39*(2), 203–218.

Doll, B., Spies, R., Strasil, E., LeClair, C., Fleissner, S., & Kurien, S. (2006, March). *Successful student study: Precursors to academic, social and behavioral success.* Paper presented at the annual convention of the National Association of School Psychologists, Anaheim, CA.

Doll, B., & Yoon, J. (2010). The current status of youth prevention science. In B. Doll, W. Pfohl, & J. Yoon (Eds.), *Handbook of youth prevention science* (pp. 1–18). New York: Routledge.

Downer, J. T., Rimm-Kaufman, S. E., & Pianta, R. C. (2007). How do classroom conditions and children's risk for school problems contribute to children's engagement in learning? *School Psychology Review, 36,* 413–432.

DuPaul, G. J., & Weyandt, L. L. (2006). School-based intervention for children with attention deficit hyperactivity disorder: Effects on academic, social, and behavioural functioning. *International Journal of Disability, Development and Education, 53*, 161–176.

Dweck, C. S., & Master, A. (2009). Self-theories and motivation: Students' beliefs about intelligence. In K. R. Wentzel & A. Wigfield (Eds.), *Handbook of motivation at school* (pp. 123–140). New York: Routledge.

Dwyer, K. P. (2002). Mental health in the schools. *Journal of Child and Family Studies, 11*, 101–111.

Eddy, J. M., Reid, J. B., & Fetrow, R. A. (2000). An elementary school-based prevention program targeting modifiable antecedents of youth delinquency and violence: Linking the Interests of Families and Teachers (LIFT). *Journal of Emotional and Behavioral Disorders, 8*(3), 165–176.

Elias, M. J., & Tobias, S. E. (1996). *Social problem solving: Interventions in the schools*. New York: Guilford Press.

Elias, M. J., Zins, J., Weissberg, R., Frey, K., Greenberg, M., Haynes, N., et al. (1997). *Promoting social and emotional learning*. Alexandria, VA: Association for Supervision and Curriculum Development.

Elliott, S. N. (1988). Acceptability of behavioral treatments in educational settings. In J. C. Witt, S. N. Elliott, & F. M. Gresham (Eds.), *The handbook of behavior therapy in education* (pp. 121–150). New York: Plenum Press.

Elliott, S. N., & Von Brock Treuting, M. (1991). The Behavior Intervention Rating Scale: Development and validation of a pretreatment acceptability and effectiveness measure. *Journal of School Psychology, 29*, 43–52.

Erchul, W. P., & Martens, B. K. (2002). *School consultation: Conceptual and empirical bases of practice* (2nd ed.). New York: Plenum.

Faber, A., & Mazlish, E. (1995). *How to talk so kids can learn*. New York: Rawson Associates.

Fan, X., & Chen, M. (2001). Parental involvement and students' academic achievement: A meta-analysis. *Educational Psychology Review, 13*, 1–22.

Fantuzzo, J. W., & Rohrbeck, C. A. (1992). Self-managed groups: Fitting self-management approaches into classroom systems. *School Psychology Review, 21*, 255–263.

Fast, L. A., Lewis, J. L., Bryant, M. J., Bocian, K. A., Cardullo, R. A., Rettig, M., et al. (2010). Does math self-efficacy mediate the effect of the perceived classroom environment on standardized math test performance? *Journal of Educational Psychology, 102*, 729–740.

Finn, J. D. (1998). Parental engagement that makes a difference. *Educational Leadership, 55*, 20–24.

Flay, B. R., & Allred, C. G. (2003). Long-term effects of the Positive Action® program. *American Journal of Health Behavior, 27*, S6–S21.

Flay, B. R., Allred, C. G., & Ordway, N. (2001). Effects of the Positive Action program on achievement and discipline: Two matched-control comparisons. *Prevention Science, 2*, 71–89.

Fredricks, J. A., Blumenfeld, P. C., & Paris, A. H. (2004). School engagement: Potential of the concept, state of the evidence. *Review of Educational Research, 74*, 59–109.

Frey, K. S., Hirschstein, M. K., & Guzzo, B. A. (2000). Second Step: Preventing aggression by promoting social competence. *Journal of Emotional and Behavioral Disorders, 8*, 102–112.

Frisby, B. N., & Martin, M. M. (2010). Instructor–student and student–student rapport in the classroom. *Communication Education, 59*(2), 146–164.

Garrity, C., Jens, K., Porter, W., Sager, N., & Short-Camilli, C. (1997). *Bully-proofing your school: A comprehensive approach for elementary schools*. Longmont, CO: Sopris West.

Glasser, W. (1969). *Schools without failure*. New York: Harper & Row.

Greenberg, M. T., Kusche, C., & Mihalic, S. F. (1998). *Blueprints for violence prevention: Promoting alternative thinking strategies*. Boulder: University of Colorado, Institute of Behavioral Science, Center for the Study and Prevention of Violence.

Greenwood, C. R. (1991). Longitudinal analysis of time, engagement and achievement in at-risk versus nonrisk students. *Exceptional Children, 57*, 521–535.

Greenwood, C. R., Maheady, L., & Delquadri, J. C. (2002). Classwide peer tutoring programs. In M. R. Shinn, H. M. Walker, & G. Stoner (Eds.), *Interventions for academic and behavior problems: II. Preventive and remedial approaches* (pp. 611–649). Bethesda, MD: National Association of School Psychologists.

Gregory, A., & Rimm-Kaufman, S. (2008). Positive mother–child interactions in kindergarten: Predictors of school success in high school. *School Psychology Review, 37*(4), 499–515.

Gresham, F. M. (1986). Conceptual issues in the assessment of social competence in children. In P. Strain, M. Guralnick, & H. Walker (Eds.), *Children's social behavior: Development, assessment and modification*. New York: Academic Press.

Gresham, F. M., Sugai, C., & Horner, R. H. (2001). Interpreting outcomes of social skills training for students with high-incidence disabilities. *Exceptional Children, 67*, 331–344.

Grolnick, W. S., Friendly, R. W., & Bellas, V. M. (2009). Parenting and children's motivation at school. In K. R. Wentzel & A. Wigfield (Eds.), *Handbook of motivation at school* (pp. 279–300). New York: Routledge.

Gropeter, J. K., & Crick, N. R. (1996). Relational aggression, overt aggression, and friendship. *Child Development, 67*, 2328–2338.

Gutkin, T. B., & Curtis, M. J. (2009). School-based consultation: The science and practice of indirect service delivery. In T. B. Gutkin & C. R. Reynolds (Eds.), *The handbook of school psychology* (4th ed., pp. 591–635). Hoboken: Wiley.

Hamre, B. K., & Pianta, R. C. (2001). *STARS: Students, teachers and relationship support*. Lutz, FL: Psychological Assessment Resources.

Hamre, B. K., & Pianta, R. C. (2005). Can instructional and emotional support in the first-grade classroom make a difference for children at risk of school failure? *Child Development, 76*(5), 949–967.

Hardre, P. L., & Reeve, J. (2003). A motivational model of rural students' intentions to persist in, versus drop out of, high school. *Journal of Educational Psychology, 95*(2), 347–356.

Hawkins, J. D., Catalano, R. F., Morrison, D. M., O'Donnell, J., Abbott, R. D., & Day, L. E. (1992). The Seattle Social Development Project: Effects of the first four years on protective factors and problem behaviors. In J. McCord & R. E. Tremblay (Eds.), *Preventing antisocial behavior: Interventions from birth through adolescence* (pp. 139–161). New York: Guilford Press.

Hawkins, J. D., Smith, B. H., Hill, K. G., Kosterman, R. F. C., Catalano, F. C., & Abbott, R. D. (2003). Understanding and preventing crime and violence: Findings from the Seattle Social Development Project. In T. P. Thornberry & M. D. Krohn (Eds.), *Taking stock of delinquency: An overview of findings from contemporary longitudinal studies* (pp. 255–312). New York: Kluwer Academic/Plenum Press.

Haynes, N. M., Emmons, C., & Comer, J. P. (1993). *Elementary and middle school climate survey*. New Haven, CT: Yale University Child Study Center.

Hayvren, M., & Hymel, S. (1984). Ethical issues in sociometric testing. The impact of sociometric measures on interactive behavior. *Developmental Psychology, 20*, 844–849.

High, B. (2008). Bully police USA: Does your state have an anti-bully law? Retrieved December 23, 2008, from *www.bullypolice.org*.

Hintze, J. M., & Matthews, W. J. (2004). The generalizability of systematic direct observations across time and setting: A preliminary investigation of the psychometrics of behavior observation. *School Psychology Review, 33*, 258–270.

Hoagwood, K., & Johnson, J. (2003). School psychology: A public health framework I. From evidence-based practices to evidence-based policies. *Journal of School Psychology, 41*, 3–21.

Hoover-Dempsey, K. V., Walker, J. M. T., Sandler, H. M., Whetsel, D., Green, C. L., Wilkins, A. S., et al. (2005). Why do parents become involved?: Research findings and implications. *Elementary School Journal, 106*, 105–130.

Hughes, J., & Kwok, O. (2007). Influence of student–teacher and parent–teacher relationships on lower achieving readers' engagement and achievement in the primary grades. *Journal of Educational Psychology, 99*(1), 39–51.

Hughes, J. N., Wu, W., & West, S. G. (2011). Teacher performance goal practices and elementary students' behavioral engagement: A developmental perspective. *Journal of School Psychology, 49*, 1–23.

Individuals with Disabilities Education Improvement Act of 2004, H. R. 1350, 108th Congress.

Ingersoll, R. M., & May, H. (2011, September). The minority teacher shortage: Fact or fable. *Kappan*, pp. 62–65.

Irvin, L. K., Horner, R. H., Ingram, K., Todd, A. W., Sugai, G., Sampson, N. K., et al. (2006). Using office discipline referral data for decision making about student behavior in elementary and middle schools: An empirical evaluation of validity. *Journal of Positive Behavior Interventions, 8*, 10–23.

Jimerson, S. R., Egeland, B., Sroufe, L., & Carlson, B. (2000). A prospective longitudinal study of high school dropouts: Examining multiple predictors across development. *Journal of School Psychology, 38*(6), 525–549.

Jinks, J., & Lorsbach, A. (2003). Introduction. Motivation and self-efficacy belief. *Reading and Writing Quarterly, 19*, 113–118.

Joët, G., Usher, E. L., & Bressoux, P. (2011). Sources of self-efficacy: An investigation of elementary school students in France. *Journal of Educational Psychology, 103*(3), 649–663.

Johnson, D. W., Johnson, R. T., & Anderson, D. (1983). Social interdependence and classroom climate. *Journal of Psychology, 114*, 135–142.

Joussemet, M., Koestner, R., Lekes, N., & Houlfort, N. (2004). Introducing uninteresting tasks to children: A comparison of the effects of rewards and autonomy support. *Journal of Personality, 72*(1), 139–166.

Juvonen, J. (2007). Reforming middle schools: Focus on continuity, social connectedness, and engagement. *Educational Psychologist, 42*(4), 197–208.

Juvonen, J., Nishina, A., & Graham, S. (2006). Ethnic diversity and perceptions of safety in urban middle schools. *Psychological Science (Wiley-Blackwell), 17*(5), 393–400.

Kam, C., Greenberg, M. T., & Kusché, C. A. (2004). Sustained effects of the PATHS curriculum on the social and psychological adjustment of children in special education. *Journal of Emotional and Behavioral Disorders, 12*, 66–78.

Kamps, D. M., Greenwood, C., Arreaga-Mayer, C., Veerkamp, M. B., Utley, C., Tapia, Y., et al. (2008). The efficacy of classwide peer tutoring in middle schools. *Education and Treatment of Children, 31*(2), 119–152.

Katz, I., Kaplan, A., & Gueta, G. (2010). Students' needs, teachers' support, and motivation for doing homework: A cross-sectional study. *Journal of Experimental Education, 78*, 246–267.

Kendall, P. C., & Braswell, L. (1985). *Cognitive-behavioral therapy for impulsive children.* New York: Guilford Press.

Kennedy, C. H. (2005). *Single case designs for educational research.* Boston: Allyn & Bacon.

Kesner, J. E. (2000). Teacher characteristics and the quality of child–teacher relationships. *Journal of School Psychology, 38*(2), 133–149.

Kettler, T., Shiu, A., & Johnsen, S. K. (2006). AP as an intervention for middle school Hispanic students. *Gifted Child Today, 29*(1), 39–46.

Kiresuk, T. J., Smith, A., & Cardillo, J. E. (1994). *Goal attainment scaling: Applications, theory and measurement.* Hillsdale, NJ: Erlbaum

Knitzer, J. (2005). Advocacy for children's mental health: A personal journey. *Journal of Clinical Child and Adolescent Psychology, 34*(4), 612–618.

Koplow, L. (2002). *Creating schools that heal.* New York: Teachers College Press.

Kortering, L. J., & Braziel, P. M. (2002). A look at high school programs as perceived by youth with learning disabilities. *Learning Disability Quarterly, 25*, 177–188.

Kosse, S., & Doll, B. (2006, March). *A comparison of traditional student assistance teams and response to intervention.* Paper presented at the annual convention of the National Association of School Psychologists, Anaheim, CA.

Kratochwill, T. R. (2008). Best practices in school-based problem-solving consultation: Applications in prevention and intervention systems. In A. Thomas & J. Grimes (Eds.), *Best practices in school psychology* (5th ed., pp. 1673–1688). Bethesda, MD: National Association of School Psychologists.

Kusché, C. A., & Greenberg, M. T. (1994). *The PATHS curriculum.* Seattle: Developmental Research and Programs.

Kyriakides, L. (2005). Evaluating school policy on parents working with their children in class. *Journal of Educational Research, 98*(5), 281–298.

Ladd, G. W. (2005). *Children's peer relations and social competence: A century of progress.* New Haven, CT: Yale University Press.

Ladd, G. W., Herald-Brown, S. L., & Kochel, K. P. (2009). Peers and motivation. In K. Wentzel & A. Wigfield (Eds.), *Handbook of motivation at school* (pp. 323–348). New York: Routledge.

Lane, K., Pierson, M. R., & Givner, C. C. (2003). Teacher expectations of student behavior: Which skills do elementary and secondary teachers deem necessary for success in the classroom? *Education and Treatment of Children, 26*(4), 413–430.

Lau, S., & Nie, Y. (2008). Interplay between personal goals and classroom goal structures in predicting student outcomes: A multilevel analysis of person–context interactions. *Journal of Educational Psychology, 100*, 15–29.

Levy, I., Kaplan, A., & Patrick, H. (2004). Early adolescents' achievement goals, social status, and attitudes towards cooperation with peers. *Social Psychology of Education, 7*, 127–159.

Li, K., Washburn, I., DuBois, D. L., Vuchinich, S., Ji, P., Brechling, V., et al. (2011). Effects of the Positive Action programme on problem behaviours in elementary school students: A matched-pair randomised control trial in Chicago. *Psychology and Health, 26*(2), 187–204.

Liaupsin, C., Umbreit, J., Ferro, J., Urso, A., & Upreti, G. (2006). Improving academic engagement through systematic, function-based intervention. *Education and Treatment of Children, 29*, 573–591.

Linares, L. O., Rosbruch, N., Stern, M. B., Edwards, M. E., Walker, G., Abikoff, H. B., et al. (2005). Developing cognitive-social-emotional competencies to enhance academic learning. *Psychology in the Schools, 42*(4), 405–417.

Linnenbrink, E. A. (2005). The dilemma of performance-approach goals: The use of multiple goal contexts to promote students' motivation and learning. *Journal of Educational Psychology, 97*, 197–213.

Linnenbrink, E. A., & Pintrich, P. R. (2003). The role of self-efficacy beliefs in student engagement and learning in the classroom. *Reading and Writing Quarterly, 19*, 119–137.

Lochman, J. E., Powell, N. R., Boxmeyer, C. L., & Baden, R. (2010). Dissemination of evidence-based programs in the schools: The Coping Power Program. In B. Doll, W. Pfohl, & J. Yoon (Eds.), *Handbook of youth prevention science* (pp. 393–412). New York: Routledge.

Lochman, J. E., Wells, K. C., & Lenhart, L. A. (2008). *Coping power: Child group facilitator's guide.* New York: Oxford University Press.

Locke, E. A., & Latham, G. P. (2002). Building a practically useful theory of goal setting and task motivation: A 35-year odyssey. *American Psychologist, 57*(9), 705–717.

Lorsbach, A. W., & Jinks, J. (1999). Self-efficacy theory and learning environment research. *Learning Environments Research, 2,* 157–167.

Luellen, W. S. (2003, February). The effectiveness of social skills training for children with disturbed peer relationships: A review of meta-analyses. *NASP Communiqué, 31*(5), 38–39.

Machen, S. M., Wilson, J. D., & Notar, C. E. (2005). Parental involvement in the classroom. *Journal of Instructional Psychology, 32*(1), 13–16.

Malecki, C. K., & Elliott, S. N. (2002). Children's social behaviors as predictors of academic achievement: A longitudinal analysis. *School Psychology Quarterly, 17,* 1–23.

Martens, B. K., & DiGennaro, F. D. (2008). Behavioral consultation. In W. P. Erchul & S. M. Sheridan (Eds.), *Handbook of research in school consultation* (pp. 147–170). New York: Taylor & Francis Group/Routledge.

Masten, A. S. (2001). Ordinary magic: Resilience processes in development. *American Psychologist, 56,* 227–238.

Masten, A. S., Hubbard, J. J., Gest, S. D., Tellegen A., Garmezy, N., & Ramirez, M. (1999). Competence in the context of adversity: Pathways to resilience and maladaptation from childhood to late adolescence. *Development and Psychopathology, 11,* 143–169.

Mathur, S. R., Kavale, K. A., Quinn, M. M., Forness, S. R., & Rutherford Jr., R. B. (1998). Social skills interventions with students with emotional and behavioral problems: A quantitative synthesis of single-subject research. *Behavioral Disorders, 23,* 193–201.

May, S., Ard, W., Todd, A. W., Horner, R. H., Glasgow, A., Sugai, G., et al. (2003). *Schoolwide information system.* Eugene: Educational and Community Supports, University of Oregon.

McDermott, P. A., Mordell, M., & Stoltzfus, J. (2001). The organization of student performance in American schools: Discipline, motivation, verbal learning, and nonverbal learning. *Journal of Educational Psychology, 93*(1), 65–76.

Menesses, K. F., & Gresham, F. M. (2009). Relative efficacy of reciprocal and nonreciprocal peer tutoring for students at-risk for academic failure. *School Psychology Quarterly, 24*(4), 266–275.

Merrell, K. W., Carrizales, D. C., Feuerborn, L., Gueldner, B. A., & Tran, O. K. (2007a). *Strong Kids—grades 3–5: A social emotional learning curriculum.* Baltimore: Brookes.

Merrell, K. W., Carrizales, D. C., Feuerborn, L., Gueldner, B. A., & Tran, O. K. (2007b). *Strong Kids—grades 6–8: A social-emotional learning curriculum.* Baltimore: Brookes.

Merrell, K. W., Gueldner, B. A., & Tran, O. K. (2008). Social and emotional learning: A school-wide approach to intervention for socialization, friendship problems, and more. In B. Doll & J. A. Cummings (Eds.), *Transforming school mental health services* (pp. 165–185). Thousand Oaks, CA: Corwin Press/National Association of School Psychologists.

Metcalf, L. S. (2008). *Counseling toward solutions* (2nd ed.). New York: Wiley.

Middleton, M. J., & Midgley, C. (2002). Beyond motivation: Middle school students' perceptions of press for understanding in math. *Contemporary Educational Psychology, 27,* 373–391.

Miserandino, M. (1996). Children who do well in school: Individual differences in perceived competence and autonomy in above-average children. *Journal of Educational Psychology, 88,* 203–215.

Mitchem, K. J., Young, K. R., West, R. P., & Benyo, J. (2001). CWPASM: A Classwide Peer-Assisted Self-Management Program for general education classrooms. *Education and Treatment of Children, 24,* 111–141.

Multon, K. D., Brown, S. D., & Lent, R. W. (1991). Relation of self-efficacy beliefs to academic outcomes: A meta-analytic investigation. *Journal of Counseling Psychology, 18,* 30–38.

Murphy, J. J. (2008). *Solution-focused counseling in schools* (2nd ed.). Alexandria, VA: American Counseling Association.

Murphy, P. S. (2002). *The effect of classroom meetings on the reduction of recess problems: A single case design.* Unpublished doctoral dissertation, University of Denver, Denver, CO.

Murray, C., & Malmgren, K. (2005). Implementing a teacher–student relationship program in a high-poverty urban school: Effects on social, emotional, and academic adjustment and lessons learned. *Journal of School Psychology, 43,* 137–152.

Murray, C., & Murray, K. (2004). Child level correlates of teacher-student relationships: An examination of demographic characteristics, academic orientations, and behavioral orientations. *Psychology in the Schools, 41*(7), 751–762.

National Association of School Psychologists. (2006). *School psychology: A blueprint for training and practice III.* Bethesda, MD: Author. Retrieved January 13, 2012, from *www.nasponline.org/resources/blueprint/finalblueprintinteriors.pdf.*

National Association of School Psychologists. (2010). *Principles for professional ethics.* Bethesda, MD: Author. Retrieved January 12, 2012, from *www. nasponline.org/standards/2010standards/1_%20 ethical%20principles.pdf.*

National Association of School Psychologists. (2012). *School–family partnering to enhance learning: Essential elements and responsibilities* [NASP position statement]. Bethesda, MD: Author. Retrieved July 5, 2012, from *www.nasponline.org/about_ nasp/positionpapers/home-schoolcollaboration. pdf.*

National Parent–Teacher Association. (1997). *National standards for parent/family involvement programs.* Chicago: Author.

National Research Council and Institute of Medicine. (2004). *Engaging schools: Fostering high school students' motivation to learn.* Committee on Increasing High School Students' Engagement and Motivation to Learn; Board on Children, Youth, and Families; Division of Behavioral and Social Sciences and Education. Washington, DC: National Academies Press.

Newman, D. A., Horne, A. M., & Bartolomucci, C. L. (2000). *Bully busters: A teacher's manual for helping bullies, victims, and bystanders.* Champaign, IL: Research Press.

Nickolite, A., & Doll, B. (2008). Resilience applied in schools: Strengthening classroom environments for learning. *Canadian Journal of School Psychology, 23*(1), 94–113.

Noblit, G. W., Dwight, L. R., & McCadden, B. M. (1995). In the meantime: The possibilities of caring. *Phi Delta Kappan, 76,* 680–684.

No Child Left Behind (NCLB) Act of 2001, Pub. L. No. 107-110, § 115, Stat. 1425 (2002).

Odom, S. L., Hanson, M., Lieber, J., Diamond, K., Palmer, S., Butera, G., et al. (2010). In B. Doll, W. Pfohl, & J. Yoon (Eds.), *Handbook of youth prevention science* (pp. 413–432). New York: Routledge.

Olweus, D., Limber, S., & Mihalic, S. F. (1999). *Blueprints for violence prevention, book nine: Bullying prevention program.* Longmont, CO: Center for the Study and Prevention of Violence.

Osher, D., Bear, G. G., Sprague, J. R., & Doyle, W. (2010). How can we improve school discipline? *Educational Researcher, 39,* 48–58.

Osher, D., & Kendziora, K. (2010). Building conditions for learning and healthy adolescent development: A strategic approach. In B. Doll, W. Pfohl, & J. Yoon (Eds.), *Handbook of youth prevention science* (pp. 121–140.) New York: Routledge.

Osterman, K. F. (2000). Students' need for belonging in the school community. *Review of Educational Research, 70,* 323–367.

Otis, N., Grouzet, F. M. E., & Pelletier, L. G. (2005). Latent motivational change in an academic setting: A 3-year longitudinal study. *Journal of Educational Psychology, 97,* 170–183.

Pajares, F., & Miller, M. D. (1994). The role of self-efficacy and self-concept beliefs in mathematical problem-solving: A path analysis. *Journal of Educational Psychology, 86,* 193–203.

Pajares, F., & Schunk, D. H. (2001). Self-beliefs and school success: Self-efficacy, self-concept, and school achievement. In R. J. Riding & S. G. Rayner (Eds.), *Self-perception* (pp. 239–265). Westport, CT: Ablex.

Pajares, F., & Schunk, D. H. (2002). Self and self-belief in psychology and education: A historical perspective. In J. Aronson (Ed.), *Improving academic achievement: Impact of psychological factors on education* (pp. 3–21). San Diego, CA: Academic Press.

Palmer, S. B., & Wehmeyer, M. L. (2003). Promoting self-determination in early elementary school: Teaching self-regulated problem-solving and goal-setting skills. *Remedial and Special Education, 24,* 115–126.

Parker, J. G., & Asher, S. R. (1993). Friendship and friendship quality in middle childhood: Links with peer group acceptance and feelings of loneliness and social dissatisfaction. *Developmental Psychology, 29,* 611–621.

Pastorelli, C., Caprara, G. V., Barbaranelli, C., Rola, J., Rozsa, S., & Bandura, A. (2001). The structure of children's perceived self-efficacy: A cross-national study. *European Journal of Psychological Assessment, 17,* 87–97.

Patrikakou, E. N., & Weissberg, R. P. (2000). Parents' perception of teacher outreach and parent involvement in children's education. *Journal of Prevention and Intervention in the Community, 20,* 103–119.

Paul, K. (2005). *SchoolMaps: A reliability and validity study for a secondary education school climate instrument.* Unpublished doctoral dissertation, University of Nebraska–Lincoln.

Pellegrini, A. D. (2002). Rough-and-tumble play from childhood through adolescence: Development and possible functions. In P. K. Smith & C. H. Hart (Eds.), *Blackwell handbook of childhood social development* (pp. 437–453). Malden, MA: Blackwell.

Pellegrini, A. D. (2005). *Recess: Its role in education and development.* Mahwah, NJ: Erlbaum.

Pellegrini, A. D., & Bartini, M. (2000). A longitudinal study of bullying, victimization, and peer affiliation during the transition from primary to middle school. *American Educational Research Journal, 37,* 699–726.

Pellegrini, A. D., & Blatchford, P. (2000). *The child at school: Interactions with peers and teachers*. London: Arnold.

Peña, D. C. (2000). Parent involvement: Influencing factors and implications. *Journal of Educational Research, 94*, 42–54.

Pianta, R. C. (1999). *Enhancing relationships between children and teachers*. Washington, DC: American Psychological Association.

Pianta, R. C. (2001). Implications of a developmental systems model for preventing and treating behavioral disturbances in children and adolescents. In J. A. Hughes, A. M. LaGreca, & J. C. Conoley (Eds.), *Handbook of psychological services for children and adolescents* (pp. 23–41). Oxford, UK: Oxford University Press.

Pianta, R. C., & Hamre, B. K. (2001). *STARS: Students, teachers and relationship support—consultant's manual*. Lutz, FL: Psychological Assessment Resources.

Pianta, R C., & Walsh, D. J. (1996). *High-risk children in schools: Constructing sustaining relationships*. New York: Routledge.

Pintrich, P. R. (2000). Multiple goals, multiple pathways: The role of goal orientation in learning and achievement. *Journal of Educational Psychology, 92*, 544–555.

Pintrich, P. R. (2003). A motivational science perspective on the role of student motivation in learning and teaching contexts. *Journal of Educational Psychology, 95*, 667–686.

President's Commission on Excellence in Special Education. (2002). *A new era: Revitalizing special education for children and their families*. Washington, DC: U.S. Department of Education.

Pullin, D. C. (2008). Assessment, equity, and opportunity to learn. In P. A. Moss, D. C. Pullin, J. P. Gee, E. H. Haertel, & L. J. Young (Eds.), *Assessment, equity, and opportunity to learn* (pp. 333–351). New York: Cambridge University Press.

Quinn, M. M., Kavale, K. A., Mathur, S. R., Rutherford Jr., R. B., & Forness, S. R. (1999). A meta-analysis of social skill interventions for students with emotional or behavioral disorders. *Journal of Emotional and Behavioral Disorders, 7*, 54–64.

Randi, J., & Corno, L. (2000). Teacher innovations in self-regulated learning. In M. Boekaerts, P. R. Pintrich, & M. Zeidner (Eds.), *Handbook of self-regulation*. New York: Academic Press.

Rathvon, N. (2003). *Effective school interventions: Strategies for enhancing academic achievement and social competence*. New York: Guilford Press.

Reeve, J. (2002). Self-determination theory applied to educational settings. In E. L. Deci & R. M. Ryan (Eds.), *Handbook of self-determination research* (pp. 183–203). Rochester, NY: University of Rochester Press.

Reeve, J. (2006). Teachers as facilitators: What autonomy-supportive teachers do and why their students benefit. *Elementary School Journal, 106*(3), 225–236.

Reeve, J., & Halusic, M. (2009). How K–12 teachers can put self-determination theory principles into practice. *Theory and Research in Education, 7*, 145–154.

Reeve, J., Jang, H., Carrell, D., Jeon, S., & Barch, J. (2004). Enhancing students' engagement by increasing teachers' autonomy support. *Motivation and Emotion, 28*, 147–169.

Reschly, A. L., & Christenson, S. L. (2006). Prediction of dropout among students with mild disabilities: A case for the inclusion of student engagement variables. *Remedial and Special Education, 27*, 276–292.

Reynolds, C. R., & Kamphaus, R. W. (2004). *Behavior assessment system for children* (2nd ed.). Bloomington, MN: Pearson Assessments.

Riley, P. (2011). *Attachment theory and the teacher–student relationship: A practical guide for teachers, teacher educators and school leaders*. New York: Routledge.

Rimm-Kaufman, S. E., Curby, T., Grimm, K., Nathanson, L., & Brock, L. (2009). The contribution of children's self-regulation and classroom quality to children's adaptive behaviors in the kindergarten classroom. *Developmental Psychology, 45*(4), 958–972.

Rohrbeck, C. A., Ginsburg-Block, M. D., Fantuzzo, J. W., & Miller, T. R. (2003). Peer-assisted learning interventions with elementary school students: A meta-analytic review. *Journal of Educational Psychology, 95*, 240–257.

Rosenfield, S. (2008). Best practices in instructional consultation and instructional consultation teams. In A. Thomas & J. Grimes (Eds.), *Best practices in school psychology* (5th ed., pp. 1645–1660). Bethesda, MD: National Association of School Psychologists.

Rudasill, K. M., Reio, T. G., Stipanovic, N., & Taylor, J. E. (2010). A longitudinal study of student–teacher relationship quality, difficult temperament, and risky behavior from childhood to early adolescence. *Journal of School Psychology, 48*, 389–412.

Rutter, M. (2010). Child and adolescent psychiatry: Past scientific achievement and challenges for the future. *European Child and Adolescent Psychiatry, 19*, 689–703.

Ryan, A. M., Patrick, H., & Shim, S. (2005). Differential profiles of students identified by their teacher as having avoidant, appropriate, or dependent help-seeking tendencies in the classroom. *Journal of Educational Psychology, 97*(2), 275–285.

Ryan, A. M., Gheen, M. H., & Midgley, C. (1998). Why do some students avoid asking for help?: An examination of the interplay among students' academic efficacy, teachers' social–emotional role, and the classroom goal structure. *Journal of Educational Psychology, 90,* 528–535.

Ryan, A. M., & Pintrich, P. R. (1997). "Should I ask for help?": The role of motivation and attitudes in adolescents' help seeking in math class. *Journal of Educational Psychology, 89*(2), 329–341.

Salisbury, C., Gallucci, C., Palombaro, M. M., & Peck, C. A. (1995). Strategies that promote social relations among elementary students with and without severe disabilities in inclusive schools. *Exceptional Children, 62,* 125–137.

Schonert-Reichl, K. A. (1993). Empathy and social relationships in adolescents with behavioral disorders. *Behavior Disorders, 18,* 189–204.

Schunk, D. H. (2003). Self-efficacy for reading and writing: Influence of modeling, goal setting, and self-evaluation. *Reading and Writing Quarterly, 19,* 159–172.

Schunk, D. H., & Ertmer, P. A. (2000). Self-regulation and academic learning: Self-efficacy enhancing interventions. In M. Boekaerts, P. R. Pintrich, & M. Zeidner (Eds.), *Handbook of self-regulation* (pp. 631–649). San Diego: Academic Press.

Schunk, D. H., & Meece, J. L. (2006). Self-efficacy development in adolescence. In F. Pajares & T. Urdan (Eds.), *Self-efficacy beliefs of adolescents* (pp. 71–96). Greenwich, CT: Information Age.

Schunk, D. H., & Pajares, F. (2005). Competence perceptions and academic functioning. In A. J. Elliot & C. Dweck (Eds.), *Handbook of competence and motivation* (pp. 85–104). New York: Guilford Press.

Schunk, D. H., & Pajares, F. (2009). Self-efficacy theory. In K. R. Wentzel & A. Wigfield (Eds.), *Handbook of motivation at school* (pp. 35–53). New York: Routledge.

Severson, H. H., Walker, H. M., Hope-Doolittle, J., Kratochwill, T. R., & Gresham, F. M. (2007). Proactive, early screening to detect behaviorally at risk students: Issues, approaches, emerging innovations, and professional practices. *Journal of School Psychology, 45,* 193–223.

Sharkey, J. D., Furlong, M. J., & Yetter, G. (2006). An overview of measurement issues in school violence and school safety research. In S. R. Jimerson & M. J. Furlong (Eds.), *Handbook of school violence and school safety: From research to practice* (pp. 121–134). Mahwah, NJ: Erlbaum.

Sheridan, S. M. (1997). Conceptual and empirical bases of conjoint behavioral consultation. *School Psychology Quarterly, 12,* 119–133.

Sheridan, S. M., Eagle, J. W., Cowan, R. J., & Mickelson, W. (2001). The effects of conjoint behavioral consultation: Results of a four-year investigation. *Journal of School Psychology, 39,* 361–388.

Sheridan, S. M., & Kratochwill, T. R. (2008). *Conjoint behavioral consultation: Promoting family–school connections and interventions.* New York: Springer.

Sheridan, S. M., & Steck, M. (1995). Acceptability of conjoint behavioral consultation: A national survey of school psychologists. *School Psychology Review, 24,* 633–647.

Shih, S. S. (2005). Role of achievement goals in children's learning in Taiwan. *Journal of Educational Research, 98,* 310–319.

Shim, S., Ryan, A. M., & Anderson, C. J. (2008). Achievement goals and achievement during early adolescence: Examining time-varying predictor and outcome variables in growth-curve analysis. *Journal of Educational Psychology, 100*(3), 655–671.

Short, R. J., & Strein, W. (2008). Behavioral and social epidemiology: Population-based problem identification and monitoring. In B. Doll & J. A. Cummings (Eds.), *Transforming school mental health services* (pp. 23–42). Thousand Oaks, CA: Corwin Press/National Association of School Psychologists.

Shure, M. B. (1997). Interpersonal cognitive problem solving: Primary prevention of early high-risk behaviors in the preschool and primary years. In G. Albee & T. Gullotta (Eds.), *Primary prevention works* (pp. 167–188). Thousand Oaks, CA: Sage.

Sierens, E., Vansteenkiste, M., Goossens, L., Soenens, B., & Dochy, F. (2009). The synergistic relationship of perceived autonomy support and structure in the prediction of self-regulated learning. *British Journal of Educational Psychology, 79,* 57–68.

Skaalvik, E. M., & Skaalvik, S. (2007). Dimensions of teacher self-efficacy and relations with strain factors, perceived collective teacher efficacy, and teacher burnout. *Journal of Educational Psychology, 99*(3), 611–625.

Slavin, R. E., & Madden, N. A. (2001). *Success for all: Research and reform in elementary education.* Mahwah, NJ: Erlbaum.

Smith, S. W., Daunic, A., & Miller, D. M. (2002). Conflict resolution and peer mediation in middle schools: Extending the process and outcome knowledge base. *Journal of Social Psychology, 142*(5), 567–586.

Song, S. Y., & Sogo, W. (2010). A hybrid framework for intervention development: Social justice for bullying in low resource schools. In B. Doll, W. Pfohl, &

J. Yoon (Eds.), *Handbook of youth prevention science* (pp. 307–326). New York: Routledge.

Song, S. Y., & Stoiber, K. (2008). Children exposed to violence at school: Understanding bullying and evidence-based interventions. *Special Issue on Children Exposed to Violence, Journal of Emotional Abuse, 8,* 235–253.

Squires, D. A., & Joyner, E. T. (1996). Time and alignment: Potent tools for improving achievement. In J. P. Comer, N. M. Haynes, E. T. Joyner, & M. Ben-Avie (Eds.), *Rallying the whole village: The Comer process for reforming education* (pp. 98–122). New York: Teachers College Press.

Stern, M. (1999). *Unique Minds Program for children with learning disabilities and their families.* West Vancouver, BC: Unique Minds Foundations.

Sugai, G., & Horner, R. (2001, June). *School climate and discipline: Going to scale.* Paper presented at the National Summit on the Shared Implementation of IDEA, Washington, DC.

Sugai, G., & Horner, R. H. (2006). A promising approach for expanding and sustaining schoolwide positive behavior support. *School Psychology Review, 35*(2), 245–259.

Sugai, G., Horner, R. H., & Gresham, F. M. (2002). Behaviorally effective school environments. In M. R. Shinn, H. M. Walker, & G. Stoner (Eds.), *Interventions for academic and behavior problems: II. Preventive and remedial approaches* (pp. 315–350). Bethesda, MD: National Association of School Psychologists.

Sugai, G., Horner, R. H., & McIntosh, K. (2008). Best practices in developing a broad-scale system of support for school-wide positive behavior support. In A. Thomas & J. P. Grimes (Eds.), *Best practices in school psychology* (Vol. 3, pp. 765–780). Bethesda, MD: National Association of School Psychologists.

Suldo, S. M., Friedrich, A. A., White, T., Farmer, J., Minch, D., & Michalowski, J. (2009). Teacher support and adolescents' subjective well-being: A mixed-methods investigation. *School Psychology Review, 38*(1), 67–85.

Sungur, S., & Senler, B. (2010). Students' achievement goals in relation to academic motivation, competence expectancy, and classroom environment perceptions. *Educational Research and Evaluation, 16*(4), 303–324.

Sutherland, K. S., & Wehby, J. H. (2001). The effect of self-evaluation on teaching behavior in classrooms for students with emotional and behavioral disorders. *Journal of Special Education, 35,* 161–171.

Swearer, S. M., & Espelage, D. L. (2011). Expanding the social–ecological framework of bullying among youth: Lessons learned from the past and directions for the future. In D. L. Espelage & S.

M. Swearer (Eds.), *Bullying in North American schools* (2nd ed., pp. 3–10). New York: Routledge.

Telzrow, C. F., McNamara, K., & Hollinger, C. L. (2000). Fidelity of problem-solving implementation and relationship to student performance. *School Pychology Review, 29,* 443–461.

Tollefson, N. (2000). Classroom applications of cognitive theories of motivation. *Educational Psychology Review, 12,* 63–83.

Tran, O. K., & Merrell, K. W. (2010). Promoting student resilience: Strong Kids social and emotional learning curricula. In B. Doll, W. Pfohl, & J. Yoon (Eds.), *Handbook of youth prevention science* (pp. 273–285). New York: Routledge.

Treptow, M. A., Burns, M. K., & McComas, J. J. (2007). Reading at the frustration, instructional, and independent levels: The effects on students' reading comprehension and time on task. *School Psychology Review, 36*(1), 159–166.

Tsai, Y., Kunter, M., Lüdtke, O., Trautwein, U., & Ryan, R. M. (2008). What makes lessons interesting? The role of situational and individual factors in three school subjects. *Journal of Educational Psychology, 100*(2), 460–472.

Turner, J. C., Midgley, C., Meyer, D. K., Gheen, M., Anderman, E. M., Kang, Y., et al. (2002). The classroom environment and students' reports of avoidance strategies in mathematics: A multimethod study. *Journal of Educational Psychology, 94,* 88–106.

U.S. Bureau of the Census. (2004). *U.S. interim projections by age, sex, race, and Hispanic origin.* Retrieved May 4, 2008, from *www.census.gov/ipc/www/usinterimproj.*

U.S. Department of Education. (1999). *Twenty-first annual report to congress on the implementation of the Individuals with Disabilities Act.* Washington, DC: Author.

U.S. Department of Education, Office of Special Education and Rehabilitative Services. (2010). *29th annual report to Congress on the implementation of the Individuals with Disabilities Education Act, 2007, Vol. 1.* Washington, DC: Author.

U.S. Department of Health and Human Services. (1999). *Mental health: A report of the Surgeon General.* Rockville, MD: Author.

Usher, E. L., & Pajares, F. (2006). Sources of academic and self-regulatory efficacy beliefs of entering middle school students. *Contemporary Educational Psychology, 31,* 125–141.

Vadasy, P. F., Jenkins, J. R., Antil, L. R., Phillips, N. B., & Pool, K. (1997). The research-to-practice ball game: Classwide peer tutoring and teacher interest, implementation, and modifications. *Remedial and Special Education, 18,* 143–156.

Vansteenkiste, M., Simons, J., Lens, W., Sheldon, K. M., & Deci, E. L. (2004). Motivating learning, performance, and persistence: The synergistic role of intrinsic goals and autonomy–support. *Journal of Personality and Social Psychology, 87,* 246–260.

Vansteenkiste, M., Timmermans, T., Lens, W., Soenens, B., & Van den Broeck, A. (2008). Does extrinsic goal framing enhance extrinsic goal oriented individuals' learning and performance? An experimental test of the match-perspective vs. self-determination theory. *Journal of Educational Psychology, 100*(2), 387–397.

Von Brock, M. B., & Elliott, S. N. (1987). Influence of treatment effectiveness information on the acceptability of classroom interventions. *Journal of School Psychology, 25,* 131–144.

Walker, H. M., Colvin, G., & Ramsey, E. (1995). *Antisocial behavior in school: Strategies and best practices.* Pacific Grove, CA: Brooks-Cole.

Walker, H. M., & Severson, H. H. (1992). *Systematic screening for behaviour disorders.* Longmont, CO: Sopris West.

Walker, H. M., Severson, H. H., Naquin, F., D'Atrio, C., Feil, E. G., Hawken, L., et al. (2010). Implementing universal screening systems within an Rti-PBS context. In B. Doll, W. Pfohl, & J. Yoon (Eds.), *Handbook of youth prevention science* (pp. 96–120). New York: Routledge.

Webster-Stratton, C., Reid, M. J., & Hammond, M. (2001). Social skills and problems solving training for children with early-onset conduct problems: Who benefits? *Journal of Child Psychology and Psychiatry, 42,* 943–952.

Weisz, J. R., & Gray, J. S. (2008). Evidence-based psychotherapy for children and adolescents: Data from the present and a model for the future. *Child and Adolescent Mental Health, 13,* 54–65.

Wentzel, K. R. (1991). Social competence at school: The relation between social responsibility and academic achievement. *Review of Educational Research, 61,* 1–24.

Wentzel. K. R. (1993). Does being good make the grade?: Social behavior and academic competence in middle school. *Journal of Educational Psychology 85*(2), 357–364.

Wentzel, K. R. (2002). Are effective teachers like good parents?: Interpersonal predictors of school adjustment in early adolescence. *Child Development, 73,* 287–301.

Wentzel, K. R. (2009). Students' relationships with teachers as motivational contexts. In K. R. Wentzel & A. Wigfield (Eds.), *Handbook of motivation at school* (pp. 301–322). New York: Routledge.

Wentzel, K. R., Barry, C. M., & Caldwell, K. A. (2007). Friendships in middle school: Influences on motivation and school adjustment. *Journal of Educational Psychology, 96,* 195–203.

Wentzel, K. R., & Watkins, D. E. (2002). Peer relationships and collaborative learning as contexts for academic enablers. *School Psychology Review, 31,* 366–377.

Werner, E. E. (2013). What can we learn about resilience from large-scale longitudinal studies? In S. Goldstein & R. B. Brooks (Eds.), *Handbook of resilience in children* (pp. 87–104). New York: Springer.

Wilson, D. B., Gottfredson, D. C., & Najaka, S. S. (2001). School-based prevention of problem behaviors: A meta-analysis. *Journal of Quantitative Criminology, 17,* 247–272.

Witt, J., LaFleur, L., Naquin, G., & Gilbertson, D. (1999). *Teaching effective classroom routines.* Longmont, CO: Sopris West.

Ysseldyke, J., Burns, M., Dawson, P., Kelley, B., Morrison, D., Ortiz, S., et al. (2006). *School psychology: A blueprint for training and practice, III.* Bethesda, MD: National Association of School Psychologists.

Zajac, R. J., & Hartup, W. W. (1997). Friends as coworkers: Research review and classroom implications. *Elementary School Journal, 98,* 3–13.

Zimmerman, B. J. (2000). Attainment of self-regulation: A social cognitive perspective. In M. Boekaerts, P. R. Pintrich, & M. Zeidner (Eds.), *Handbook of self-regulation* (pp. 13–39). San Diego, CA: Academic Press.

Zimmerman, B. J., Bandura, A., & Martinez-Pons, M. (1992). Self-motivation for academic attainment: The role of self-efficacy beliefs and personal goal setting. *American Educational Research Journal, 29,* 663–676.

Zimmerman, B. J., Bonner, S., & Kovach, R. (1996). *Developing self-regulated learners: Beyond achievement to self-efficacy.* Washington, DC: American Psychological Association.

Zimmerman, B. J., & Schunk, D. H. (2008). Motivation: An essential dimension of self-regulated learning. In D. H. Schunk & B. J. Zimmerman (Eds.), *Motivation and self-regulated learning: Theory, research, and applications* (pp. 1–30). Mahwah, NJ: Erlbaum.

Zins, J. E., Weissberg, R. P., Wang, M. C., & Walberg, H. J. (2004). *Building academic success on social and emotional learning.* New York: Teachers College Press.

Zullig, K. J., Koopman, T. M., Patton, J. M., & Ubbes, V. A. (2010). School climate: Historical review, instrument development, and school assessment. *Journal of Psychoeducational Assessment, 28*(2), 139–152.

Index

Page numbers in italics indicate figures or tables.